Building America
The Democratic Promise
of Public Work

Building America
The Democratic Promise of Public Work

Harry C. Boyte and Nancy N. Kari

Temple University Press
Philadelphia

Temple University Press, Philadelphia 19122

Copyright ©1996 by Temple University

Published 1996

Printed in the United States of America

⊛ The paper used in this publication meets the requirements of the
American National Standard for Information Sciences—Permanence of
Paper for Printed Library Materials, ANSI Z39.48-1984

Text design by Karen White

Library of Congress Cataloging-in-Publication Data

Boyte, Harry Chatten. 1945–
    Building America : the democratic promise of public work / by
Harry C. Boyte and Nancy N. Kari.
        p.   cm.
    Includes bibliographical references and index.
    ISBN 1-56639-457-0 (hardcover). — ISBN 1-56639-458-9 (paper)
    1. Public service employment—United States.   2. Volunteer
workers in community development—United States.   I. Kari,
Nancy N., 1947– . II. Title.
    HD5713.6.U54B69   1996
    331.12'042'093—dc20   96-13030

To Janet Chatten Ferguson and Betty and Harold Newland

For Wise Counsel

And Lifetimes of Productive Work

From Which We Have Drawn Inspiration

Freedom's Plow

A long time ago, but not too long ago,
ships came from across the sea
Bringing Pilgrims and prayer-makers,
Adventurers and booty seekers,
Free men and indentured servants,
Slave men and slave masters, all new—
To a new world, America!

With billowing sails the galleons came
Bringing men and dreams, women and dreams.
In little bands together,
heart reaching out to heart,
Hand reaching out to hand,
They began to build our land.
Some were free hands

Seeking a greater freedom,
Some were indentured hands
Hoping to find their freedom,
Some were indentured hands
Guarding in their hearts the seed of freedom.
But the word was there always
     FREEDOM.

Down into the earth went the plow
In the free hands and the slave hands,
In indentured hands and adventurous hands,
Turning the rich soil went the plow in many hands
That planted and harvested the food that fed
And the cotton that clothed America.
Clang against the trees went the ax in many hands
That hewed and shaped the rooftops of America.
Splash into the rivers and the seas went the boat-hulls
That moved and transported America.
Crack went the whips that drove the horses
Across the plains of America.
Free hands and slave hands,
Indentured hands, adventurous hands,
White hands and black hands
Held the plow handles,
Ax handles, hammer handles,
Launched the boats and whipped the horses
That fed and housed and moved America.
Thus together through labor
All these hand made America.

                              —Langston Hughes

Verses from "Freedom's Plow" in *Selected Poems of Langston Hughes* (New York: Random House, 1990), pp. 291–293.

CONTENTS

Acknowledgments   xi

Introduction   1

Chapter 1: Meanings of Citizenship   13

Chapter 2: The New Democracy   33

Chapter 3: Rural Democracy   56

Chapter 4: People's Institutions   78

Chapter 5: Making a New Deal   95

Chapter 6: The New Gentry and the Loss of Public Space   111

Chapter 7: Citizenship Schools   130

Chapter 8: A Nation Divided   148

Chapter 9: Turning Our Jobs into Public Work   164

Chapter 10: A Commonwealth of Freedom   189

Appendix: Public Work   201

Notes   214

Index   246

ACKNOWLEDGMENTS

Building America is about public work. It is also a product of public work that we have done together and with other people.

In one sense, the work that created the seedbed for the book began in late 1986 in a conversation Harry Boyte had with Harlan Cleveland, then Dean of the Humphrey Institute of Public Affairs. Harlan's stellar accomplishments—former U.S. Ambassador to NATO, Dean of the Maxwell School, President of the World Academy of Art and Science, among other things—are embodied in a certain civic flair. "There is something wrong with American politics," he observed. "People are going to make useful observations about the causes. I want you to look at what might be done to solve the problem." Harlan Cleveland's challenge led to the creation of a network of remarkable colleagues with whom we have worked on democracy's dilemmas for the last nine years. The major base of this effort has been the Center for Democracy and Citizenship at the Humphrey Institute, and its predecessor, Project Public Life, formed by Harry with Nan and others in the late 1980s. Harry Boyte codirects the Center with Edwin Fogelman, Chair of the Department of Political Science at the University of Minnesota.

In another sense, the book stems from questions raised by Nan Kari's work over a number of years, questions that sensitized her to the need for public work. The word *anger* descends from the old Norse word *angr,* meaning a sense of grief at lost or unrealized possibility. This well describes Nan's stance toward her professional background in occupational therapy. As we describe in Chapter 9, occupational therapy is a profession once grounded in deep concern for the meaning and liberating possibilities of work. In recent decades these larger insights have been eclipsed by reductionistic ways of thinking about human potential. Nan has struggled with how democratic possibilities in health professions and higher education might be liberated and developed. In this quest much of her work has been done in association with the Center. It has informed the Center's theory and practice, especially raising the thorny issues of how professionals might rethink their everyday work in more democratic and interactive ways.

The aim throughout has been to develop ways to re-engage ordinary citizens in public life and to renew civic cultures in institutions and communities. We claim responsibility for the conclusions and errors we have drawn from these experiences. But many partners and colleagues across the nation have contributed valuable ideas and insights.

Early on, E. J. Dionne argued for creating a network of extensive experimental projects in a limited but diverse cluster of settings. In this fashion, he suggested, we would be able to draw out key themes and lessons, making comparisons across environments and contexts. It was sound and wise counsel.

Dorothy Cotton, former Director of the Citizenship Education Program of the Southern Christian Leadership Conference during the southern civil rights movement, has been an inspiration and a source of advice throughout. Dorothy brought her vision of "citizenship education" in its richest, fullest sense. Popular civic education needs to have a deep grounding in the culture, traditions, and ways of life of ordinary people. Peg Michels, for a time codirector of Project Public Life, contributed the fine eye of an organizer who cares deeply about the power of ideas to awaken civic spirit. Nan Skelton, now Director of Training and Youth Development at the Center, has enormously enriched our strategic thinking, as well as our youth initiatives.

We have worked closely with a network of "partners" involved directly in civic experiments associated with the Center. We have also benefited greatly from the ideas and feedback of many others with whom we have been in ongoing conversation. A full listing is noted in Chapter 9. Here, we want to acknowledge the contributions of Melissa Bass, Rebecca Breuer, Gil Clary, David Cohen, Mary Dietz, Dennis Donovan, Sara Evans, James Farr, Kate Hogg, Pam Hayle, Juan Jackson, Carol McGee Johnson, John Kari, Paul Light, Tony Massengale, Judy Meath, Deborah Meier, Miaisha Mitchell, William Schambra, Tim Sheldon, Carol Shields, and Gerald Taylor. At the Humphrey Institute, John Brandl, John Bryson, Bill Diaz, Robert Kudrle, Sam Myers, Joe Nathan, Barbara Nelson, Tim Penny, G. Edward Schuh, and Vin Weber among others have created a lively interdisciplinary and bipartisan climate for our work.

The New Citizenship, a national initiative to strengthen citizen–government partnership in America coordinated by the Center, formed an important base of experience from which we have also drawn. We want especially to acknowledge Carmen Sirianni who served as the Research Director of the New Citizenship/American Civic Forum. Sirianni now edits an on-line service, Civic Practices Network, that allows the exchange and analysis of civic experiments and stories.

A number of institutions and associations have been helpful in the New Citizenship. William Galston, formerly deputy assistant of domestic policy in the White House, helped to open many doors in the federal government. Bill's extraordinary commitment to citizenship and his wide-ranging knowledge of political theory and practices alike made this partnership with the White House a formative and crystallizing experience for the Center's evolving theory. Benjamin Barber, director of the Whitman Center at Rutgers, has been a colleague from the beginning. Ben, along with Will Marshall, president of the Progressive Policy Institute, helped to coauthor the *Civic Declaration*, a widely endorsed national call for citizenship which Harry coordinated. The *Civic Declaration* introduced some of our ideas about public work to a national audience. The Kettering Foundation, which published the *Civic Declaration* as an occasional paper, has been a source of insight and a forum for debate of these ideas over many years. We especially want to thank David Mathews, Suzanne Morse, Harold Saunders, Estus Smith, William Winter, and David Brown.

The efforts of the New Citizenship led to a session with President Clinton, Vice President Gore and other leaders of the administration at Camp David on the future of democracy and citizenship, held January 14, 1995. There, Harry Boyte presented some of the themes and examples of public work.

This book project has enlisted many friends and family, whom we also wish to acknowledge. From the beginning, we used what we called "the mom test": our mothers, Betty Newland (Nan's) and Janet Ferguson (Harry's), judged whether the writing sounded too academic or stilted. We are not sure that we always measured up, but their commentary, prods, challenges, and criticisms were extraordinarily valuable. Their exemplary lives of productive, creative, determined work have also partly inspired this book. We dedicate *Building America* to Betty and Harold Newland and to Janet Ferguson.

Other family members and friends gave extensive feedback. We want to thank especially John Kari and Judy Meath who also read the manuscript cover to cover. John offered insights for potential application of these ideas, and support for the importance of the project.

Judy's critical eye caught many flaws in the argument and anticipated potential misunderstandings that readers might have. Gar Alperovitz, Michael Ames, Dorothy Cotton, John de Graaf, Lary May, Harold McDougall, Elizabeth Minnick, Christy Myers, Scott Peters, Carmen Sirianni, Nan Skelton, and Gerald Taylor all provided feedback on various chapters.

We also want to acknowledge Scott Peter's highly creative and detailed labors as a Graduate Research Assistant with the Center over the past three years. Scott's research into the largely forgotten democratic traditions of land-grant education and his discovery of the fertile thought and life work of Liberty Hyde Bailey, in particular, created a vital resource for the Center as well as for this book. Along the way, the book crept into many other events. Harry's morning running group in St. Anthony Park, St. Paul, heard many stories of public work. Bon Hwan Kim, Director of the Korean Youth Cultural Center, reflected on public work and its potential to bridge searing racial divisions in Los Angeles at a lunch, when Harry and his daughter Jae, were on a visit to Korea Town.

Our children were deeply engaged, while they also gave us space and time for writing. Craig Evans Boyte shared many conversations about public work on a European trip with Harry in the summer of 1995. Ana Kari encouraged her mother, while remembering "many loud kitchen conversations" over the summer. Jonathan Kari helped with interviews and engaged in an ongoing conversation about the Civilian Conservation Corps. Jae Boyte-Evans helped with a workshop on public work in Korea Town and furnished her strong opinions throughout the writing.

Our ideas about work and democracy are most importantly the product of a partnership many years in the making. They have been strengthened and nourished by joint writing projects, presentations, and visits to monuments of American democracy. Nan brings a long-term exploration of practical and theoretical questions that concern the transformation of professional and therapeutic cultures. Her talents as an organizer have crafted environments in which ideas can be tested. Nan also has a passion for spare, focused argument. Harry's long-time work has been about the practical theory of democracy: How ordinary people develop the confidence skills, and capacities for shaping the world. His writing and interviews over the years brought a multitude of voices to the development of the theory of public work.

Introduction

It may seem for a moment that the world of labor is just a world of toiling units, each bearing the burden of its own life. But this is only a fragment of the truth. Our inventions, our just laws, our system of jurisprudence, our agricultural methods, all the things that contribute to the ease and safety of human life have been won for us by the desperate struggle, "the agony and bloody sweat" of a vast succession of obscure as well as illustrious ancestors. There would be no Wealth but for the Commonwealth.

Joseph Wood, "Wealth and the Commonwealth"[1]

*P*ublic work, work that makes things of value and importance in cooperation with others, is the taproot of American democracy. Linking everyday work to democracy gives work larger meaning and makes citizenship serious.

Work of significance—in offices and schools, factories and farms, government agencies or inner-city neighborhoods—has been the way diverse people have forged connections with each other and addressed the nation's problems. Through such work people gain visibility, authority, and larger intellectual horizons. People become creators of their communities, stakeholders in the country, and guardians of the commonwealth through common work.

Building America is a first look at the relationship between work and democracy across the sweep of American history. Abraham Lincoln's idea of work-centered government, the instrument of common purpose, remained vibrant well into the 1940s. Belief in the dignity of labor and in work as a source of power fueled popular reform movements for change. For instance, in the first decades of the twentieth century a massive country life movement in rural America called for renewal of democracy in rural life. As a counter to widespread changes in farming, movement leaders argued that agriculture had long been an example of "democratic public work." The nation needed to remember farming's larger meaning, rather than succumb to the blandishments of those who perceived farming simply as a commercial enterprise.

During the Great Depression, themes of the dignity of labor inspired broad movements like union organizing in basic industry. Many of Roosevelt's New Deal programs promoted public work. Millions of poor and unemployed youth put their talents to work in the

Civilian Conservation Corps, building dams and bridges, planting forests, and preventing soil erosion. Public work infused institutions of many kinds, stretching from local communities to the federal government, creating a sense of wide popular ownership. Well into the 1940s, themes of work also filled popular culture—Will Rogers movies, post office art, and Langston Hughes's poetry, all were redolent with images of productive labor.

People without formal credentials or higher education felt their work mattered on the larger stage. College graduates also understood the larger civic meanings and implications of their professional careers. Citizenship was embedded in university and college missions and mainstream practices, as John A. Hannah, president of Michigan State University, illustrated eloquently in 1944:

> Our colleges should not be content with only the training of outstanding agriculturists, or engineers, or home economists, or teachers, or scientists, or lawyers, or doctors, or veterinarians—it is not enough that our young people be outstanding technicians. The first and never-forgotten objective must be that every human product of our educational system must be given that training that will enable him [sic] to be an effective citizen, appreciating the opportunities, and fully willing to assume his responsibilities in a great democracy.[2]

Historically, colleges and universities claimed responsibility for developing civic leadership that could sustain a democratic society. They expressed such concern especially through tying students' future careers to active citizenship.

Yet in our time, such perspectives in higher education are virtually absent. Colleges today buzz with talk about the importance of teaching civic values through activities like community service, but there is very little discussion of the relationship between work and citizenship and democracy. John Hannah's warnings about the dangers of excessively narrow disciplinary and technical training appear all too prophetic. As one federal employee told us in the New Citizenship research project that we undertook with the White House and a variety of civic organizations, "we've lost the 'civil' in civil service."

This loss reflects the crisis of work and its meanings in our age. Today, people are supposedly "overworked." In fact, work has become simply a means to an end—one "has to work" to feed the family, to pay for the vacation, to survive economically. Few worksites discuss the larger significance of what one makes or produces.

We are convinced that in fact people are "underworked." However, many hours, work has lost its tie to larger public purposes, challenges, and possibilities. Work's dignity, meaning, and importance have disappeared from view. With this disappearance, people become outsiders. Politics is left to special interests and professionals. Democracy is troubled. The commonwealth itself becomes invisible. When work is not understood in its broadest terms, fundamental questions vital to a democracy are not raised. What is wealth? What is produced? Who produces it?

America's Civic Crisis and the Limits of Democratic Theory

> [In a "free society] social relations would be directly modeled upon the organization of labour; men would group themselves in small working collectivities . . . it is a fine sight to see a handful of workmen in the building trade, checked by some difficulty, [who] ponder the problem each for himself, make various suggestions for dealing with it, and then apply unanimously the method conceived by one, who may or may not have any official authority . . . at such moments, the image of a free community appears.
>
> Simone Weil, "On the Portrait of a Free Society"[3]

Simone Weil points to a key dimension of work: its potential to democratize power relationships. Work can provide a way for people to bring authority and to have power beyond simply their formal position or role. As we have lost larger meanings and purposes of work as a society, we have lost critical tools for people to participate as confident, powerful actors in the affairs of the public world. By the mid-1990s, many observers express alarm at the state of things in America. "They're way beyond angry," pollster Frank Luntz told *Newsweek* senior editor Joe Klein, describing "middle Americans" he surveyed. "They're hopeless. That's the big change and the big danger; they've lost hope."[4]

The federal government stood at the bottom in polling about faith in major American institutions, with only 8 percent expressing "a great deal of confidence." According to a *New York Times* poll in August, 1995, "frustration runs deep, perhaps deeper than any other time in modern American history." Seventy-nine percent of the public, the highest in several decades, believed that the government is pretty much "run by a few big interests looking out for themselves." Fifty-eight percent of those polled believed that people like themselves "had little to say about what the government did."[5]

Resentment of politics, politicians, and government is the tip of a larger iceberg of general discontent, anger about every institution, and fear for the future. Government "of the people" depended on a widespread producer culture. The effects of the loss of such a culture are evident in many other settings as well. Scholars have documented the symptoms, but they have not understood the causes.

Harvard social scientist Robert Putnam found that Americans' affiliations with civic institutions with a face-to-face quality—from churches to service groups like Kiwanis and PTAs—have declined over the last generation. In an essay called "Bowling Alone," in the magazine *Journal of Democracy,* Putnam pointed out that though more Americans were bowling—no mean statistic, since more Americans bowl each year than vote—far more were bowling by themselves. Bowling league participation had sharply declined. The industry was alarmed because alleys gain most profit from concession sales of products like beer and pretzels, consumed mostly as a social activity. Putnam had other worries. In the 1960s, he observed, two-thirds of the public expressed trust of other citizens, whereas one-third was distrustful. By the 1990s, figures had reversed themselves: Two-thirds distrusted other people.[6]

Such civic disaffection, in turn, exacerbates other dangerous trends: sharp social and cultural divisions; growing economic discrepancies; and a wide pattern of group demands for rights and resources with little corresponding commitment to responsibilities and contributions. "Everyone wants everything, and no one wants to pay for it," one retired factory foreman told the *New York Times* during the 1993 health care debate.

A curious paradox exists. For all of our problems and fears as a nation, civic energy abounds. Americans are not uncaring or apathetic about public affairs. In fact, a rich array of civic work in many diverse settings is evident across the country. Yet, if creative public activity is all around us, why haven't its possibilities and its full significance been widely understood?

A veritable growth industry of articles and books has diagnosed democracy's ills in recent years. Current writings on democracy point to special-interest money in politics, the posturing of elected officials on inflammatory issues, and the collapse of "mediating" political institutions like parties and unions to explain the crisis in politics. More generally, social critics trace the decline of participation in voluntary groups and communal life to factors like television, suburbanization, a culture of individualism, and two-job households. Almost without exception, current writers separate "citizenship" from work, worksites, and people's identities as "producers." Many writers, in fact, argue that work itself is the major problem: Americans are too busy to volunteer, the argument runs. Women have left community activities and entered the paid workforce. When citizenship is equated with voluntarism, it loses its seriousness and power. It becomes what one does after hours and on the side.

Contemporary writings about citizenship and democracy have documented a series of alarming trends, but their neglect of work leads to serious limitations in proposals for remedy. Pointing to problems with elections and governmental institutions leads to calls for election and campaign finance reform or "reinventing government" to make it more responsive to "customers." Those who identify declining participation in voluntary groups and a growing climate of rancor and incivility as the central problems call for measures to stimulate a sense of "community." Efforts such as community service, proposals for better public dialogue, and opportunities for public discussion forums reflect this thinking. These are worthy ideas. But they miss the point of work.[7]

The customary way intellectuals, academics, political observers, and politicians themselves characterize concepts like "citizenship" is much more shallow than the civic efforts that are emerging across America. Conventional terms used to describe citizen activity are inadequate: *volunteerism, deliberative democracy, citizen participation, civil society*, or the recent term used to describe the sum total of civic interactions, *social capital*. These terms simply do not begin to convey the richness or name the importance of what citizens are doing. Moreover, they largely focus on process, separating citizen effort from what is actually created or produced of value.

Work is not beside the point. It is at the center of citizenship. Worksites are not irrelevant; they are critical. Returning work—paid and unpaid—to the center of discussion about democracy opens up enormous new possibilities for democratic renewal. It also highlights major obstacles to change and unearths a history which has been largely forgotten. It points to the need for a more adequate and extensive way of thinking theoretically about the democratic possibilities of work.

Democratic theory of any use is never created in a vacuum. It needs grounding in experience, practical experiment, and real-world settings that reflect the diverse challenges and possibilities of the public world. It evolves as it is constantly tested. Traditions of thinking about public topics over the centuries and contemporary university-based research are of use in this process. But practical experiences and experiments are the touchstone of effective theory that guides practical action.

Here current academic discussions are of relatively little value. Contemporary theory is largely concerned with historical analysis, on the one hand, and questions of institutional design, formal structure, and theories of knowledge on the other hand. The authors of the *Federalist Papers* are, in an important way, emblematic. From the vantage of most theorizing in our time, the question is, what kind of institutional and formal arrangements serve democracy best?[8]

In contrast, the tradition of democratic theorizing that we find most useful in American history takes quite a different tack. Practical democratic theory looks at questions of civic action and civic capacity: What forms of education, popular organization, relationships, and cultural practices cultivate the confidence, spirit, and skills that citizens need for effective action and participation in governance? How do citizens come to understand their efforts in relation not only to immediate interests but also to the longer range "commonwealth" of interests in the society as a whole?

From this perspective, theory looks quite different than what is traditionally included in mainstream intellectual discussion. Conventional positions of all kinds are too narrowly framed. Many of the most important thinkers about democratic action are excluded. These include, in our view, literary figures such as Herman Melville, Langston Hughes, Zora Neal Hurston, and Ralph Ellison. More generally, standard listings of political theorizing simply drop out most of those who have had useful things to say about how citizens best develop the skills and capacities for effective "public work." Thomas Jefferson and John Dewey in America—or an occasional theorist from abroad such as Simone Weil, who made a rare but crucial connection between work and freedom—make the grade. But key practical theorists of democratic action such as Frances Willard, W. E. B. Du Bois, Jane Addams, Liberty Hyde Bailey, Saul Alinsky, Ella Baker, and, in our time, Ernesto Cortes, Gerald Taylor, and Deborah Meier would rarely if ever find mention in academic treatments.

We seek to continue the tradition of practical democratic theory. We are convinced that America has been a remarkable seedbed of democratic experiment in the last generation, in a fashion little understood, whose broad lessons have been largely unexplored. *Building America* draws not only on a wide-ranging analysis of diverse civic practices but also builds on our work at the Center for Democracy and Citizenship in a variety of settings over the past nine years. The lessons of civic work in communities for overcoming America's growing racial divide are described in Chapter 8. Our own work in thinking about how "jobs" might be translated into work with broader public meaning, as well as examples from other environments, are described in Chapters 9 and 10.

Out of all of these past and present experiences a basic theme emerges: Productive labor is at the heart of American democracy in ways that have not been well theorized. This is summed up in the idea of "public work."

Public work is a term that only a few American intellectuals have used. It has been far more widely employed by ordinary people.[9] *Public work* is a term that we find resonates widely with activists from the 1930s and 1940s. Interestingly, it has been a term commonly used by blue-collar workers in the South who move from farms or family to work in the textile mill, factories, and mines. Although the term has not been widely used in a theoretical sense, in fact it has a particular and powerful usefulness in our time. Explicit discussion of public work in its different meanings provides us a vehicle and means for reintroducing the civic overtones and meanings of labor. It is a way to help regrow a sense of productive work and its tie to democracy that has been lost.[10]

The concept of public work is associated with a constellation of other insights and themes. For instance, it is connected to the idea that democratization depends on people's own, largely self-directed learning, drawing strongly from people's cultures, traditions, and ways of life but also informed by larger civic concepts and lessons. Put differently, this means a focus on the development of the civic capacities of individuals, institutions, and communities. "Public leadership development" (in contemporary language)—or popular civic education—is central to building a democracy. In turn, the key to such development is reconfiguring jobs as public work.

Building America lifts up the richness of public work evident today and provides a lens for seeing contemporary work in larger terms. It also begins a conversation about an approach to democratic theory grounded in people's labor and everyday lives.

The Reemergence of Public Work in the 1990s

Teaching should be in public, open, available to criticisms. It should serve the broadest purposes like democracy and citizenship. It has to convey that it matters. It has to engage intellectual capacities. We build public relationships through teaching and through focus on the craft of teaching. Good teaching is good public work.

Deborah Meier, Director, Central Park East Schools

Public work begins where people are in everyday environments. It requires building capacities for public life. Deborah Meier uses the term *good public work* to explain the broad changes in schools and other social environments that have taken place in the Central Park schools of East Harlem. There, almost all students—mainly kids from poor, working-class and minority inner-city neighborhoods—graduate from high school. Eighty percent go on to college. Meier stresses the multidimensionality of public work. The concept of public work suggests the importance of work's larger civic purposes. The Central Park East schools form a learning environment in which all are understood to be coproducers of education. Students, parents, community members, and support staff have critical roles, in addition to teachers. Moreover, the schools have a well-developed understanding that it is the common investment in the work itself that provides the key bridge across otherwise sharp lines of division. "For people to stay at the table, in the face of all the arguments and conflicts, requires important work in which all have a strong stake," Meier observes.

The Central Park schools pose as their core questions, "Who cares?" and "Why does it matter?" Connecting individual concerns and actions to questions about the relationship of education to democracy teaches people to think differently about the meaning of their work. In this way, work acquires a larger purpose.[11]

Public work is emerging in many arenas besides secondary education—in health care settings, in higher education, in approaches to youth development, and within professions such as journalism. Obstacles and opportunities for reconfiguring work are discussed in Chapter 9.

Building America is an interpretive essay meant to spark discussion and further investigation. It is not an exhaustive treatment. It suggests some lessons from environments in which public work has flourished and others in which it is being reborn.

In the book, as well as in our efforts with the Center for Democracy and Citizenship, we focus in particular on the renewal of public work in low-income and blue-collar communities, in professionalized service institutions where expert–client patterns have replaced productive public interactions, and on the interactions between such communities and such institutions. The emphasis is based on our analysis of how "civic muscles" have been eroded over the last several decades.

We have been interested in those institutions and networks that make up what the political theorist Michael Walzer has recently termed "meat and potatoes pluralism."[12] These connected local work, involving face-to-face relationships, with large worlds of policy and politics at every level of government. Churches and synagogues, voluntary associations, community centers, settlement houses, ethnic groups and newspapers, popular education movements and local schools, trade unions and political parties formed the heart of popular democratic politics well into the 1940s. These networks furnished the means through which millions of ordinary people could shape the larger society. They created partnerships with government and businesses. And they were sustained, in large part, by practices of public professionalism which have now disappeared. We are convinced that it is this kind of erosion of civic life and spirit that has most dramatically led to the loss of civic power and capacity for action. Renewal of public work in such settings for the twenty-first century is key to the reinvigoration of democracy.

In many cases, our treatment is only suggestive. Even more to the point, large continents of American worksites and contexts that are critical to a revived civic culture remain to be explored.

The development of a broad philosophy of public work will need to draw from a myriad of cultural traditions that are not taken up here, from Latino to Asian, Native American to Caribbean. Most of our stories are drawn from European American and African American history and contemporary experiences. A philosophy of public work asks, what do America's diverse cultures contribute or potentially contribute to the American commonwealth through work? This is a considerably different framework than the often sentimentalized language of "celebrating diversity."

An evolving philosophy of the democratic possibilities of work will need to explore in much greater detail many other topics beyond those treated here. For instance, many religious traditions powerfully uphold the dignity and worth of labor. The concept of public work needs to be informed by different religious teachings and perspectives. Further, examples of public work by groups named in terms of their deficiencies—the "frail elderly," people with "disabilities," or "children at risk"—have much to contribute.

Finally, the civic meanings of work need to be explored far more extensively in the private sector. Corporations once were seen as creations of "the commonwealth," in the terminology of the Massachusetts Supreme Court in the nineteenth century. Today, some businesses have begun to recognize the limits of the bottom line as a way to understand business success and employee motivation.

Although at an early stage of theorizing, we are nonetheless convinced that concepts and practices of public work provide extraordinary tools for democratic renewal. Work is something everyone does; it is commonplace, and therefore inclusive of many different interests, cultures, perspectives, and viewpoints when its public possibilities are drawn out.

Public has three strands of meaning, all of which contribute to the usefulness of the concept of public work: *Public* is a diverse group acting together—a public; *public* is a quality of space that is open, visible, and accessible to view; and, finally, *public* suggests broad purposes of general importance, for example in public goods or public interests.

In the first case, when a diverse public acts, there are multiple possibilities for changing and democratizing power relationships, as Simone Weil observed. Thus, for instance, groups excluded from public life in American history—slaves, the landless and poor, women, and diverse ethnic groups—have been able to make claims for full participation on the basis of their contributions through work.

Second, public space, which includes diverse perspectives and wide visibility, can generate often remarkable transformations in identity and character. In public spaces people can learn new ways of thinking. They understand their own histories in more complex ways as they encounter others' stories. Finally, the larger stage of being in public provides opportunities for integration of older understandings of the self with new capacities and challenges.

Third, as people come to focus on larger public purposes through their work, they develop what the philosopher Hannah Arendt called "care for the world." Indeed, it was Adam Smith, father of modern economics, who observed that narrow self-interests could never be sufficient for the challenges of a "great society": "The last duty of the commonwealth is that of erecting and maintaining those public institutions and those public works which, though they may be in the highest degree advantageous to a great society, are, however, of such a nature that the profit could never repay the expense to any individual or small number."[13]

Further, through work embued with larger public purposes, people develop an unmistakable sense of freedom and of creation. For instance, for participants in the southern civil rights movement of the 1960s, the movement's "freedom language" came not only from its challenge to the patterns of segregation, which prevented blacks from exercising full civil rights. Freedom, as it was talked about continuously in civil rights songs, sermons, and the everyday work of the movement, also meant the liberating, exhilarating realization that people were involved in changing their communities and the nation as a whole; they were "co-creators" of history.[14]

It is in this spirit that we offer a practical theory about the tradition and practices of public work in America. Whatever our disagreements as citizens, we share a common destiny as Americans. All can participate in public work; all can ask questions about the larger meaning of our nation and how we might contribute to its renewal in a time of crisis.

CHAPTER 1

Meanings of Citizenship

In a neighborhood dispute there may be stunts, rough words, and even hot insults. But when a whole people speaks to its government, the dialogue and the action must be on a level reflecting the worth of that people and the responsibility of that government.

> Martin Luther King, Jr., and other civil rights leaders, explaining the nonviolent purpose of the March on Washington, 1963[1]

*A*mericans in the mid-1990s are angry and disgusted at politicians. People also give abundant evidence of deep worry about the country's basic directions.

Yet simple anger at politicians lets us off the hook. As a pundit once put it, we get the government we deserve. In our time, politics and public affairs are seen as the work of politicians. Citizens' roles in public life are secondary: consumers, complaining clients, special interest advocates, or volunteers who "help out" but make few serious decisions. Unless we take citizenship seriously, few things are likely to change.

The irony of democracy is that its decline at home is paralleled by its emulation around the world. We face a mountain of challenges as a nation that politics is not adequately addressing. We have a crisis on our hands. But the proposed solutions address symptoms, not the root problem.

Conservatives argue for term limits on the grounds that politicians have forgotten their status as ordinary people. Groups like Common Cause propose campaign reform as a way to limit the role of large sums of money in politics. Others argue for change in the media coverage of elections, in order to address the dilemma that public relations gimmicks have replaced conversation among citizens in campaigns.

Each of these are efforts to fix the governmental machinery and make important suggestions. But our real crisis is the disengagement of ordinary people from productive involvement in public affairs.

The role of ordinary citizens in public life has been debated from the beginning of the Republic. For example, James Madison believed that public affairs ought to be the domain of politicians and government officials. In his *Federalist Paper #10*, Madison argued that deliberations of representatives, "a chosen body of citizens," are "more consonant to the public good than if pronounced by the people themselves." He gave title to officeholders. This continues to be the standard, formal definition of public life.

Thomas Jefferson had a far different understanding of public life—one that was reflected in the Ninth and Tenth Amendments to the Constitution, reserving all powers not specifically assigned to officials to the citizens themselves:

> Where everyman is . . . participator in the government of affairs, not merely at an election one day in the year but every day . . . he will let the heart be torn out of his body sooner than his power be wrested from him by a Caesar or a Bonapart.[2]

Whatever Madison's hopes for an enlightened and virtuous political class that would wisely and independently represent the varying interests on behalf of the whole country, in fact Americans interacted constantly with government. Ordinary people worked vigorously on public problems in farms, workplaces, and local communities, in schools, religious congregations, voluntary organizations, and other settings not formally part of the political system. Through common work they gained a sense of their stake in government and their roles in public life. Such broad patterns of civic action contributed to the self-definition of government employees and officials themselves as citizens. These dynamics are reflected in Abraham Lincoln's famous formulation at Gettysburg: government *of* the people, *by* the people, and *for* the people.

The loss of the idea that public affairs originates from the people means that we lose our stake in the nation. We become outsiders and tourists of the age. Further, a corruption of our deepest ideals occurs. At Gettysburg, Lincoln described democratic government as conceived in and dedicated to liberty. He saw, "the great and good work" of saving the Union as ushering in a new birth of freedom.[3]

Freedom for Lincoln was inextricably tied to work. It meant the right to be in control of one's own labor. Hence his abhorrence of slavery. Freedom also was the experience that citizens gained as they set about the work of self-governance. Thus, free labor, understood both individually and collectively, was the way people *became* citizens—accountable participants in building the country.

In place of government *of* the people and *by* the people, today we focus on government *for* the people whose primary responsibility is to provide services. From a nation of free citizens, we have become a nation of individualists and consumers for whom liberty means the right to be left alone and the right to choose among brands of toothpaste.

Many dynamics contribute to the erosion of public work by citizens, from mass communications and the emergence of the corporate economy to changing patterns of work. Our reliance on others to solve problems is directly related to the rise of scientific knowledge and credentialed expertise. Experts themselves have found their scope of initiative severely constricting. Our pervasive consumer culture is a potent force in shaping our identities as Americans. But perhaps least noted and most central is this: We have few visible examples of citizens engaged in serious public work that is named as such. We have even less discussion of what the lessons and implications of such efforts are for a complex, modern, technological society.

"Public work" is work by ordinary people that builds and sustains our basic public goods and resources—what used to be called "our commonwealth." It solves common problems and creates common things. It may be paid or voluntary. It may be done in communities. It may be done as part of one's regular job. In fact, adding public dimensions to work—recognizing the larger potential meaning and impact of what one does as a teacher or nurse, as a county extension agent or a computer programmer or a machinist or a college professor or anything else—often can turn an unsatisfying "job" into much more significant "work." The story of the two bricklayers who were asked what they were doing conveys this sense. One said, "building a wall." The other said, "building a cathedral."

In the fullest sense of the term, public work takes place not only with an eye to public consequences, it also is work "in public"—work that is visible, open to inspection, whose significance is widely recognized. And it is cooperative civic work of "a public": a mix of people whose interests, backgrounds, and resources may be quite different.

Public work focuses attention on a point that we have largely lost in our age of high technology: We help to build the world through our common effort. What we have built and created we can also recreate. Thus, public work suggests new possibilities for democracy.

Rebuilding the Walls

You see the trouble we are in: Jerusalem is in ruins, its gates have been burned down. Come, let us rebuild the walls of Jerusalem and suffer this indignity no longer . . . "Let us start!" they exclaimed. "Let us build;" and with willing hands they set about the good work.

Nehemiah 2:17–18

The Old Testament Book of Nehemiah, a political and social reformer who led his people during exile, tells a story of public leadership and the work of a people. In late-twentieth-century America, Nehemiah has become a symbol for inner-city community efforts to rebuild neighborhoods once thought lost to urban decay.

East Brooklyn Churches (EBC) is a community organization affiliated with a national network of community groups called the Industrial Areas Foundation. The Industrial Areas Foundation, or IAF, includes the largest community groups in the country, most often based in low income communities and organized around churches.

EBC had successes in the impoverished neighborhoods of the East Brooklyn area of New York. EBC members forced clean-ups in local food stores, pressured the city to install hundreds of street signs, renovated local parks, and worked to clean up vacant lots. Slowly through common work they forged a sense of solidarity and potency.

In the early 1980s, they took on a project to build houses on a scale that dwarfed any other low-income development effort in the country. EBC envisioned construction of 5,000 single-family, owner-occupied housing units designed for lower- to middle-income buyers, to rise in the midst of the decimated and mostly black neighborhoods of East Brooklyn. The obstacles were tremendous. Drug dealers ruled the streets. Block after block had been bulldozed into rubble, like a vast war zone. Middle-income families had fled. Prior efforts at revitalization had failed. But they had confidence from earlier successes. "We are not a grassroots organization," thundered the Reverend Johnny Ray Youngblood, a key leader in the organization. "Grass roots are shallow roots. Grass roots are fragile roots. *Our* roots are deep roots.

Our roots have fought for existence in the shattered glass of East New York." EBC turned to housing out of the conviction that only widespread home ownership could create the kind of "roots" essential for renewed community pride and freedom from fear. Teaming up with a well-known *Daily News* columnist and former developer, I. D. Robbins, they adopted his controversial argument that for half the cost of high-density, high-rise apartments, it would be possible to build large numbers of single-family homes that could create stable neighborhoods.

They named their undertaking the "Nehemiah Homes," recalling the Old Testament leader who gained permission from the King of Persia in 446 B.C. to go back to Jerusalem in order to rebuild the walls of the city which had lain in ruins for one hundred years. "The story connected our work to something real, not something bogus," explained Mike Gecan, organizer for the East Brooklyn Churches. "It got it out of the "housing" field and the idea that you have to have a bureaucracy with 35 consultants to do anything. It made it a 'non-program,' something more than housing." Or as one EBC leader, Celina Jamieson, emphasized, "We are more than a Nehemiah Plan. We are about the central development of dignity and self-respect."[4]

East Brooklyn community residents found in Nehemiah powerful parallels to their own situation. Rich with passion and politics, the story makes the point that even a divinely inspired leader has trouble in such work. Large-scale projects are messy, complex undertakings. In the biblical narrative, workers faced divisions, doubts, and jealousies. At the same time, however, their efforts generated pride and accomplishment partly through their very visibility. The people recovered their dignity in view of often envious neighbors:

> When Sanballat heard that we were rebuilding the walls, he flew into a rage, beside himself with anger . . . "What are these pathetic Jews trying to do? . . . Do they think they can put new life into these charred stones, salvaged from the heaps of rubble?" Tobiah the Ammonite was standing beside him. "Let them build," he said. "A jackal jumping on the wall will soon knock the stones down again." . . . [Yet the people] worked with all their hearts.

Nehemiah 3:33–38

The story illustrates the motivating power of a public arena which holds various groups accountable. Divisive factions were called to answer for their actions in front of the whole people. Thus, when Nehemiah heard complaints about unjust practices among the nobles who were making excessive profit from the poor, he called for a public assembly:

> When I heard [the peoples'] complaints . . . I was very angry.. . . Summoning a great assembly to deal with them, I said to them, "to the best of our power we have redeemed our brother Jews . . . and now you in turn are selling our brothers." . . . They were silent and could find nothing to say. . . . "What you are doing . . . is wrong." They replied, "We will make restitution."
>
> Nehemiah 5:6–12

The narrative combines a story of remarkable democratic leadership by Nehemiah himself, who rolled up his sleeves and got to work, with a covenant made by the people to work together to restore what had been lost. Many participated. Forty groups are named including merchants, priests, governors, nobles, members of the perfume and goldsmiths' guilds, and women. Builders faced discouragement, ridicule, even threats to their lives. They posted guards when warned of conspiracy. They prayed. The walls rose.

Like its biblical predecessors, East Brooklyn Churches involved many different tasks. People in the churches stuffed envelopes, organized community meetings on the building plans, negotiated with city officials and did many other things. What distinguished Nehemiah from "voluntarism" or "helping out" was not the specific tasks but the character of the effort as a whole: Nehemiah was about changing a whole community. To accomplish this required that people developed power and authority in new ways.

East Brooklyn Churches' Nehemiah Project faced many parallel obstacles. Although the group had commitments from an impressive array of churches and other financial backers, the project's success depended on city funding for a loan pool. When then-Mayor Edward Koch refused to meet with them, project leaders held a press conference that made public the mayor's indecision.

The community's efforts so far had been visible mainly to itself. But this press conference marked a significant transition in which the importance of larger recognition and a sense of public importance became vivid: The work of East Brooklyn Churches moved to a larger public stage that impacted the whole city of New York. That evening the local CBS affiliate showed film clips of the desolate area, while an announcer read from the Book of Nehemiah: "You see the trouble we are in, how Jerusalem lies in ruins with its gates burned. Come, let us build the wall of Jerusalem, that we may no longer suffer disgrace."

Viewers were outraged. The following day Mayor Koch, declaring himself the new Nehemiah, pledged his full support for the effort. He gave Nehemiah speeches for several months thereafter. At the groundbreaking of the first Nehemiah homes, thousands of Poles and Italians and other ethnics from Catholic parishes in Queens turned out to join an interfaith religious celebration demonstrating widespread support of the extraordinary community effort. Nearly 3,000 homes have been built to date.

Ultimately, the success of the Nehemiah Plan led to the only major national federal housing legislation during the Reagan years, which provides financial aid for inner-city owner-occupied homes.

Nehemiah seems at first glance the kind of inspiring story of voluntary community effort that we hear of now and then in the news—like those featured in a *Newsweek* cover story on "Everyday Heroes" at the end of May, 1995. "Individual efforts to reverse the tide often feel like a thousand points of light in a million pools of darkness," the story read. But it sought to convey hope through multiple examples of renewed civic spirit. "People still care about each other more than we give them credit for," it continued. "Charitable giving is down slightly, but the communal spirit is still strong. . . . Intergenerational volunteerism is growing rapidly. Businesses are pitching in as never before." The magazine cites examples of businesses that close for a day so that their employees can volunteer. Journalistic features like *Newsweek's* describe remarkable stories of voluntary effort.[5] But the problem is that they neglect the tie between citizenship and work.

Specifically, in the Nehemiah Project the success came not only from community volunteers who saw their work in public terms but also from professionals who worked differently than normal professional patterns, in broader, more interactive ways. The developer I. D.

Robbins, housing experts, ministers, church officials, and, most dramatically, television journalists—all did public work.

Across the course of American history, citizenship as public work has changed people's sense of themselves and the larger political culture, alike.

Citizenship as Public Work

American citizenship in its most expansive sense is understood as public work: visible effort on common tasks of importance to the community or nation, involving many different people. This older view of citizenship is grounded in people's everyday workplaces and living environments. Public work is always subject to argument and interpretation. Public work makes things. It builds things. It creates social as well as material culture.

Our most common associations with the idea of public work are public "works," in which the focus is on the products themselves. Public works include water mains and roads, sewer systems and bridges, and other parts of the infrastructure. Cities have departments of public works. Franklin Roosevelt's New Deal organized a Public Works Administration.

Public works also extend beyond function and usefulness. Public works can express the grandeur, the beauty, even the highest aspirations of a civilization. In the United States, San Francisco's Golden Gate Bridge is a public work, as are the majestic figures carved from Mount Rushmore. The Lincoln and Jefferson Memorials grace the capital, conveying our democratic traditions. Though public works of cultural and social nature may seem more difficult to identify than roads and public buildings, they are nonetheless a vital part of our environment. Music, dance, and art, like other cultural practices, can be public works.

When the emphasis is simply on the product, then regardless how grand the creation or how noble the aspiration, democracy is not part of the equation. The work activity itself—those who do it and how it is done—remain hidden and in the background.

In fact, public work understood simply as products may convey the opposite of democracy. Public works can conjure up the image of oppressed and brutalized masses, like the Hebrews enslaved in Egypt, or "coolie labor"—the abused Chinese workers who built the American railroads. The invisibility of work in those grand public creations highlights a painful contrast: Although the importance of the thing itself may be recognized on the largest public stage, those who create the thing may be rendered insignificant in comparison. "It's the not-recognition by other people," Mike Lefevre told Studs Terkel for his book, *Working*. "To say a woman is *just* a housewife is degrading. It's also degrading to say *just* a laborer. Somebody built the pyramids. Pyramids. Empire State Building—these things don't just happen. There's hard work behind it."[6]

When "public work" as a term first appeared in America, it had a broader range of associations than it does today. Public work was understood to create public goods, even if by private businesses and corporations, that were thus subject to public deliberation. Farmers, artisans, merchants, and others often saw their work in more public terms than is now common.

The rulings by Lemuel Shaw, Chief Justice of the Massachusetts Supreme Court from 1830 to 1860, were particularly important in this regard. Shaw, known for his "commonwealth" legal theory, which held that government was the agent of the people to be used for the good of the country as a whole, expanded the concept of "eminent domain" on the basis of public work. Eminent domain justified government action to appropriate private property or control aspects of its use (like environmental impact today) for the sake of a larger public good. In 1836 he argued that even though railroads were constructed at private expense, acts of the legislature intended to promote public improvements for the railroads were legitimate. "The work is not less a public work; and the public accommodation is the ultimate object." Shaw's concept of public work led him to affirm rights of legislatures to regulate certain businesses. This became the foundation of twentieth-century business regulations.[7]

Today it takes conscious effort to make visible one's labor. Economic, social, and technological changes of the last half century account for the difficulty in understanding the public dimensions of work. Workplaces divide roles into smaller and smaller areas of responsibility. Narrow job descriptions separate work from larger purpose. Work isolates workers from each other. The growing trend of subcontracting work to people not associated directly with the institution threatens further isolation. As the nature of the economy has shifted from manufacturing to service and information systems, the visible, "public" nature of the products that workers create becomes more difficult to identify. Finally, the important work today in our society is considered to be the work of professionals, experts, and technicians, whose own work is generally cut off from a sense of larger purpose. Manual labor is devalued, and its attention to craft has been largely forgotten.

Work done by a mix of people around recognized public tasks of significance has dropped out of sight. Yet Mike Lefevre's anger at the devaluation of manual labor is a reminder that public work has been a vibrant theme in American history.

Public work is work *for* the public. It is also work *of* the public and *by* the public. It brings to the fore questions of responsibility, reciprocity, civic dignity, and accountability. The problem is that this understanding of citizenship has largely disappeared.

The Crisis of Citizenship

America faces problems on many fronts—from homelessness to deteriorating schools, from violence to teen pregnancy—problems that cannot be adequately addressed without substantial engagement by the general citizenry.

As recently as the 1960s, a deeper sense of citizenship was widespread. People could be challenged to think of the larger, long-range consequences of their efforts. Martin Luther King's famous "I Have a Dream" speech in front of the Lincoln Memorial captured this sense. In the program notes for that day, King and other leaders urged marchers to resist the efforts of those who promoted violence, in the language of the frontispiece of this chapter.

This kind of civic dignity has eroded. In our fieldwork in the past nine years at the Center for Democracy and Citizenship, we have seen many examples of people who have learned to act on problems that they were initially unable to imagine addressing.

For people to come to a view of themselves as active, effective citizens means most importantly realizing that civic action is simply hard work that can produce results. It is unpredictable. It means dealing with people who make us uncomfortable. It involves learning to think strategically, taking into account dynamics of power, interest, and the long-range consequences of one's action. Civic action on public questions rarely comes out entirely as we imagine, nor does it produce all the results that we might hope for. At the same time, it can have a catalytic effect, generating new sources of energy that are unanticipated.

It is possible to evaluate the impact of civic action. At the Center for Democracy and Citizenship, for instance, we use four categories to assess the impact of public work. First, public work builds tangible things of general usefulness, whose value can be measured. Second, public work can build capacities among individuals of all ages, and it also can strengthen institutional capacities for collaborative effort, both of which can be assessed. Thus in the Nehemiah story, churches strengthened their civic capacities because they learned to cooperate across denominational lines, and to work with many government agencies, businesses, and banks.

Third, public work can bring to the forefront new resources for problem solving. A public-work frame shifts thinking from a scarcity mindset, which assumes a relatively static understanding of resources, to a much more dynamic and multi-dimensional view of power sources. When addressing questions of crime and violence prevention, for example, resources are enormously multiplied when the question shifts from "How do we provide more police?" or "How can we create a stronger sense of community?" to "What can many different kinds of people and institutions contribute to creating a safe environment?"

Finally, attention to creating a larger culture of public work highlights the importance of assessing how well lessons from the work itself are integrated into the collective memory of a community. What has been the impact on ongoing education, media, arts and culture, and other ways a community has of passing on its public knowledge?

Effective citizenship thus depends on people thinking of themselves as productive: people who can build things and do things; people who come up with ideas and resources; people who are bold; people who are accountable. The problem is that today there are few places where people can develop these capacities. Instead, people have learned to expect to get things from the government and to demand that experts fix things.

In our youth and citizenship efforts, we regularly ask groups of young people and adults what to do about critical issues that they care about. They have ideas, but regularly they look to professionals and the government to solve their problems.

In one session, a group of deaf youngsters listed dozens of problems, from discrimination to phones that were unusable and teachers who did not know sign language. Afterwards, the two social workers with the group told our workshop leader that in more than twenty years of combined work with the deaf, they had never heard *anyone* ask hearing-impaired teenagers what they themselves could do about the problems that they experience.

Deaf youngsters dramatically illustrate "clienthood": Most disability programs view those whom they serve as people at risk, in need of help. The idea that people with disabilities might be capable of creative problem solving—and accountability for their actions—is not normally part of the training that professionals receive.

Civic Identity

The way people imagine what they can and ought to do powerfully shapes how they act. Think for a moment about the multiple functions of professional identities—whether as an occupational therapist or college professor of English, engineer or chemist. Professional identities define actions and behaviors. They develop through a long socialization process including formal credentialing, continuing education, and a system of rewards. Identities carry a set of ethical expectations. They pattern relationships with coworkers, other professions, and with clients. Professional identities structure ways of naming problems and planning strategies for action. Particular patterns of power, usually unnamed, operate in all of this.

In the 1990s the civic dimension of one's identity (that is, how work is tied to the rest of society) as a professional, or as a young person, parent, community member, factory worker, or almost anything else, is given little thought at all. This does not mean that people are apathetic about public affairs. It simply means that people see themselves largely as outsiders and observers in this arena, and they see their work as isolated from larger problems and purposes.

Currently, there are two dominant definitions of citizenship, neither of which has much to do with acting on demanding public problems.[8]

The first view of citizenship is what we learn in civics. The center of attention is on formal government: how a bill becomes law; how to vote; how to make one's views known to legislators. This perspective structures programs like the Youth in Government efforts of the YMCA or the civic education programs of the League of Women Voters. It also is the basis for grassroots lobbying which, over the years, has brought a broad range of groups into politics. During the sixties, "citizen participation" became the touchstone of many government programs. A number of training centers, across the political spectrum, developed to teach what had been the skills of elite groups of lobbyists.

Grassroots organizations continue to teach political skills to thousands of civic leaders. The problem is that simply expanding the number of players in the political game has done little to change the nature of the game itself. We have an explosion of demands and strategies aimed at winning resources and rights. Essentially, in these roles people are cast as client-consumers, asking the government for benefits. We have also seen, simultaneously, the fracturing of civic culture. A mood of rancor is widespread in America as a result. This has led to another version of citizenship that calls for renewed civility and community spirit.

In contrast to the government-centered approach, the second view of citizenship emphasizes a democracy of shared values and understandings achieved through a deliberative process. Those who promote this perspective stress a balance between responsibilities and individual rights. Above all, in this view, the purpose of politics should be to pursue the "common good." Responsibility, mutual regard, and understanding of difference are key outcomes.

Robert Bellah and his colleagues articulate this version in their best-selling 1986 book, *Habits of the Heart*. The book struck a nerve with many Americans because it vividly describes the loss of human connection and community that many experience. Its solutions are based on a proposition about people's moral interconnectedness.

Generosity of spirit is thus the ability to acknowledge an interconnectedness—one's debts to society—that binds one to others whether one wants to accept it or not. It is also the ability to engage in the caring that nurtures that interconnectedness. It is a virtue that everyone should strive for . . . a conception of citizenship that is still alive in America.[9]

New strategies for civic education have evolved reflecting this perspective, like the community service movement in K-12 education. Following Bellah's themes, community service projects in grade schools and high schools justify outcomes like "teaching skills of caring," "improving self-esteem," "heightening personal sensitivity," and "developing personal belief in the ability to make a difference."

A myriad of other practical initiatives have developed that reflect a similar meaning of citizenship. White House conferences on character building; national initiatives for parental responsibility; a veritable industry of "multicultural" programs on college campuses that teach prejudice reduction; proposals for more civil public discourse; and a seemingly endless number of conflict resolution consultants—all convey this outlook. Voluntarism itself (which has become virtually synonymous with this definition of "active citizen") embodies this spirit when it emphasizes voluntary action as mainly helping others. Voluntarism is today symbolized by a heart.

The idea of a more caring, morally interconnected society is important. Values of personal responsibility and concern for others are elementary ingredients of any functioning civic culture. The problem is that the call for community comes without much sense of how to achieve it other than exhortation to act on behalf of the "common good."

Public work highlights the reality of the conflict-filled nature of public affairs. Public life, even in the most harmonious of cases, is filled with diverse interests, antagonisms, disagreements, and unbalanced power relationships. Calls to care for each other easily purify citizenship. They substitute mutual care and individual responsibility for practical work on common tasks.

Citizenship in these terms can become a mile wide and an inch deep. When the tie between work and civic effort is severed, there is a dramatic loss of accountability and the idea of sustained commitment. The City Cares network, begun in 1986, reflecting the ironies of our age, provides a case in point. "From Atlanta and Miami to San Diego and Seattle, a new brand of youthful volunteerism is flourishing," reported *The New York Times.* "[It is] devoted to providing varied, flexible and guilt-free opportunities for young professionals to serve their communities." *The Times* describes how the network creates opportunities for volunteerism made easy. "If someone wakes up on Saturday morning in a mood to paint an elementary school, all she or he has to do is show up. If he had to head into the office or chooses to play tennis instead, no one calls to harangue him." One young woman, while sorting cans of corn for a food bank remarked, "If I don't show up for a month, no one's going to think I let them down."[10]

When citizenship lacks acknowledgment of the hard work required to impact the world, citizens inevitably become distanced from serious engagement in public affairs. Citizenship communicates an understanding of public identity, how people see their roles and range of action, and what they imagine themselves doing and as capable of doing. Today, the dominant approaches to citizenship lack substantial content for action.

Beyond Civics and Community

The idea of public work offers a different strategy for overcoming divisions among diverse groups of Americans than what is conventionally used by those who call for harmony and renewal of community spirit. Public work allows groups to put aside divisions for the sake of combined effort toward common ends. We can recognize the need to work with others whom we do not like, whom we do not agree with, and whom we see as far different than those in our own community when there are larger public purposes.

Citizenship of this kind is crucial today. The problem in America is often not so much the lack of morality as it is contending versions of morality. Blacks in South Chicago and white ethnics in Cicero, for instance, likely have different views of racial justice, based on different experiences. Seeking consensus may deepen the divide, not bridge it.

Work on common problems certainly raises value questions. Public life has pragmatic, problem-solving dimensions that bring together people with very different conceptions of what is just and right. It is more about taking action than it is about achieving consensus. Few causes lend themselves to the dramatic, wide moral agreement that civil rights or women's participation in public life achieved in the 1960s and 1970s.

On most pressing issues, values—what people care about most strongly—cannot be assumed before the fact. Rather, meaning and value are constantly reworked or created anew in the process of the work itself. In America's immensely diverse culture, it is only through the ongoing work of people with different perspectives that we can bring back traditions of the "commonwealth," a conception of shared life based on the things we make, which requires continual creation.

Public work teaches a different, richer, more complex view of "truth." At its best, it produces a collective wisdom and judgment, rather than individual opinion. It acknowledges that there are many different points of view and ways of thinking about things in public life. Rarely can a single viewpoint profess answers for the whole.

Public work generates new sources of energy. It brings together people, resources, and groups who may never have imagined working together. By creating new working relationships, it also changes the dynamics of power, often in significant ways.

The value of common work is evident throughout American history. The Civilian Conservation Corps (CCC) in the New Deal, for example, taught young men how to work together in spite of their diversity. The Corps was seen not simply as a jobs program. Rather it represented a national response to urgent public needs through the mobilization of the amateur labor of ordinary citizens. The CCC enrolled almost 3 million young men, mostly from poor, rural backgrounds, in an array of public projects that built a remarkable legacy for the nation. As important as anything was the experience of the public dimension that connected people beyond their immediate backgrounds and neighborhoods. Al Hammer of Minnesota recalls, "The CCC got people like me out into the public. I hadn't gotten out much and this gave me a chance to meet and work with people different than me from all over the country—farm boys, city boys, mountain boys, all worked together. I was a farm kid. I didn't know how other people lived or what other people thought about the world. In the CCC we didn't have a choice, we had to work together and get to know each other."[11]

Here and there, examples of public work in recent years have created bridges across bitter divisions. In several cities, a movement called Common Ground has brought together activists on both sides of the abortion controversy. It poses an alternative to the win-lose quality of conventional approaches.

The Common Ground Association in St. Louis began after an intense public controversy, following a challenge to a court decision which upheld a Missouri abortion law that restricted access to abortion. Activists from respective sides began working on issues of mutual concern: adoption, foster care, and the securing of adequate services and counseling for women and children. David Cohen of the Advocacy Institute, a citizen training center, served as an advisor throughout. Such public work relationships only can develop, in Cohen's view, if people have sufficient confidence to enable them to tackle public problems through a problem-solving, win-win approach. "It requires skills of actively listening to others with different views, the ability to take advantage of opportunities to address issues, and respect for confidentiality as the discussions and negotiations develop."[12]

Finally, public work in our time suggests fundamentally different understandings of work itself, in which professional and other work roles are basically recast. Expertise becomes something that is part of a larger citizen effort, not the solution to problems. In Tomah, Wisconsin, a public health project dealing with underage drinking found that the concept of public space where public work can take place was useful in generating productive relationships. In the process, the effort reshaped the ways a number of professionals thought about their work.

Jeanne Carls, the organizer of the project in Tomah, created a strategy team that involved a wide range of groups and interests that had never worked together before—police, merchants, bar owners, church leaders, parents, teenagers, as well as professionals in public health and treatment fields. "You tell people, there are going to be many different people coming together who you may have thought would never be at the same table, but can see the need to work on the same issue," Carls recounted. "It was like bringing two lions to the table in some cases. People would sit across the table and never say anything to each other directly. But they all had a strong interest in youth, and youth issues. As meetings progressed, you could see that each was beginning to look at what others could contribute in a new way."

Health care workers, city officials, and other citizens came to see themselves in a cooperative public process, not as professionals who alone were responsible for solutions. Dave Berner, the city manager, said that typically in his job, "people will come up to me—perhaps with a petition—and say, 'we want you to fix this issue. Could you bring this up at the city council?' " But the project on teenage drinking entailed a different approach in which he was one player among many. "I bring some specific skills and knowledge, like how things are really decided in city politics. But many others make contributions as well. In the last couple of years I have changed the way I think about my job."[13]

Public work in all of these cases generates a larger sense of significance and visibility. As Gerald Taylor, an organizer on the national staff of the Industrial Areas Foundation puts it, "Public work gives people the understanding that they are rewriting the history of their cities."[14]

Renewing democracy will mean that examples such as these are multiplied many times over, in many different settings. This will require that a variety of institutions create spaces for public work from the federal government to local schools, from YMCAs and YWCAs to 4-H clubs to professional associations, colleges, and the media. It will also require careful attention to lessons learned.

Public work is not an ideology or a blueprint, but it does provide a framework rich with resources for democratic action. Public work highlights the elemental fact that we all constantly participate in sustaining and creating our environments—our local institutions, our jobs, and workplaces, and on the larger scale, our government and politics.

Despite fragmentation and discouragement in America today, there are also openings for a renewal of public work. As traditional bureaucratic ways of addressing our public problems obviously do not work, people search for approaches that do. The very proliferation of information, facts, data, and knowledge that is part and parcel of the new "information society" demands something more. People are coming to recognize the need for public judgment in decision making, for a different kind of professionalism, for changes in institutions.[15]

The powerful meaning of citizenship conveyed by the idea of public work is the promise for democracy. It calls forth forgotten but rich and durable American identities of the citizen as producer. These have always existed in different forms—even in the midst of the most consumer-driven decades, like the 1950s, as we will see. It also recalls the legacy of a varied tradition of education for public life—from farmers institutes and labor education programs to urban settlements, from land-grant colleges to grassroots citizenship schools in the civil rights movement. These are what we have to build on, if we are to bring democracy to life again.

CHAPTER 2

The New Democracy

Experience proves that the very men whom you entrust with the support and defense of your most sacred liberties are frequently corrupt . . . if ever therefore your rights are preserved, it must be through the virtue and integrity of the middling sort, as farmers, tradesmen, & c. who despise venality and best know the sweets of liberty.

"Publius," for Philadelphia artisans, 1772 [1]

*T*he Working People's Social Science Club' was organized at Hull House in the spring of 1890 by an English workingman," writes Jane Addams in her autobiographical account of the famous settlement house. "For seven years it held a weekly meeting." The evenings were highly charged with intense conversation. "The enthusiasm of this club seldom lagged," Addams writes. "Its zest for discussion was unceasing." Participants insisted on questions of the most substantial and serious nature. "Everything was thrown back upon general principles and all discussion save that which 'went to the root of things' was impatiently discarded as an unworthy, halfway measure." With such spirit, the group's intent remained clear throughout. "Any attempt to turn it into a study or reading club always met with the strong disapprobation of the members."[2]

Nineteenth-century America created forums for public talk and work like this in a myriad of settings and cultures. These served as schools for citizenship. Ordinary people developed in them an assertiveness and self-confidence, as well as skills.

Americans' challenge to custom and hierarchy left foreign visitors aghast. White "lower classes . . . have a tendency to be saucy and insolent," said one. Charles Augustus Murray observed that there was no proper sense of title at all. Upon first acquaintance, "farm-assistants and labourers called me 'Charlie,' " whereas the tavern owner expected to be called "General" and a local handyman "Colonel." "Everybody talks to you," complained Charles Dickens. Commonly, Europeans described the penchant of Americans to talk to strangers. "Wherever you go, you are surrounded by men (who never saw you before in their lives) who immediately have a thousand questions," said one newcomer. "Diffidence," said another, "is scarcely to be met with in the United States." The country, he groused, "greatly promotes fluency of speech."[3] Accounts like these give us a glimpse of the great democratic conversation that filled the nineteenth century.

American democracy gave its distinctive stamp to an ancient tradition. Democracy acquired an indelible connection to work and was expressed in many forms of public life, from economic associations to public debating clubs, from voluntary organizations to groups that agitated for moral renewal and education reform. These created an historical legacy of democracy of larger meaning than we have today. The wider aims of public work were especially described by the language of the commonwealth.

Democracy as an idea was the extraordinary achievement of the Greeks. Democracy means simply that "political power is exercised by the people." Early on, the Greeks—most explicitly the Athenians—in response to the possibilities and challenges of their time, crafted a public sphere. Citizens were free men from all economic and social backgrounds who came together to address common problems. The freedom and power that flowed from their experience of collective self-determination have echoed across the centuries.

A modern lens highlights the sharp exclusions and limits of Greek democracy. Women, slaves, youth, and non-Athenians were consigned to private existence, *idion*. (This is the root of our word idiot). Feminists have argued persuasively that the sharp separation between public sphere, *polis*, and private life, *oikos*, was possible precisely because women were consigned to the *oikos*, and largely barred from the public world.[4]

The deliberations of Greek citizens in the public domain were not inclusive. They did not address many issues. Matters of work were largely excluded from public life. Most citizens were hardworking, but according to Greek historian Christian Meier, from the vantage of the *polis*, work was looked on with relative disdain because it was a necessity, full of hardship. In part, this attitude conveyed the way the aristocracy had always viewed labor. Aristocrats themselves took matters one step further, viewing work with frank disgust. Aristotle, reflecting such a view, termed work a "curse."[5]

Questions of the *oikos*, or household management and social patterns, were also not subject to public discussion. Rather, in the Assembly Athenians deliberated on what were considered public things, or the "commonwealth": laws, public works projects, food supplies, matters of foreign policy, and war.

Thus, the public sphere existed in a society full of undemocratic features. Its range of topics was limited. But in many ways, its democratic equality was all the more dramatic because of the contrasts. Greek writers and orators, playwrights, and poets make vivid the intense seriousness with which citizens took on their public roles. For Greek citizens, involvement in public life offered visibility, recognition, and freedom. Citizens acted together on the great topics of their time. Pericles in his famous Funeral Oration praised the remarkable fighting spirit of Athenian democrats, who defeated the soldiers of authoritarian Sparta. "Only among us is a man who takes no part [in political affairs] called, not a quiet citizen, but a bad citizen."[6]

Different societies create democracies with different faces. A people's cultural traditions, history, and aspirations, all influence democracy's shape and character. In the nineteenth century, America offered wide-open social and physical frontiers—free spaces in which to build a new country. In the process of nation building in the decades after the Revolution, Americans also transformed their understandings of citizenship and public life from something that mainly elite members of the gentry engaged in, as leisure time activities, into a part of everyday experience.

Formal institutions like governments or established churches were relatively weak. Places for public conversation and action abounded. Ordinary Americans claimed the ideas of citizenship, public affairs, and politics, once beyond their reach, and spread a new democracy throughout the country.

The uniqueness of nineteenth-century American democracy was especially its tie to work. Democratic ideas of freedom and independence were made practical through the notion that citizens (free white men) owned their own labor. Most were self-employed farmers and artisans. They owned their own tools. They could determine what they produced. Strong individualistic identities developed around their craft as a result. Growing from such experiences of self-direction, working men also made collective decisions about their lives. Thus American democracy, acquired a practical, down-to-earth quality. Through a language of the commonwealth it also conveyed larger, even luminous dimensions when people were able to connect their daily labor to building America.

Civic Virtue

Throughout millennia, those who looked to Greek and Roman republics for models of active citizenship believed leisure, not work, was essential to "civic virtue." Gentlemanly virtue depended on several criteria: the ability to escape normal constraints of labor; a cultured and cosmopolitan outlook; an avoidance of corruptions of the marketplace and profit-making; and a particular distancing of one's immediate self-interests. Civic-minded gentlemen devoted themselves instead to public service without any thought of their personal gain.

America's educated and established leaders reflected this viewpoint during the Revolution and afterward. On his way to become minister to Great Britain, John Adams's conviction about the honor of a gentleman led him to refuse his turn at the pump when the boat was in danger of sinking and passengers were asked to help. In Adams's view "it was not befitting a person who had public status" to do such manual labor.[7]

During the Revolution, educated, elite leaders hoped that their view of citizenship—public service concerned only with the "public good," not individual gain or self interest—might spread to some degree among the "middling" levels of society. To many England seemed "one mass of corruption" and "tottering on the brink of destruction," whereas America was a land where the "ancient English tradition of liberty" might still survive through dedication to the public welfare. As the Trenton *New Jersey Gazette* put it:

> Here Governments their last perfection take.
> Erected only for the People's sake:
> Founded no more on Conquest or in blood,
> But on the basis of the Public Good.[8]

Yet most established leaders quickly became disillusioned with the plain people, their intelligence and their motivations. Men like John Adams and James Madison largely abandoned earlier hopes that people below them in the social order might come to see civic involvement as they had hoped they would. The Articles of Confederation, the nation's first constitution, seemed to produce constant bickering and divisions among the states. Events like Shay's Rebellion in Massachusetts, in which farmers sought to overthrow a government they viewed as all too much like the British, alarmed many large landowners and affluent merchants. By the 1780s, elites increasingly worried about the "chaos" and disorder engendered by decentralized government and the popular participation of groups of mechanics, artisans, small farmers, and other independent craftsmen in any sort of public affairs.

The Constitution and the Federalist argument resulted, based on the belief that civic virtue—concern for the general interests and the commonweal—was in short supply among the general population. By the time of the early 1790s, during debates over adoption of the Constitution, John Adams vigorously disputed the natural inclination of citizens to put the commonweal over private interests: "Not only a majority, but almost all, confine their benevolence to their families, relations, personal friends, parish, village, city, county, province. . . . Very few, indeed, extend it impartially to the whole community." Alexander Hamilton put it even starker terms: "*Every man* ought to be supposed a *knave;* and to have no other end, in all his actions, but *private interest.* By this interest we must govern him; and, by means of it, *make him cooperate to public good,* not withstanding his insatiable avarice and ambition."[9]

Voices of the gentry were not the only party in the conversation, however. Their view of public service and leisure came under unrelenting criticism and popular scorn in the late eighteenth and early nineteenth centuries. As the historian Gordon Wood has put it, "when [classical ideals of disinterested civic virtue] proved too idealistic and visionary, [Americans] found new democratic adhesives in the actual behavior of plain ordinary people."[10]

Urban artisans and working people, as well as farmers, stressed labor as a source of public virtue far different than leisure. Thomas Paine, especially, among Revolutionary leaders drew his inspiration from the common sense and dedication to liberty he believed resided among artisans, farmers, and other "middling sorts." Paine was a eloquent spokesman for those like Publius who begins this chapter.

As early as the 1760s, mechanics in Charleston, South Carolina, responded to William Henry Drayton, a wealthy planter who thought them unfit to participate in government on the grounds that they lacked education in the liberal arts. Most everyone, they replied, could be said to have a measure of common sense. But perhaps Mr. Drayton was an exception, "his upper works being damaged by some rough treatment of the person who conducted his birth" in a way that "cannot be compensated by all the learning of the schools." Mr. Drayton, despite what they termed "his great condescension," might "allow us a place amongst human beings." But mechanics were considerably more valuable than that. In fact, they merited the designation of "the most useful people in a community." In contrast, they asked if Mr. Drayton could "claim any merit from his possessing an estate not obtained or obtainable by his own industry?"[11]

By the 1790s, Jeffersonians described the Federalist gentry as reared "in idleness, dissipation, and extravagance," whereas they claimed they represented instead, "the industrious part of the community." America, in their view, was divided between those who work, on the one hand, and those who "live on the stock of the community, already produced, not by *their labor* but obtained by their *art* and *cunning* or that of their ancestors" on the other hand. According to William Manning, a self-taught New England farmer, the nation faced a struggle between "those that Labour for a Living and those that git a Living without Bodily labour." The latter included "the merchant, phisition, lawyer & divine, the philosipher, and school master, the Juditial & Executive Offers & many others."[12]

America reveled in work from the vantage of many foreign visitors. One Scotsman arriving at Eastport, Maine, expressed shock that dock workers "did not walk quietly and soberly up the gangway with the heavy packages or wheelbarrows; they leaped, jumped, ran . . . all rushing up with their burdens and flying down for a fresh load."[13]

The down-to-earth quality of American democracy reflected the fact that it was an overwhelmingly agricultural society. Nine out of ten people lived on the land in 1790. In 1860, eight out of ten continued to live in nonurban areas, farms or villages with less than 2,500 population. "In countries thinly inhabited, or where people live principally by agriculture, as in America, everyman is in some measure an artist," declared Noah Webster in the late eighteenth century. "He makes a variety of utensils, rough indeed, but such as will answer his purpose—he is a husbandman in summer, and a mechanic in winter." The tie to land and everyday production created an exemplary model for work centered democracy in subsequent generations.[14]

In politics, the rising tide and common experience of feeling that valued productive labor over the leisured gentry swept the country. Merchants, small artisans, manufacturers, and mill workers, all were angered by the contempt of a gentry who labeled them "commoners." Men like Christopher Leffingwell, a manufacturer in Connecticut, and Joseph Williams, the richest man in Norwich, despite their wealth, had also felt scorned by the gentry. Thus they made alliances with artisans as part of the "laboring interest" who supported "the general or common interest" of the whole community against those they considered aristocrats and unproductive parasites.[15]

The argument that work can be for the public good gave visibility to the civic contributions of many outside the formal political arena. Figures such as Benjamin Franklin—inventor, printer, editor, as well as public statesman—became the archetypal example of civic "hero." Indeed, in America public service and profit making were not necessarily mutually exclusive. In fact, the linkage was often valued. Only in the United States, argued Francis Grund, a European observer, had labor become fully respectable; only here was "industry an honor, and idleness a disgrace." Similarly the Frenchman Michel Chevalier observed that in England, businessmen worked only in the mornings. The rest of the day they posed as gentlemen. In contrast, "the American of the North and the Northwest whose character sets the tone in the United States is permanently a man of business, he is always the Englishman of the morning." Alexis de Tocqueville found it amazing that not only was work itself "honorable," but "work specifically to gain money" was honorable. In Europe, he wrote, there were "hardly any public officials who do not claim to serve the state without interested motives. Their salary is a detail to which sometimes they give a little thought and to which they always pretend to give none."[16]

Thus, by the early decades of the nineteenth century, the broad array of those who linked "productive labor" to democracy had carried the day, at least in rhetoric. Elites that did not spend time in gainful employment did not advertise the fact. Even southern plantation owners heralded their hard work—though their aristocratic pretensions also fueled conflict.

Yet American democracy, like the Greek *polis,* existed in the midst of a surrounding environment of exclusions and inequalities, the consequences of which we still struggle with. A focus on work brings with it, in fact, possibilities for new exclusions. Full citizens are those whose work is visible, valued, and self-directed. The exclusions from a democracy based on work, as well as its inclusions, are useful in highlighting the meanings and implications of "public work."

In starkest terms, the story of African American slaves illustrates the importance of some significant measure of self-direction and autonomy in public work. Slaves did not own their own labor. Black men and women also did not have access to the formal political world of white men. Thus they lacked the ability to negotiate democratic rights. Their roles in the more general public arena were brutally circumscribed—they appeared in the balconies and on the margins, in subservient roles.

Slaves were far from being simply victims, but their own work life and social activities were largely invisible. Only in subterranean places, on the margins of plantations and after hours, did blacks engage in self-directed work. There, in a sense, they created alternative public arenas where they were visible to each other, if not to dominant whites. John Vlach describes the free spaces created within the rigid confines of plantation life. "Slaves did not move through the plantation in the same way as whites, nor were they expected to." Slaves were not expected to conform to the manners and customs of white society—they escaped, in a fashion, the formality that so defined southern civility. Slaves gardened and planted crops, created their own handicrafts, tools, buildings, and other products. And they found spaces for their own worship: From Christianity which was taught to them as an effort to break blacks from African cultural traditions, they forged their own distinctive language of religion, aimed at freedom. "Understood to be a servant people, their place was defined as both away from and outside of . . . the formality that planters had so carefully laid out. They were under control but they were not totally coerced by that control," says Vlach.[17]

Women constituted a second exclusion from American democracy, in a way that illustrates the importance of public spaces for public work. Women's work, although valued, was not the same as men's self-directed work, precisely because it occurred in the private sphere, and thus was far less visible. Their world of work was largely defined by boundaries of household and family relations, or at least by domestic identities. European visitors, especially women, often remarked on the sharp divisions between the sexes and the relative exclusion of women from formal public life.

Yet as with blacks the patterns were complex. Though excluded from formal politics and defined in subordinate ways in many public arenas, women also created out of their domestic roles and identities distinctive public spaces of their own. These included wide-ranging networks of religious associations, voluntary groups, moral reform efforts, and education campaigns. There was constant argument and conflict across the whole society over women's public activities. As one minister put it in 1859, seeking (unsuccessfully) to prohibit women from forming a women's prayer group, "who knows what they would pray for if they did it by themselves?"[18]

In nineteenth-century America the fusion of democracy and work was a radical conceptual change. This was the first time people's everyday lives, once thought private affairs, were connected to the public realm in ways that generated a wide sense of participation and stake in public life. At the same time, such a tie was fraught with complexities. Work-centered democracy, in sum, raised new questions of power. It put on the public table new topics and concerns. Work also made connections between individuals and small groups and larger communities and the nation as a whole. These issues, in turn, were expressed and argued out in the language of the commonwealth.

Taking Care of the Commons

Today *commonwealth* is a musty, forgotten term. It brings to mind the old governments of the British empire, perhaps, or the states of Massachusetts, Virginia, Kentucky, and Pennsylvania, all of which are called "commonwealths." But in the eighteenth and nineteenth centuries and through the 1930s in America, the term *commonwealth* had vibrant power. It was both a description of what American democracy *was* and, simultaneously, it was a dramatic, compelling vision of what it could be and should become. The commonwealth was created by public work, and thus popular and lower-class groups could claim central standing and authority.

Commonwealth, like democracy, public life, and citizenship, had associations that made it powerful for both educated elites and the popular classes. But these associations were quite different. For educated leaders, "commonwealth" summed up the classical tradition of government responsive to citizens. For popular groups, the term conveyed a much more down-to-earth notion of "the commons," those basic public goods in which all had a stake and which all needed to help build and preserve.

Commonwealth was a term for the Greek *polis,* the Roman republic, and the Italian city states of the Renaissance. In the American colonies, it conveyed the struggles against the British monarchy for expanded rights. "Commonwealth" had early become identified with the concept of the public, the established and recognized body of citizenry. In this way it connected to the idea of republican government in which "the whole people" had voice. By the seventeenth century, commonwealth customarily meant the idea of government *of* and *by* free citizens, instead of the crown. Thus, the Parliamentary act of May 19, 1649, ending the monarchy declared "That the People of England . . . shall henceforward be Governed as a Commonwealth and Free State." Thus, during the American Revolution commonwealth suggested a republican government—a popular alternative to the monarchy. John Adams urged that every state declare itself a commonwealth, and four eventually did so officially.

Even more important than the associations with political tradition and theory, commonwealth had power for farmers, artisans, small business, and others through its association with the idea of common (public) work. "Commonwealth" meant simply what one took care of collectively.[19]

This association drew on old traditions. In English history, deliberation by villagers about the exercise of the rights and upkeep of common lands, footpaths, farm lands, and fishing areas, as well as maintenance of common buildings like the village church, gave middle-level peasantry a constant, daily schooling in rough democracy. Sometimes village communities collaborated with lords, sometimes they engaged in bitter struggle with them. But there was customarily space for regular deliberation over commons issues. Male villagers regularly promulgated laws, sometimes in joint consultation with lords. Churches, as community centers, were especially important to the commons. Village churches provided space for multiple purposes: feasts and celebrations, public deliberation, refuge from raids, dances, marketplace, and sometimes even theater for pagan plays. As Edward Miller and John Hatcher have put it, Parishioners "were called on to keep the nave in repair, the churchyard in good order, to provide many items of equipment including . . . bells for the steeple, a pyx, a Lenten veil, a font, a bier for the dead, a vessel for holy water and certain other items of equipment." Churches were supported through taxes and tithes of corn, garden produce, and livestock, as well.[20]

Traditions of the commons were transplanted to the colonies with the first European settlers of the seventeenth century. Indeed, immigrants left England and other nations in some cases partly out of distaste for the spreading practices of "engrossing," that saw the gentry seize common lands by force or purchase. New England settlers typically created a pattern of one "house lot" from one to ten acres for each family, with shares in the common lands of pasture, wood, and meadow. A separate land was set aside for the church and meeting house, often adjoining the town green, or commons, "which provided a kind of physical axis of the community and served other community functions—militia muster, farmers market, even in some places, common pasture."[21]

In the first settlements, most crops were grown in common fields, but the soil and weather in New England proved not to be as favorable to single-crop planting, and soon individual planting of a variety of crops became the norm. Continuing immigration into towns also created sharp political tensions: Were newcomers to get a share in the commons, for instance? Did they receive land for a household lot— the very symbol of citizenship in English society? The commons, in short, was an object of constant debate, discussion, and conversation.

These practices of collective effort to build and sustain things of value to communities expanded throughout the nineteenth century and came to include social welfare, in addition to material public works. This dynamic created the vast and rich array of formal and informal associations that observers like Alexis de Tocqueville said was most typically American. Practices of concern for the community and national welfare on broad topics involved many groups with seemingly quite different aims. For instance, the Women's Christian Temperance Union (WCTU) of the late nineteenth century sought to control the "demon rum." Yet it combined moral reform agitation with communal problem-solving efforts. Its slogan was "Do-Everything." By 1889, WCTU activities in Chicago included nurseries, Sunday schools, an industrial school, a homeless shelter, a free medical dispensary, and a lodging for poor men.[22]

These efforts often gave groups who had been excluded from public arenas a new sense of their power. As Frances Willard, the WCTU's guiding force, put it:

> Perhaps the most significant outcome of this movement was the knowledge of their own power gained by the conservative women of the Churches. They had never even seen a 'woman's rights' convention,' and had been held aloof from the 'suffragists' by fears as to their orthodoxy; but now there were women prominent in all Church cares and duties eager to clasp hands for a more aggressive work than such women had ever before dreamed of undertaking.[23]

These traditions of public work for the commons also generated a vibrant culture of public talk.

Public Talk

America overflowed with public talk. Foreign observers were constantly struck by contentious street corner debates, public disputations, political festivals, and democratic self-education movements.

John Adams, with his patrician gaze, nonetheless conveyed a confidence in such talk in a letter to his wife, Abigail, in 1776. "Time has been given for the whole People, maturely to consider the great Question of Independence and to ripen their Judgments, dissipate their Fears, and allure their Hopes, by discussing it in News Papers and Pamphletts, by debating it, in Assemblies, Conventions, Committees of Safety and In-spection, in Town and County Meetings, as well as in private Conversations."[24]

The view of the citizenry as a deliberative, talking body produced large civic education movements through the nineteenth century.

Voluntary citizen organizations played a key role in public education. Public libraries created through citizen efforts, for example, were justified as "arsenals of democracy." In the early 1830s, John Holbrook's Lyceum Movement created adult learning centers in order to provide forums for citizens to discuss public affairs. By 1837, the movement included an estimated 3,000 towns. After the Civil War, the Chatauqua Assembly movement continued this legacy, eventually including 15,000 "home study circles" for discussion of public affairs. Similarly, university extension programs, adopted from England in the 1880s, were designed to promote better rural citizenship, as well as improved farming. In poor and immigrant communities, institutions like the Workmen's Circle and settlement houses educated citizens to current public issues.

More generally, public language assumed the common sense and intelligence of ordinary people and challenged the pretensions of any who spoke in arcane fashion. Medical advice was a good illustration. "No discovery can ever be of general utility while the practice of it is kept in the hands of a few," wrote William Buchan, whose *Domestic Medicine* became a standard popular guide from the late eighteenth through the mid-nineteenth centuries. Buchan subtitled his work as "an attempt to render the Medical Art more generally useful, by showing people what is in their own power both with respect to the Prevention and Cure of Diseases." Buchan argued that "every thing valuable in the practical part of medicine is within reach of common sense." John C. Gunn's *Domestic Medicine,* published in 1830, followed in this vein. Gunn proposed that Latin words for common medicine were intended "to *astonish the people*" and aid in deception and fraud. "The more nearly we can place men on a level of equality in point of *knowledge,* the happier we would become in a society with each other, and the less danger there would be of *tyranny.*"[25]

At the same time, Americans valued common sense. Many artisans, mechanics, and others who named themselves freethinkers simultaneously held that engagement with large ideas must infuse everyday life. They believed that working people could realize democratic possibility only as they became free in their thinking from the control of unreflected convention—religious orthodoxy, traditionalism, or deference to political authority. Such convictions spawned a wide variety of workers' education movements, debating societies, and other organizations dedicated to the legacy of Thomas Paine. For instance, by the 1830s, New York had become a center of free thought activity, with organizations like the Society of Free Inquirers, the Temple of Arts, the Minerva Institution, and the Institution of Practical Education proliferating. Their vision, writes the historian, Sean Wilentz, was "a world turned upside down where men [*sic*] would truly be able to think, reflect, and act for themselves, free of aristocratic and religious tyranny: Where one would find according to a freethinkers' toast 'soldiers at the plow, kings in the mines, lawyers at the spinning genney, and priests in heaven.' "[26]

Democratic manners and common work were distinctive features of public life in nineteenth-century America. As the society changed, another aspect of the commonwealth tradition of public work also shaped the country. Commonwealth was not only a descriptive term. It also conveyed an ideal. The commonwealth was a vision of a future society of equality and justice. Its spirit had contagious effect. It inspired a myriad of struggles against exclusions and injustices of all kinds.

The Cooperative Commonwealth

From the beginning of the nation and before, those who challenged authority, the rich and powerful, often used a language of commonwealth to describe their aims. During the Revolutionary period, the commonwealth concept of property—the notion that property is created through common work—served as rallying cry for many. Thus, in the midst of the economic crisis in Philadelphia in 1779, artisans challenged Robert Morris, a wealthy merchant, for shipping grain outside the city. In view of the local scarcity of bread, they argued that Morris's property rights to use his ship were held in check by the social origins of property and the needs of the community. "We hold that [the shipyard workers] and the state in general have a right in the service of the vessel," they argued, "because it constitutes a considerable part of the advantage [the workers] hoped to derive from their labours." Property is subject to the commonwealth, they continued: "The *property* of the vessel is the immediate right of the owners," but "the service of it is the right of the community collectively with the owners."[27]

In Rhode Island, a series of fierce battles between farmers and mill owners took place over farmers' common-law right "to enter the close of his neighbor, for the purpose of abating or removing the cause of injury" when owners built dams and thus damaged the fishing in the rivers, long regarded as a commons. In 1773, petition campaigns and agitation by backcountry farmers upriver from Pawtucket Falls caused the General Assembly to enact a law with the title, "An act making it lawful to break down and blow up Rocks at Pawtucket Falls to let fish pass up." In 1785, the Assembly limited the rights of sawmill owners to the Pawtucket River valley to dam the rivers during the spring runs.

In other parts of the state, however, farmers were not as successful. Sixty-six farmers from Cranston and Warwick petitioned the Assembly on the ground that dams and commercial fishermen's nets were preventing alewives from spawning, adding that "before said obstructions said fish were taken in great plenty and were of infinite advantage to the Poor and middling sort of People." They claimed an "unalienable right" to fish in the rivers, but the Assembly ruled against them. Throughout this period in successful struggles and defeats alike, farmers found in the commonwealth vocabulary of the Revolution a way to frame their tangible concerns.[28]

These traditions of commonwealth property shaped American legal theory as well. Lemuel Shaw, Chief Justice of the Massachusetts Supreme Court from 1830 to 1860, drew on these ideas of collective well-being and the social nature of property in his commonwealth theory of jurisprudence. He held that government was the agent of the people to be used for the good of the country as a whole. Shaw taught that "all property . . . is derived directly or indirectly from the government, and held subject to those general regulations that are necessary to the common good and general welfare."[29]

Throughout the nineteenth century, groups such as the poor, slaves, immigrants, and women all were able to draw on this repertoire of images about work and the commonwealth to press their causes and demands for fuller participation. After the Civil War, a range of radicals and reformers used a vocabulary of commonwealth to challenge large-scale systems of concentrated power. Thus, former slaves proposed a distribution of land—"40 acres and a mule"—that would allow them full rights as citizens. Frances Harper, a nineteenth-century African American poet, challenged the nation to live up to its ideals of freedom. In 1875 she wrote that, "The great problem to be solved by the American people is this: Whether or not there is strength enough in democracy, virtue enough in our civilization and power enough in our religions to have mercy and deal justly with four millions of people lately translated from the old oligarchy of slavery to the new commonwealth of freedom."

Language of freedom such as that used by Harper provided a tremendously powerful resource for freed slaves to press their claim for education, for land, and for political rights. Even though their fullest hopes were not to be realized, the vocabulary of a commonwealth of freedom contributed to important victories, like the Fourteenth Amendment which became the touchstone for subsequent generations of civil rights agitation and litigation.[30]

Women's rights crusaders envisioned a "maternal commonwealth" as an alternative to the male-dominated public world, which they argued was increasingly brutal and corrupt. Similarly, labor organizers called for a "cooperative commonwealth" where small producers and cooperative enterprise would replace the new trusts and corporations.[31]

A striking feature of these commonwealth movements was their often relatively diverse and pluralist quality. The concept of labor for the commonwealth—and challenges to those who would undermine or threaten the dignity and independence of such labor through unfair labor practices or insufficient compensation—provided a way for people to imagine working with people in common cause across considerable ideological and cultural division.

Late-nineteenth-century populism, for instance, was a movement largely based on small farmers. They fought what they saw as the dangers that rails, merchants, and others posed to family farming. The populists were not free of the prejudices woven through the dominant political culture—indeed, racial animosities, especially, proved a fatal line of division in the face of a determined assault in the South.

For a decade, however, populism's demands for public control over levers of community and economic life like the rails and the money supply helped to create a public space. The movement was far more tolerant of difference than either the dominant culture or political movements that aimed at conversion to a single truth. The populist movement's main base was white family farmers, but it also attracted support from African American tenants and landowners, urban professionals and intellectuals, women's suffragists, ethnic communities, Hispanics in the Southwest, railroad workers, and a variety of others. This wide mix of interests found some common ground in the aspiration of broad democratic control over economic power.

Similarly, the Knights of Labor, the populists' labor ally, created a wide-ranging and pluralist movement of workers in the 1880s. It included factory workers, farmers, professionals and small merchants—almost everyone was eligible, except lawyers. Its strength, wrote the Boston *Labor Leader,* was found "in the fact that the whole life of the community is drawn into it, that people of all kinds are together."[32]

Thus the language of the commonwealth helped people develop tools and programs of democratic change in two ways. In the first place, it allowed working people of many backgrounds, trades, cultures, and settings to point to and make visible the importance of their labor—to make it public. The language of the commonwealth also highlighted important sources of inequality or threat to productive labor and the larger public interest. Although this tradition has greatly weakened in our time, it retains a subterranean power on the basis of these two components.

Today it takes conscious, artful effort to retrieve public work and its larger meanings and resonances. The commonwealth language in recent years has provided resources to accomplish this task. The commonwealth holds within itself the labor that creates and sustains "the commons," thus making visible that work helps illustrate and substantiate the idea of commonwealth as well. It can reveal larger purposes and significance of work, by bringing to center stage the very meaning of wealth and progress. These issues are highlighted in the modern commonwealth story of Seattle's Lake Union.

A Commonwealth Retrieved

Seattle, Washington, today at first sight seems overwhelmingly oriented to the future, not the past. The airport reflects advanced technology, with cavernous spaces and automated trains. The drive into the city curves like spaghetti past the "space needle," left over from a

World's Fair, and takes one into glass and steel canyons at the city's center.

But there remains an older heritage alive beneath the modern gloss. On a clear day, the stunning natural beauty of the city is augmented by an abundance of trees and public gardens filled with scotch broom, purple heather, foxglove, daffodils, rhododendron, and forsythia. Similarly, the richly textured human environment mingles old-fashioned scenes with landmarks of change. Seattle is a city of neighborhoods, many still bearing the names of original ethnic villages: Greenwood, Belltown, Ballard, and Fremont, all of which joined together at the turn of the century.

The waterfront is the city's focal point. Sailboats are everywhere alongside trawlers, ferries, and tugboats. The Pike Place Market in the city's central district has retained the sort of jumbled, crazy-quilt diversity and informality that downtown San Francisco has lost. Merchants from dozens of nationalities display wares and foods: Alex's Phillipine Cuisine; Hassan Brothers; and the Athenian, where old retired sailors from the low-income housing project across the street gather and sip coffee. There are fruit and vegetable and fish stalls selling hundreds of different goods, from garlic to Alaskan crabs.

Whatever the complexities of progress in Seattle, the city retains a balance with its older traditions that many communities have lost. How was this accomplished? Part of the answer lies in the successful efforts of Terry Pettus, a long-time newspaper man and activist who kept alive a vision of public work for "the commonwealth," long after it disappeared in the country as a whole.

In the 1920s, Terry Pettus and his wife, Berta, moved to Seattle, where Pettus became a newspaperman and well-known writer. Over the next two decades, Pettus was a leading figure in many popular movements: the fight for public utilities and rural electrification; efforts to achieve the referendum; a campaign to win industrial accident insurance and old-age pensions. At the heart of each, in his view, was the notion of the whole, the common good.

In the mid-1930s, labor unions, farmers, and neighborhood groups came together during the Great Depression in a new political movement to press their interests. Calling themselves the Washington Commonwealth Federation, they drew on older currents of radicalism. Organized by precincts, the Commonwealth Federation in the late 1930s and 1940s became the dominant force in the state Democratic Party, sending several congressmen to Washington, at times controlling the state legislature.[33]

However, in the early 1950s, the mood of the country changed sharply as charges of subversion were leveled against radicals and reformers of all kinds. Pettus, target of FBI investigations, was convicted under the Smith Act and spent six months in jail before his conviction was overturned. Once free, he decided to retire after a life-career as a journalist and activist. He wrote mystery novels. Retirement lasted a decade.

In 1933, Terry and Berta had purchased and moved into a houseboat on Seattle's Lake Union. At that time, over a thousand houseboats were moored close together along the lake near the center of town. Houseboaters paid dirt cheap rents for moorage. From the beginning, the houseboaters included an interesting mix of people. Boatyard workers, sailors, students, and bohemians mingled with retired radicals from the revolutionary union, Industrial Workers of the World. Large numbers of the city's poor, who could scarcely afford to live anywhere else, also lived in the houseboat area. Along the shores, speakeasies and brothels were scattered through the small shacks and apartments. "It was a breeding ground for nonconformity," wrote Howard Droker, who authored a history of the houseboats.[34]

From the beginning of the settlement by Europeans, and arguably of Indians as well, Lake Union was a "working lake." In the 1870s, barges carrying coal and lumber crossed the water, heading from the nation's interior to the rail lines on the western shore. In those years, much of the shoreline retained its natural quality. Wildlife on the waterfront was plenty. A hunter killed a cougar there in 1870.

In the first years of the great boom in immigration, which increased the city's size from 3,533 in 1880 to 237,194 in 1910, streetcars and rail lines made the lake accessible from all the surrounding villages. In the twentieth century, boat works and dry docks appeared along the shore, servicing water vessels of all kinds. Along with the expanding commercial activity came the first houseboaters.

City officials had long looked askance at the floating community as a "health hazard." At the same time, real estate developers had coveted the lakeshore. They exerted growing pressure on the city to take action. In 1962, the city administration moved vigorously to evict boaters, in order to acquire the land to erect apartment buildings and other development projects along the lakefront.

A major complaint against the houseboats in the 1960s was sewage pollution on the lake. Few knew that in fact the city of Seattle itself dumped raw sewage into Lake Union through thirteen sewer lines. The boaters' contribution was minuscule—something like one-half of 1 percent of the total. Houseboaters knew they could never win by debating percentages, or claiming "less responsibility" than others, so they turned the issue on its head. To the consternation of the city, they demanded that they be permitted to pay for sewer lines to their boats. The Floating Homes Association, the houseboaters group, held workshops on how to weld pipes and how to hook up sewer lines. In the process they found new allies, like the city's health department.

Most thought the rugged individualists of Lake Union could never be organized, but Pettus understood the power of a larger vision. "People will fight for their existence, if not for abstractions," he explained. The Floating Homes Association formed to solidify the houseboat community. But instead of banding together to fight city hall, they redefined the issue. They tied their own fate to the future of the city as a whole. "We knew we could never win if the issue was simply the survival of the houseboats," said Pettus.

Drawing on the commonwealth legacy which had shaped Pettus's politics for decades, Pettus and his neighbors described the problem in commonwealth terms. They created a broad vision of Lake Union as the commonwealth of the people of Seattle—"a gift to us from the Ice Age." Key to the strategy was connecting the heritage of the city and the lake to the idea of practical work.

They created a public conversation about control over the future in a variety of ways. As the campaign developed, houseboaters connected the idea of the lake as an environmental resource with the concept of the lake as working lake, a lake *of* and *for* public work. Its multiple uses—recreation, commerce, residency—all were interconnected. The process of the campaign itself was diverse public work. Houseboaters sponsored tours. They led in the building of a public park. They created social events and festivals. They made alliances across the city. They made the lake, its legacy, and its symbolism come alive.

Citizen action had dramatic effect. By late 1963, the city, responding to the association's remarkable popular support, initiated a study that called for protection of the lake. With such a statement, the association was able to block industrial use of a large area; press the city to acquire 23 acres to create a public park; and inspire the state legislature to pass one of the nation's strongest shoreline management control acts on new development. Terry Pettus helped write the legislation.

By the early 1970s, the spirit of the houseboaters' victory energized a number of other citizen efforts. The historic Pike Place Market was saved from the developers when a local architect and friend of Pettus's, Victor Steinbrueck, framed the controversy in broad commonwealth language. He touted the market as an irreplaceable part of the city's heritage.

At the decade's end, Seattle had achieved national recognition as a pioneer in a number of neighborhood-based programs and participatory civic initiatives, most of which could trace their roots one way or another to the Lake Union fight which drew directly on the commonwealth vision that Terry Pettus reinvigorated. Even traditional establishment leaders who fought the community activists acknowledged the benefits. "Seattle had a major era of citizen participation," said James Ellis, a man sometimes called the informal leader of the city's elite. As a result, "there was an incredible flowering in the city."[35]

The houseboaters' greatest contribution was to make Lake Union take on a much larger meaning as symbol of people's work and connection, the city's diverse interests, and its future possibilities. In the process they retrieved the nineteenth-century traditions of public work and commonwealth, and also changed and adapted them for a radically different environment. This adaptive, innovative quality was the essence of the "portable democracy" that Americans created in the nineteenth century. Where people and their work went, so went the opportunity for democratic creativity. For Americans, democracy was not confined to institutional structures; rather it was something they carried with them. It became a way of life.

Such a democracy, because it was incorporated into people's identities and it was tied to the skills of their everyday work, meant that the people themselves were the ultimate producers. Portable democracy created the capacity for people to change and rebuild the commons, as well as preserve and enhance it.

Public work, as expressed and elaborated in the nineteenth-century tradition of the commonwealth, most simply conveyed the idea of common work on things people needed to do together. It embodied the democratic spirit of American manners and talk. And it created a culture and a wide-ranging process of citizenship education through which people sought to understand, define, and gain control over technical progress and wealth itself.

These ideas had powerful roots in rural and agricultural life. In the twentieth-century they flowed into a large movement to revitalize democracy on the land that sought to tame the forces of science and technology overwhelming the nation.

CHAPTER 3

*R*ural Democracy

It is not sufficient to train technically in the trades and crafts and arts to the end of securing greater economic efficiency. This may be accomplished in a despotism and result in no self-action on the part of the people.

Every democracy must reach far beyond what is commonly known as economic efficiency and do everything it can to enable those in the background to maintain their standing and their pride and to participate in the making of political affairs.

Liberty Hyde Bailey, *The Holy Earth*, 1915[1]

*I*n the nineteenth century, American democracy was rooted in rural life and agriculture. Based on widespread patterns of family farming, in farms that were often roughly equal in size, people developed self confidence. They learned independence and self-reliance and, simultaneously, the cooperative ethic that comes from working with neighbors on common projects. They saw the visible products of their own labor take shape, and also felt themselves contributing to the larger community and to the nation. Farming created an American iconography, the image of the producer, the proud yeoman farmer, at the center of our democracy.

Dramatic changes over the past hundred years have transformed rural life and American society broadly. The nation became urban, industrial, and characterized more by mass consumer culture than by images of the producer. The nation's public affairs and institutional life started being guided by a professional class that used science and its applications as justification for its authority and as the tools of its trade.

Science at the turn of the twentieth century was a force that seemed revolutionary in its potential to end human suffering, create abundance, dispel bigotry and prejudice, and bring enlightenment. Almost all who believed in American democracy shared an unbounded optimism about the liberation that the scientific outlook heralded. Yet over time, this promise revealed its limits. Most Americans were relegated by those who spoke in the name of science to the backwaters of ignorance and superstition. The fallacies of a one-dimensional view that adhered to scientific "truth" as the singular legitimate form of knowledge in human affairs became evident in a technical language increasingly denuded of diverse perspectives and experiences.

The result has been that increasingly products themselves and the machines and technical processes associated with their making and marketing have taken on a life of their own. They have moved to the center stage of our society. The actual labor, physical labor and even most mental labor in this age of the "smart machine," embodied in products, have shifted to the background.

In cultural terms, farms and rural areas came under an unrelenting attack as backward and unsophisticated. Literary figures like Hamlin Garland in his travel log, *Main-Travelled Roads* (1891), depicted rural men and women as living in culturally barren landscapes, surrounded by piles of manure, and buried under massive mortgages. The National Education Association report on rural schools in 1897, prepared by the leading school administrators of the day, scoffed at the one-room country school, once the very symbol of America's democratic education.[2]

In such a context it has taken skill, energy, and creativity to make ordinary people's work *public*—visible and valued—in any setting. Yet, as we will argue in Chapters 3 and 4, people have been far from simple victims or objects of such processes. In rural America, the "country life" movement in the early decades of the twentieth century mounted a powerful alternative to the supposedly sophisticated opinion of its time. Colleges and universities like Cornell, with missions that centered on "education for citizenship" and strong rural outreach programs, played key roles in this movement. They charged their students to go out and participate in the great work of revitalizing rural democracy. Such democracy, in the movement's terms, did not deny the value of science or technology; rather it liberated their potential. It lent them richer meaning by placing them at the service of communities and citizens.

For a time, the practical vision of rural life as an indispensable foundation of democracy itself had remarkable power and appeal. It enlisted support from prominent figures like Theodore Roosevelt. It formed the foundation for the national cooperative extension system. It left a legacy of education and a model of government practice that show signs of reviving once again in systems like cooperative extension.

Rural democracy may seem distant at first in our time. But it recalls practices in rural areas that are still close to the surface of memory.

Rural Democracy

Daniel Kemmis, former Speaker of the Montana House of Representatives, grew up in a small town in the eastern part of the state in the 1950s. Kemmis likes to tell a story that he sees as conveying "the politics of cooperation," an understanding of a community-based public work forged out of the necessities of rural survival.

When he was a child, the wind blew down the family barn. Neighbors came from around the area to help rebuild it; in a sense, every private barn was also part of the common stock of barns on which all depended. Neighbors included the family of Albert Volbrecht, whose "hat was the biggest . . . voice the loudest . . . language the foulest . . . intake of beer the most prodigious." Daniel Kemmis's mother, Lilly, did not like the Volbrechts at all. Kemmis remembers that she "would have done anything in her power to deny my brother and me that part of our education" that came from the young Volbrecht daughter, who regaled other children with ribald stories while the adults worked.

Such community-wide practices were frequent in those years. Sometimes they made public work out of a private family crisis, like a fallen barn. They also prompted joint work on a variety of community affairs, according to Kemmis, from participation in the local school board to regulating water lines and parks. Whatever the occasion, public contact was unavoidable. "In another time and place, Albert and Lilly would have had nothing to do with one another," said Kemmis. "But on those Montana plains life was still harsh enough that they had no choice. Avoiding people you did not like was not an option. Everyone was needed by everyone else in one capacity or another. If Albert and Lilly could have snubbed one another, our barn might not have been built, and neither our calves nor Albert's branded."

Personal likes and dislikes did not necessarily change much from the interactions. Kemmis's mother remained angry every time the Volbrechts came by. But the community and his family gained other things: different "slants" on the world, as Kemmis put it; awareness that people could count on others in the community whatever their personal likes; and an experience of community effectiveness in accomplishing difficult tasks.

Kemmis contrasts this story with another from Missoula in recent years. A group considering ways to raise money for a musical festival canceled their plan for an old-fashioned box lunch because of fear of a lawsuit if anyone got sick. In Kemmis's eyes, today's "litigious society" of confrontations and special interests results in "civic suffocation."[3]

There were limitations of communities like Kemmis's childhood town world that might too easily be forgotten in the glow of positive images: sharp divisions and hierarchies along lines of ethnicity and race, for instance; circumscribed roles for women; and an avoidance of discussion and debate about many controversial subjects.

Yet the appeal of Kemmis's boyhood story also cuts across many contemporary divisions of politics, race, and gender. In the memories of many people alive today—not only in rural areas and small towns but also in relatively stable ethnic communities of big cities—people learned ongoing connections and experiences of power and efficacy through work together with their neighbors in the larger community in which they lived. They developed a consciousness of mutual responsibility. They had ways to hold accountable those who were too disruptive or violent. People of different ages—the young, the middle-aged, or the elderly—interacted in a fashion that allowed the transmission of values, perspective, and wisdom across generational lines. Thus people experienced an ongoing education in common effort that broadened public affairs to much more than elections alone or the activities of government. Daniel Kemmis's story of his boyhood reminds us of a society when the ideal of "commonwealth" created through productive, public work had real power, at least on local levels.

Through the nineteenth century this was the story of the nation in significant measure. America was an overwhelmingly agricultural society. Nine out of ten people lived on the land in 1790. In 1860, eight out of ten continued to live in nonurban areas, farms or villages with less than 2,500 population. Still, in 1890, 64 percent was rural—living on farms or in small villages.[4]

Agriculture was imagined by the democratic leaders of the American Revolution as the essential basis. Yet in the late nineteenth century, the rural basis for American democracy eroded dramatically for a variety of reasons.[5]

Age of the Machine

In 1902, America fell in love with the book *The Wonderful Wizard of Oz*, which can be seen as a metaphor for the changes occurring in the nation. The Chicago rendering of this tale, a musical extravaganza opening on stage, had the longest run of any musical production up to that time in American history. By the teens, an entire Oz industry had sprung up with toys, games, coloring books, puppets, and other paraphernalia. Advertising used the familiar figures of Dorothy and Toto, the Scarecrow, Tin Man, and Lion everywhere. "Everybody's Going to the Big Store," proclaimed giant billboards for Siegel-Cooper's department store, across New York City. Leading the parade of famous persons was the Scarecrow himself.

What was behind the Oz craze? As historian William Leach has observed, in part the book's popularity testified to the masterful skill of its author, L. Frank Baum. Baum created the first "American fairy tale," in a sense. He fused the fairytale with Americana. The lonely hero in quest of a dream, helped along her journey by strange and amazing characters, wandered through enchanted forests and struggled against evil to achieve her goals. She had many good things to eat along the way. The novel brought the fairy story home: Farms in Kansas and Dorothy, the country girl; scarecrows; tricksters and snake oil salesman; and down-home humor—all were central.[6]

The book also captured popular imagination because it expressed and crystallized a powerful new culture that was spreading across the nation in the early years of the twentieth century. The *Wizard of Oz* advanced a new version of the good life in which technological wizardry and consumer goods replaced production. Dorothy in *The Wizard of Oz* wanted to go home to Kansas. In its sequel, *The Emerald City of Oz*, Dorothy brings her Aunt Em and Uncle Herald to the magic kingdom, where the narrator declares, "here everything that was dear to the little girl's heart was supplied . . . nothing so rich and beautiful could have been found in the biggest department store in America."

In the new culture, values such as the search for pleasure, comfort, and material well-being became defining features of society. Consumer culture "speaks to us," said one merchant, "only of ourselves, our pleasures, our life. It whispers, 'Amuse thyself, take care of yourself.' Is not this the natural and logical effect of an age of individualism?" This signaled a basic shift in the very understanding of individualism, however. The focus became on what one received or consumed, rather than what one produced and created.[7]

As the nation changed from a largely agricultural and rural society to an urban, industrialized nation, self-employed producers became employees of others. Technological change guided by private business and controlled by experts became the driving force. The rural world of small-scale and household production, small communities, and self-sufficiency gave way to a world of large, crowded, anonymous cities and consumer culture. Finally, a rising class of university-trained experts—engineers, technicians, doctors, lawyers, managers, professional journalists, and many others using the language and appeal of science—increasingly dominated the landscape. All these changes meant that technology and the products associated with technology took on a power and reality of their own. Correspondingly, ordinary people's labor lost ground in visibility and importance.

The changes brought noteworthy benefits for many people. Familiar worlds of communities became more unsettled, but people also gained access to new products, ideas, and goods from around the world. If science generated a rising class of experts who were often arrogant, it also conveyed powerful new insights into the universe, technological possibilities, and human experience. Finally, the urban environment created vivid public encounters with diverse viewpoints, attitudes, backgrounds, and experiences. For the middle class, especially, the urban scene was associated with a new expressiveness and public roles. For instance, women found a new voice and visibility in offices, dance halls, theater, and other settings.

Yet these gains came with costs as well. As if in eerie anticipation of the horrors of communism that were created in his name, Karl Marx had astutely described the modern factory decades before. "Men are effaced by their labor," he wrote. Workers' contributions and individuality seemed to be heading for destruction: "The individual characteristics of workers are obliterated," Marx continued. The mechanical world of machines and work schedules seemed to take on a life of its own, "quite independent of and divorced from the individuals."[8]

America had always had a fascination with technology and machines. "We live in an age of improvement," wrote Edward Everett, editor of the *North American Review* in the mid-nineteenth century. "What changes have not been already wrought in the condition of society! What addition has not been made to the wealth of nations, and the means of private comfort by the inventions, discoveries and improvements of the last hundred years!"

Progress was synonymous with America. To be opposed to it meant, somehow in our national mythology, alienation from the country. "There can be no pause," Everett expounded in the spirit of the age, "for art and science are, in themselves, progressive and infinite. . . . Nothing can arrest them which does not plunge the entire order of society into barbarism."[9]

By the later years of the century, these sentiments helped fuel a revolutionary shift toward mass communications, mass organization, and mass production. In urban areas and agricultural regions alike, the society that began to emerge was far different than what had been before.

In 1830, the nation had 23 miles of railroad track. The telegraph was first used commercially in 1847. On the threshold of the Civil War, Cyrus McCormick's Harvester Works in Chicago was, he boasted, "the largest factory of its kind in the world," with 3,500 employees. The Pullman Company, a leading American industry, employed 200 workers in its plant that built sleeping cars. In 1870, more than two-thirds of America's workers were found in agriculture, forestry, and fishing. Eighty percent of the population lived in cities or rural areas with less than 8,000 people. Government, similarly, was tiny by later standards. Only 14,000 non postal employees worked for the federal government. Capital investment per worker was $700 in manufacturing.

By 1910, only one-third of the workforce was still in farming, logging, or fishing. New York City's population had increased fourfold between 1860 and 1910; Chicago had 2.2 million people. By 1920, half the population lived in cities. With a vast stream of immigrants entering the country each year, the population doubled between 1870 and

1900. More than one-quarter of all male adults had been born overseas. Capital invested in machines and buildings per worker had risen
to more than $2,000. The total investment in manufacturing had
grown from 2.7 billion in 1879 to 20.8 billion in 1914. Hundreds of
thousands of miles of railroads and telegraphs connected the country
in transportation and communications systems that allowed a qualitatively different production process.[10]

Along with these developments came shifts in cultural attitude and
social class. Technology became a national religion. Human beings
themselves were described in mechanistic terms by a flood of writers.
Utopian novels of the late 1800s and early 1900s, like Edward Bellamy's *Looking Backward: 2000–1887* about a man who wakes up and
finds the world has changed dramatically, or Fred Clough's *The
Golden Age,* portrayed a future in which labor had virtually disappeared, replaced with machines. "On a tour of inspection the sights
they [visitors to utopia] saw were something wonderful to behold,"
wrote Clough. "Acres of wonderful machinery running noiseless and
doing perfect work." Labor- and time-saving devices freed people for
increasing leisure in these novels, and goods abounded. The under-
ground, says one citizen of utopia, is "like a gigantic mill, into the
hopper of which goods are being constantly poured by the trainload
and shipload, to use at the other end in packages of pounds and
ounces, yards and inches, pints and gallons, corresponding to the infinitely complex personal needs of half a million people."[11]

"Improved means for unimproved ends," the homespun American
philosopher Henry David Thoreau once said because he worried
about what he saw as a growing cult of efficiency. What happened
confirmed Thoreau's fears. In the early twentieth century, technological developments, the factory system, and the rising consumer culture
were managed and directed by university-trained and credentialed
experts. This class used the language of science to justify its work. "By
the 1920s," wrote the social critic Walter Lippmann, "the miracles of
science seem to be inexhaustible." Lippmann argued that "men of science should have acquired much of the intellectual authority which
churchmen once exercised."[12]

As a new class of experts emerged, new forms of hierarchy and deference also began to develop. The historian Robert Wiebe has observed that public life began to be sectioned off for the first time in

many decades. Curtained carriages, exclusive ballrooms, and detached orchestra boxes appeared. Madison Square Garden advertised itself openly as a separate place for "society."

Moreover, the rising authority of science shifted the discussion. Above all, America came to focus on "efficiency"—how things were produced or created—rather than the meaning and significance of what was produced or who produced it. This outlook destroyed many older forms of commons, like the common grazing rights throughout much of the South.[13]

In the factory, a new breed of efficiency experts followed the example of Frederick Taylor's "scientific management." Taylor divided each worker's tasks into the smallest possible component, and measured each piece to determine how it could be speeded up for maximum production. This approach, in turn, was heralded as the new standard for America. "Big things are happening in the development of this country," wrote the editors of *Harper's* in 1912. "With the spreading of the movement toward greater efficiency, a new and highly improved era in national life has begun."[14]

As machines were enthroned as kings and experts turned into their lords and ladies in waiting, others came to resemble serfs. A sprawling, desperately poor lower class of unskilled workers materialized, locked into dead-end jobs and crowded in urban ghettoes or turned into tenant farmers and sharecroppers on the land.

Movements of farmers and laborers anticipated this process in the last decades of the nineteenth century. In their view, the very identities of Americanism and the "producing classes" were at stake. The honest worker, wrote George McNeil of the Knights of Labor, is under "the iron heel of a soulless monopoly, crushing the manhood of sovereign citizens. He is now at the mercy of combinations which are in effect conspiracies against the common rights of people." Or as the Omaha Platform of the farmer's People's Party in 1892 put it, "We believe that the time has come when the railroad corporations will either own the people or the people must own the railroads."[15]

The lower class was made up especially of African Americans, Mexicans, Asians, and millions of new immigrants from eastern and central and southern Europe. In the South, former African American slaves and their descendants were systematically victimized by new statutes which legalized segregation and barred most blacks from voting. In Houston, reflecting this disenfranchisement, voting levels fell from 76 percent of the eligible voters in 1900 to 32 percent four years later.[16]

Vagrancy laws multiplied. Terms like "slum" and "poor white trash" also appeared for the first time. Anglo-Saxon became the standard. One survey of early twentieth century school books found negative stereotypes used to portray every ethnic group except the English, Germans, and Scandinavians, and the image of the Germans changed in World War I. Dirty, shiftless, smelly, dull if not backward, given to lawlessness, conniving, and of course insolent—not deferring to their "betters"—were the stock-in-trade images that immigrants and "other races" encountered in their education.[17]

In this environment, supposedly sophisticated opinion turned against rural America. Prominent clergy like Josiah Strong and Roland Hyde Hartt described rural churches as enfeebled and declining, rent with bitter rivalries, presided over by lifeless ministers. One writer in *The Atlantic Monthly* suggested that the only hope in rural areas lay in the abandonment of family farms in the open countryside, and the relocation of farmers into villages.[18]

In the face of such trends that devalued many people's labor, those with commitments to rural democracy sought to forge instruments appropriate for a new age. No one was more important or creative in this task than Liberty Hyde Bailey. Bailey helped to expand the very meaning of agricultural and land-grant education. He stressed "the great public work" of democratic renewal. He also provided a philosophical rationale for the cooperative extension system that was to reach every corner of the country.

Liberty Hyde Bailey and Land-Grant Education

American colleges and universities played important roles in democratic renewal. Many were founded with a strong civic mission, aimed at producing public leaders that were, in Jefferson's terms, examples "of talent and virtue." Nineteenth-century efforts to extend higher education to "the people" democratized this mission. In 1851, a People's College Association was formed in New York, emerging out of agrarian and labor activism. It aimed at higher education "for agriculture and the useful arts." Its meetings drew an eclectic array of reformers, including abolitionists and "Women's Rights Ladies." The movement was given impetus by the Morrill Act, passed by Congress and signed by President Lincoln in 1862. The Morrill Act promoted "the liberal and practical education of the industrial classes in the several pursuits and professions of life." It resulted in a number of new colleges, open to wider constituencies.

In the decades following the Civil War, most states established what were called "land grant" colleges, open not simply to farmers and "mechanics" but to other men as well. A second Morrill Act, passed in 1890, provided land-grant colleges with additional funds, stipulating that states have "a just and equitable division of the fund to be received under this act between one college for white students and one institution for colored students." Such measures reflected a rigid segregation that generated the "separate but equal" doctrine in the South. Whatever the irony, the funding also provided sources for black colleges—the so-called "1890 Land-Grant Colleges"—that were to be training grounds for generations of black leaders.[19]

Land-grant colleges always had a practical bent. They aimed at spreading new scientific discoveries to rural areas. This period was a time of remarkable scientific developments in farming: artificial fertilizers, the Babcock milk test, new knowledge about the transmission of diseases and the control of crop and animal diseases, treatments for hog cholera and anthrax, and the spread of new technologies like the tractor—all made a dramatic appearance.

By the 1890s, the civic mission of land-grant education came to be thought of as "extension." For decades, many land-grant colleges and other institutions had been organizing "farmers' institutes," consisting of short courses usually from two to five days. In 1899, more than 2,000 such institutes were organized, attracting over 500,000 farmers. By 1914, the number had climbed to 8,800, with more than 3 million participants.[20]

Extension work mainly meant the spread of technical and scientific knowledge, but this was not simply a one-way process. Farmers themselves often challenged the idea that university-based research and science was the only appropriate knowledge. They organized their own institutes in order to convey and help legitimize what some have called "craft based" understandings, views of what crops were best, strategies for taking care of farms that came from "collecting and systematizing" experiences of farmers themselves.[21]

Rhetoric about the democratic purposes of land-grant colleges was widespread. For instance, the Trustees of the Ohio Agricultural and Mechanical College declared in 1873 that they desired not "to educate those confided to them simply as Farmers or Mechanics, but as men, fitted by education and attainments for the greater usefulness and higher duties of citizenship." In some states, civic concerns in land-grant education were shaped by reform agitation among students and faculty involved with farmer and labor movements. In others, "citizenship training" was often simply equated with the addition of social sciences into the curriculum. Still others had a larger civic vision. Andrew White, for instance, president of Cornell University, stressed the need to teach and cultivate an ethos of public service in all students.[22]

A movement to renew "country life" developed across the rural areas of the nation in the first decades of the twentieth century with a variety of local and state groups. Protestant denominations all created departments or divisions on country life. A lively discussion about the role of land-grant education in civic development and democratic renewal spread through many colleges. It raised ideas like "the Wisconsin idea," the notion of the "democratization of knowledge," the argument that experts should be "on tap, not on top," and the proposition that "boundaries of the university are the boundaries of the state."[23]

During this period, leaders such as Liberty Hyde Bailey helped to formulate a wide-ranging philosophy which informed the movement. He stressed the importance of public work.

Bailey took over as Dean of the College of Agriculture at Cornell in 1904. He turned a struggling department into an internationally prominent institution. When he began, the student body was 252 and the faculty was 9. By 1914, the student body in agriculture had increased to 2,305, with 104 faculty and assistants.[24]

Bailey's approach was to integrate specialized knowledge into a much more comprehensive vision. "Students in agriculture are doing much more than fitting themselves to follow an occupation," he wrote. "They are to take part in a great regeneration. The student in agriculture is fitting himself for a great work."[25]

His approach challenged practices of narrow expert-led extension work. "A prevailing idea seems to be that an expert shall go into a community and give advice to the farmers on the running of their farms and on all sorts of agricultural subjects, being teacher, inspector, counselor, confessor, organizer, and guide." Bailey declared this approach was likely to fail on the face of it. Even where it effectively conveyed new information, it created dangerous dependencies, not capacities for self-action. "The re-direction of any civilization must rest primarily on the people who comprise it, rather than be imposed from persons in other conditions of life."[26]

In his view, rural communities faced many problems. Perhaps most importantly, they experienced a crisis in confidence and morale, a sense of collective victimhood constantly fed by the condescending attacks from urban elites. Above all, rural people needed to learn cooperative action. The fierce individualism common to farming had the virtues of teaching independence, self-reliance, and pride. But it also had major drawbacks. "This individualism conduces to isolation of ideas," said Bailey. "We must admit that there is now a deplorable lack of any associative effort that commands respect and puts things through." In Bailey's view, "Our present greatest need is the development of what may be called 'the community sense'—the idea of the community as a whole working together toward one work."[27]

College-based rural workers could play pivotal roles if they helped communities develop their own problem-solving capacities. Bailey continued, "Real leadership lies in taking hold of the first and commonest problems that present themselves and working them out. I like to say to my students that they should attack the first problem that presents itself when they alight from the train on their return from college. It may be a problem of roads; of a poor school; of tuberculosis; of ugly signs along the highways." The point was not simply or even mainly the specific problem. Rather, it was the fact that the public work of problem solving created opportunities to develop community capacity for self-action.

In Bailey's view this also required revitalization of every rural institution, from women's clubs to business groups, cooperative creameries to local political organizations. Above all, institutions like schools and rural churches needed to come alive with community spirit. They needed to engage their members in the problems of community life. Schools needed strong connection to rural traditions, and needed to be governed by rural people themselves instead of distant state bureaucracies. "We must outgrow the sit-still and keep-still method of school work," said Bailey. "I want to see our country school-houses without screwed down seats, and to see the children put to work with tools and soils and plants and problems." In terms similar to the philosophy of the democratic theorist John Dewey, Bailey proposed that "a child does not learn much when he is silent and inactive. Out of this work will grow the necessity of learning to read and figure and draw."[28]

Liberty Bailey was born on a farm in Michigan in an isolated area of the state. He had never seen a railroad until he was 18. An orchard farmer and then graduate of the Michigan State College of Agriculture, by the time he reached Cornell, Bailey was a world-famous horticulturist. He specialized in the evolution of dissimilar species of plants.

During the farm depression years of the 1890s, Bailey was troubled by the realization that his examination of fruit trees in western New York had failed to notice the economic devastation experienced by fruit growers themselves. In response, Bailey, his colleague George Warren, and others pioneered a new comprehensive survey approach to rural conditions. It was based on the premise "that it is impossible . . . to extend the Experiment Station and the University impulse to the people in such a manner that it shall come to them as a living and quickening force, without first studying the fundamental difficulties of the farmer's social and political environment."[29]

A comprehensive approach to rural conditions and the need for reinvigoration of rural life in the face of urban and elite condescension led Bailey to stress democratic renewal. For Bailey, science was a method for discovery, not an end in itself. He shared the faith of most intellectuals of his age that science would free humanity from "the fear of truth and the fear of dogma and the fear of nature." and that "ignorance is always bondage." He also saw resources that the city might bring to rural life: "new and large ideas, active touch with great affairs, keen business and executive ability, generosity" and other important things. But Bailey nonetheless argued strenuously that the knowledge gained from "libraries and laboratories" was limited. He stressed the need for what he called "nature study," to cultivate an appreciation for the commonplace and everyday things, as well as the beauty and curative aspects of nature. He also argued that essential democratic values were developed in rural life: "plain and frugal living of plain people." Rural life created a "school of affairs" that "deals with real, actual, essential things, problems, and events, and develops practical knowledge and ability." Finally, Bailey envisioned a larger spiritual rebirth in the nation in which rural communities would play a pivotal role.[30]

Bailey had a shrewd political sense. This proved essential for his success, because his approach to education directly confronted the rising conventional wisdom which held that academic knowledge, developed in environments detached from practical experience, was the most valid. Against the objections of many Cornell faculty who scorned the idea of expanding a "Cow College" at the university and in the face of skepticism from many urban legislators, Bailey gained state financial support sufficient to make Cornell the leading agricultural college of its time. His approach relied on a framing of agricultural education in terms of large public purposes. He sought "to lift instruction above the narrowly practical or vocational and relate it to an entire way of life," as one sympathetic journalist put it.

Turning the tables on skeptics in academia, Bailey argued that agricultural education should become the model for the rest of higher education because of its grounding in real work and its infusion with a larger public spirit. "Education by means of agriculture . . . is not merely to add one more thing to our educational institutions," he declared. "It is to re-make much of our education in a spirit of real democracy."[31]

Bailey strongly influenced Theodore Roosevelt's attitudes on rural life and farming. Roosevelt, city born and raised, had originally shown scant interest in rural life. Eventually, he came to see farmers as the central bedrock of American democracy—law-abiding, energetic and hardworking, independent, intelligent, and deeply devoted to private property, family, and community. Acting on such convictions, in 1908 Roosevelt appointed Liberty Hyde Bailey to chair the "Commission on Country Life." The commission was charged to investigate the conditions of rural life and make recommendations for rural renewal.[32]

The seven-member commission began its work on August 20, 1908, and delivered its report on January 23 of the following year. During its period of study, it mailed more than 500,000 questionnaires to farmers and others in rural areas. More than 115,000 responded. The commission got responses from 200 local meetings, held 30 public hearings across the country, and distilled commentary from thousands of letters.

The commission's report made a number of recommendations, from school improvements and road construction to cooperative action by farmers to develop their strength in the face of railroads and giant manufacturing, mining, and merchandising corporations. Most importantly, the commission proposed a national cooperative extension system that would develop rural capacities through widespread education.

The Commission on Country Life report envisioned education expressly geared to developing citizenship as well as spreading technical and scientific information. It warned vigorously against creating dependency on experts. The diverse activities it proposed—helping farmers learn the latest agricultural approaches; educating young people in 4-H clubs; organizing home economics classes for wives and other projects—all were explicitly framed in a larger context of teaching cooperative local action. They were meant to be alternatives to top-down, technical, directive government.[33]

"Care must be taken in all the reconstructive work to see that local initiative is relied upon to the fullest extent and that federal and even state agencies do not perform what might be done by the people in the communities," the report read. "Every effort must be made to develop native resources, not only of material things but of people."[34]

Thus, in the commission's view the larger end of production and farming, like science, was a democratic culture and way of life in rural areas. Such ideas created a permanent legacy of democratic thought and practice. The cooperative extension system which became the main outreach effort of land-grant colleges across the country was a main vehicle for this tradition.

Cooperative Extension

In 1909, the commission's core recommendation for a national extension system ran afoul of bitter hostility in the Department of Agriculture. The department had long been suspicious of any language of rural "democracy" and "renewal." After insisting the 115,000 questionnaires returned be stored in the department's basement, they were marked off limits. Eventually they were burned.

Roosevelt had greeted the commission's recommendations with enthusiasm. But William Howard Taft, his successor president, showed little interest in rural problems. It remained for the presidency of Woodrow Wilson to act on the commission's report.

The Smith Lever Act, passed in 1914, established the nationwide system of cooperative extension. Funds through the Department of Agriculture were matched by local and state funds. Extension created a system of county agents across the country. The bill called for "technically trained practical-minded agricultural teachers who would show the farmer and the farm woman on their own farm and in their own home how to apply the new knowledge in agriculture and home economics to their everyday problems."[35]

It also was wide in scope. "Its splendid purpose is to improve the man, enlarge his mental horizon, and give intelligent direction to his efforts . . . lighten the burdens of women, afford greater opportunities to the boys and girls upon whose shoulders soon must fall the responsibility of home and the burdens of government," orated Senator Vardaman, the chief sponsor, in ornate but revealing language.[36]

Interestingly, more than eighty years after the founding of the extension system, Seaman Knapp, a former rice farmer in Louisiana who invented what is called the "demonstration" technique of agricultural education, is often viewed as the founding father of extension. There is a Seaman Knapp Arch at the Department of Agriculture. But this construction of history suggests more about our time and the domination of a technical outlook than it reveals about the founding years of the extension system.

In the teens or twenties, few would have imagined Knapp as much more than a specialist with a good teaching technique. His teaching approach, featuring a learn-by-doing method, was useful. But Knapp had little to say about the extension system's larger meaning and philosophy. What he did say was less than helpful for any desiring to increase rural communities' capacities for public work. Knapp embodied a naive faith in science; a disdain for the intelligence of rural populations; and an often striking racism.

After his success in Terrel, Texas, where he demonstrated to initially skeptical farmers how to deal with the boll weevil, Knapp's demonstration method spread rapidly in the South and other parts of the nation. The demonstration method stressed hands-on examples and personal contact more than academic approaches. All this was useful as a teaching strategy.

Knapp's general philosophy was quite narrow, however. Though he stressed a hands-on approach to education, he also saw rural people as backward and ignorant, in need of expert tutoring. Knapp idealized the rising class of experts and scorned the Jeffersonian faith in common sense and insight of plain people. He contrasted what he called the "scrutiny of the scientists" with the outdated "philosophy of the cottage." "The masses of people fail to understand that eyes were placed on top of their shoulders to see things," he wrote. "All along life's pathways from infancy to the grave they are stumbling over the world and scolding about their bruises."

Toward poorer farmers and especially toward blacks he expressed contempt. "Where must we start?" Knapp queried in discussing extension work for black farmers. "The main point is to start at the bottom. In attempting to raise the condition of the colored man we frequently start too high up. When I talk to a negro [sic] citizen I never talk about the better civilization, but about a better chicken, a better pig, a whitewashed house."[37]

Knapp's views were common, if perhaps more elegantly phrased, in mainstream public discussion. In those years the Bailey perspective lost ground on the national scene. Yet cooperative extension continued to sustain much of his philosophy.

Intellectuals who set the tone in the teens and twenties dismissed the intelligence of ordinary citizens and rural life as a site for democracy. Instead, they sought a radical relocation of public affairs to government and experts. Thus, Herbert Croly, editor of *The New Republic,* redefined democracy away from local civic activity. He proposed what he called the "great community" of the state, arguing that democracy no longer could mean that citizens "assemble after the manner of a New England town-meeting." Instead of the communal experience of towns, the nation as a whole must be bound together by "a comprehensive social ideal," mediated by modern media. Direct civic encounter was not necessary since "the active citizenship of the country meets every morning and evening and discusses the affairs of the nation with the newspaper as an impersonal interlocutor," providing "abundant opportunities of communications and consultation without any meeting" at all.[38]

Walter Lippmann in a series of influential books—*Public Opinion,* in 1922, followed by *The Phantom Public* and *A Preface to Morals*—argued that the "mystical notion of . . . the people" simply needed discarding. "The naively democratic theory," wrote Lippmann, "was . . . [that] the opinion of the masses of persons somehow became the opinion of a corporate person called 'The People.' " The "isolated rural township" might still involve a democracy of direct discussion and problem solving. In contrast, in the "wide and unpredictable environment" of a modern, urban, industrial society, most people were simply dupes: "The number of mice and monkeys known to have been deceived in laboratories is surpassed only by the hopeful citizens of a democracy." Lippmann believed that modern society could only be managed by trained experts with life tenure; the more insulated from ordinary people the better.[39]

Agriculture itself underwent changes in the aftermath of World War I that de-emphasized rural life as a distinctive culture and stressed the business aspects of farming. What was called the "farm management" approach was spread especially by the Farm Bureau, a conservative organization of the most prosperous farmers heavily supported by agribusiness interests. Farm Bureaus devoted their efforts to advancing scientific approaches to agriculture and fighting farmer groups they saw as more activist, like the Farmers Union and the Grange. Labor-saving technologies led to significant migrations off of farms, and according to some agricultural historians, significant if unanticipated damage to soil and other natural resources. Agribusiness became a major shaper of research agendas at land-grant institutions.[40]

Despite these trends, cooperative extension retained a strong emphasis on education for rural citizenship. It continued to stress development of communities' capacities for problem solving. Russell Lord, a former extension agent and prominent journalist, argued that the influence of Bailey continued as a powerful force "in even the most rigidly formulated programs of agricultural extension." Edward Eddy, the leading historian of land-grant education through the 1950s, described the approach in this fashion: "Group effort became the accepted process of the extension method. Local programs should be locally determined and locally managed with the college acting only to suggest, guide, and standardize. In turn, it was felt that the county agent was actually much more a part of the local community than of the college."[41]

By 1929, cooperative extension had agents in more than three quarters of the nation's counties. It included 5,700 federal, state, and local employees, more than 250,000 volunteers and many millions in its clubs, committees, programs, and local groups.

Clarence Smith and Meredith Wilson, the Chief Officer and head of Extension Studies, respectively, in the Agriculture Department in 1929, described the network as combining efforts that showed "the farmer and his family and the rural community how to apply the practical results of the investigational work and studies . . . to the problems of the farm, the farm home, and the rural community," with a stress on what they called rural awakening.[42]

Ten years later, in 1939, of the 3,070 counties in the United States more than 2,900 had county agricultural agents; 929 had two; and 1,792 had "home demonstration agents"—staff who worked primarily with women homemakers.

Moreover, the New Deal programs in response to the Great Depression led to a widening of the extension system's practices. Agents helped organize communities for construction and development projects such as roads, rural electrification, cooperatives, housing efforts, and resettlement programs for poorer citizens. They conducted educational programs about New Deal policies and also catalyzed public forums and discussion groups of many kinds. One graduate dissertation from the University of Chicago in 1939, studying the depression's impact, concluded that "the county agent [had become] a part of a daring and controversial national agricultural program [that] added to, and in some sections almost completely replaced, the old type of scientific agricultural projects."[43]

Though county extension would lose much of the broader and expansive vocabulary of rural democracy over the years, it continued as a network of government workers focused on developing communities' capacities for problem solving, in a time when experts and professional systems were assuming authority for problem solving almost everywhere else. Extension thus remained a network vital in illustrating an alternative to conventional practice. The system sustained some consciousness of the ideal articulated by Liberty Bailey. It was countercultural in the technocratic world that was emerging: an example of government workers and other professionals who saw their own specialties as embedded in public work.

Through the 1930s, this philosophy of public work also had powerful urban foundations. These, like rural extension, demonstrated that even in an era of rising expertise and scientifically credentialed knowledge, people's institutions which educated for public work could be continually created and renewed.

CHAPTER 4

People's Institutions

An overmastering desire to reveal the humbler immigrant parents to their own children lay at the base of what has come to be called the Hull House Labor Museum. This was first suggested to my mind one early spring day when I saw an old Italian woman, her distaff against her homesick face, patiently spinning a thread.

. . .

Could we not interest the young people working in the neighboring factories, in these older forms of industry, so that, through their own parents and grandparents, they would find a dramatic representation of the inherited resources of their daily occupation. . . . They might also lay a foundation for reverence of the past which Goethe declares to be the basis of all sound progress . . .

Jane Addams, *Twenty Years at Hull-House*[1]

*H*ow did democracy survive the twentieth century's cataclysmic changes? How did a work-centered democratic spirit make the transition from the agrarian-based economy to one increasingly dominated by factories and mass production? These questions raise issues of democratic power as dramatic in urban areas as they were in rural America.

The transitions to urban life, especially for those from Old World peasant or rural backgrounds, were often wrenching. Perhaps most difficult was the uprootedness from an environment where the scale of everyday life seemed manageable and subject to human control. Imagine what it must have been like to step off a train or a boat into an urban tenement in New York or Chicago or Minneapolis. Adapting to relocation from the familiarity of a community where one's family had lived for generations, where daily routines were predictable, where people all spoke the same language and shared similar outlooks elicited extraordinary individual and communal responses.

The Back of the Yards area of Chicago, poignantly depicted in Upton Sinclair's *The Jungle,* formed such an immigrant community. Back of the Yards was adjacent to Chicago's stockyard district and meatpacking area. Back of the Yards filled with immigrants from Eastern and southern Europe. In the 1890s and early 1900s, Slovaks, Lithuanians, Russians, and Ukrainians joined earlier waves of English, Scots-Irish and Welsh, Germans, and Poles. Its layout, organized around the needs of industry, formed a pattern common for many industrial urban areas.

"The first thing anyone noticed about the neighborhood was the stench," writes historian Robert Slayton. Sister Mary D. recalled her arrival at the Guardian Angel Day Care Center in 1932. She had been sent up to the nursery to care for small children. "I thought they all had their pants full, excuse the expression."

The odor came from slaughterhouses and miles of pens of hogs, sheep, and cattle, mingled with garbage, fertilizer plants, vats of chemicals, piles of trash in alleys, tanneries, and a sewer known as "Bubbly Creek." Banks, rails, stockyards, and other businesses spread out around the factories. On a single day in 1920, 122,734 hogs came to the yards. As overwhelming as the stench was the power of the packinghouse industry, which overshadowed all else. By 1910, "the Yards," as the industrial complex was called, included giants like Armour and Swift and Company and many smaller firms. One Swift factory had more than 11,000 employees.[2]

Middle-class reformers viewed such areas as "the wrong side of the tracks." They portrayed Back of the Yards specifically as violent, ignorant, ugly, and, above all, simply victimized by the processes of industrialism. One English professor from the University of Chicago, seeking to kindle "the latent aesthetic interests of people in these dreary, cramped circumstances. . . . to the appeals of a simple, fine and truly great art," read to a group of working women a section from James Russell Lowell, "What is so rare as a day in June?" The women amply confirmed his suspicions of their cultural deprivation when they showed little interest.

Yet middle-class perspectives then and more recently regularly ignored the resilient ways in which people coped with radical dislocations by drawing on their own traditions, in their own ways and terms. "It never occurred to such visitors [as the English professor] that it was the question that was wrong," observes Slayton. "Ignored were the weddings, the dances in halls behind saloons, the children's games, the community patterns and the democracy that the workers and their families created. In these [things], they would indeed have found their 'truly great art.'"[3]

Such cultural traditions and communal organizations were a potent source of stability and support which helped buffer the larger world. People also built on such foundations to develop what might be called "civic muscle." Potent mediating institutions like settlement houses, unions or political parties stretched from local levels to larger worlds of public policy. With such networks and associations of popular power people were able to realize some measure of freedom that comes through self-governance. They formed public spaces which were able to sustain government by the people well into the twentieth century.

Community Roots and Public Spaces

As people adapted to and sought to bring under control the massive forces affecting urban life, they created two sorts of people's institutions: community-based groups, organized largely around cultural values and traditions; and institutions and networks with public cultures in which people from very different backgrounds worked together.

Communal networks, often isolated from the world outside the immediate neighborhood, helped organize daily life. These groups and organizations could be formal or informal: family networks, local churches and schools, mutual-aid societies, community businesses, and ethnic organizations are all examples. Forming networks of local support in a time when many felt anonymous and dehumanized in the harsh world of factory work, they sustained cultural identities and strengthened connections among people of similar backgrounds. Like Dan Kemmis's barn-raising, these local institutions generated communal obligations among neighbors.

People also created larger organizations and associations that drew upon but stretched far beyond community roots. These public spaces crossed boundaries of community, ethnicity, and particular cultural ties. They created settings where people with quite diverse interests interacted and formed bases for power with which to address common problems.

Groups like labor unions, political parties, the YMCA and YWCA, the National Association for the Advancement of Colored People (NAACP), women's suffrage groups, and other organizations for reform were spaces for public work in this sense. For instance, in the first decades of the twentieth century, women's suffrage organizations and their offspring made up diverse networks and coalitions. They not only fought for expansion of rights of formal citizenship through enfranchisement of women voters, but they also sought to teach an understanding of public affairs and citizenship as "civic housekeeping" on a range of problems. Thus, the *Woman Citizen's Library,* a 12-

volume collection of practical and theoretical material on "the larger citizenship," included among its authors leading suffragists such as Jane Addams and Cary Chapman Catt. In its 1913 inaugural edition, it declared that "the State is as real as the people who compose it. The duties of citizenship are as definite as the duties of housekeeping. Only as these self-evident facts are fully appreciated will women be able to share in those many and splendid reforms which we can see must come in our social life." The volumes included topics that ranged from the mechanics of political parties to questions of "the larger citizenship," like "the liquor traffic," "child labor," "equal pay for equal work," "schools," and "safeguarding the women immigrant." Such a view of citizenship inspired lasting, broad organizations like the League of Women Voters, the direct successor to the National American Women's Suffrage Association.[4]

Similarly, from the teens well into the 1950s, local YMCAs across the country and the YMCA Association of North America had a strong civic orientation. More than 800 "student Ys" associated with college campuses at the height of this movement sponsored a large number of civic efforts, from support for workers to public affairs forums and "citizenship camps." In the 1930s, the National Young Men's Council of the YMCA adopted as its goals "realistic education in public affairs resulting in effective participation in American democracy" and "wider participation in the civic life of the local community." As H. A. Overstreet, a leader in civic action in the Y, put the matter in 1939, "we shall restore the morale of young people precisely in the degree that year by year and day by day they learn to take part with their fellows [and] make their own judgments in company with their fellows about the matters that concern them."[5]

It is a mistake to romanticize past histories of any public spaces. However diverse, they also were fraught with various exclusions. Many women suffragists justified their efforts to secure votes for women as a buffer against dangerously radical immigrants coming to the nation. The National Board of the YMCA in 1939 declared the Y's to be a "school for democracy"; its major publication in this vein was called "Toward a Christian Democracy."

But whatever their flaws, public spaces also created environments for rendering otherwise invisible activity more apparent. They taught skills of everyday politics. At their best, they also built working relationships of respect across lines of great cultural division. In this way, they democratized hierarchical patterns of power. Moreover, they embedded questions of justice in larger frameworks of common effort.

Ethnic Communities

Historians often despair at the plight of factory workers who were caught in the clutches of unfettered industrial capitalism and, at the same time, seduced by a growing national consumer culture. Lizbeth Cohen, in her history of industrial ethnic workers between 1919 and 1939 in Chicago during what was known as "the lean years," suggests another interpretation.

Local ethnic organizations served as bases for community cohesion and adaptation to change. By the end of the 1930s, she concludes, American workers had made important though subtle shifts in how they viewed themselves and what they could accomplish through collective action.[6]

In the early 1920s, the majority of Chicago laborers and semiskilled workers in mass production were foreign born, living in isolated ethnic communities near the factories that employed them. A massive migration of blacks after World War I to Chicago from the rural South also reshaped the city.

Strong ethnic identities reflected different working-class neighborhoods, which served as buffers against powerful social changes of the 1920s and 1930s. Local ethnic cultures were reinforced by many factors: patterns of social interaction within the community; roles of the church in making links to the Old World; and the creation of mutual aid societies that assured security in times of need, among others. Thus, although factory employment attracted people to cities, it was the workers and their families, not the factory owners, who largely shaped local cultures. Community-based ethnic organizations were tools for working-class immigrants to use in this process. Several kinds of locally based organizations were especially important: self-help agencies, mutual benefit societies, and financial institutions.

Most ethnic groups developed local (and later, regional and national) self-help agencies to provide for the welfare of their communities. Generally, ethnic cultures greatly mistrusted government assistance. However, when neighbors required medical treatment that was not available through ethnic welfare services, the local precinct captain for the Democratic Party often served as a liaison between the community and the social service agency.[7] This mediating role was an important political function that helped community members negotiate unfamiliar and sometimes intimidating systems outside their neighborhoods.

The well-known journalist Mike Royko similarly described how precinct captains and ward bosses of the political machine created the connections between immigrants and the larger society. "The immigrant family looked to [the captain] as more than a link with a new and strange government." The political ward boss embodied the government. "He could tell them how to fill out their papers, how to pay their taxes, how to get a license. He was the welfare agency, with a basket of food and some coal when things got tough; an entree to the crowded charity hospital. He could take care of it when one of the kids got in trouble with the police."[8]

Other local organizations served similar self-help purposes. Mutual benefit societies—organizations providing insurance to immigrants families—were widespread. As the 1920s progressed, many ethnic mutual aid societies with shaky financial bases could not survive the demand created by widespread economic problems and competition by employers who offered better group insurance plans. But in the early years they nonetheless performed several important roles beyond providing insurance. They were links to the Old Country while reinforcing the importance of cultural traditions in America. They institutionalized a way of saving regularly for the future and for providing assistance in emergencies. They sustained and even strengthened people's belief that communities could care for each other and themselves.

Prior to World War I, workers saved money, often for future home ownership, through ethnic savings and loan associations. These democratically organized institutions were closely tied to communities in which they were located. Officers, who received minimal salaries, were elected by the membership. The associations rented space in public gathering places like churches, schools, meeting halls, even back rooms in taverns for regular meetings. Such arrangements allowed savings and loans to make investments with little overhead. Through this program, members could deposit as little as 25 cents at a time for future down-payment on land or a home, and borrow the rest at low interest.[9]

After World War I, ethnic banks grew rapidly, in part because banking practices of the general population changed dramatically. For the first time, working-class people saved and invested money at an unprecedented rate. To finance the war effort, the government had issued inexpensive bonds, called "Liberty Loans," which many citizens purchased with the idea that investing in government bonds was a patriotic act. Ethnic communities, particularly, promoted the purchase of Liberty Loans. By 1918, at the peak of bond purchasing, 46.5 percent of all subscribers were of foreign birth or parentage, although this group made up only 33 percent of the population.[10]

As the number of ethnic banks grew, they frequently became neighborhood civic centers, responding to business and social needs of the community. Bankers who knew local residents were easily accessible to workers and generally responsive to community needs. Like welfare societies and mutual benefit fraternities, ethnic savings and loan operations and banks were important mediating structures established by and accountable to local groups. All of these fraternal organizations, whatever their long-term weaknesses, helped ordinary people take care of themselves in times of need, plan for the security of their families, and save for the future.

None of this, of course, should be romanticized; fraternal organizations were often exclusive and parochial. Ethnic political bosses could create feudal strongholds. Neighborhoods like Bridgeport, the Irish enclave that produced Richard Daley and two previous mayors of Chicago, was a small town within the city, quick to threaten an errant black. Daley's boyhood club known as the Hamburgs was found by a Chicago commission to have played a major role in instigating the race riot of 1919 that left 15 whites and 23 blacks dead, after a black youth crossed the line separating the Twenty-seventh Street beach from the Twenty-ninth Street beach on Lake Michigan.

Whatever their limitations, community-based organizations nonetheless provided a scaffolding for public work—a kind of civic infrastructure that communities could draw upon in times of challenge and crisis. They also served as roots for public spaces that cut across many ethnic and community divisions.

Settlement Houses as Public Spaces

Leading American settlement houses were a potent force for social reform in the first several decades of the century. Many settlement houses formed a prototype of a people's institution with strong public dimensions. Settlement houses had both a community rootedness and an orientation to a larger world. Settlements like Hull House were also centers for political activism. All of these outward orientations and ties made settlements public spaces.

Settlement houses, established in urban areas usually in tenement districts, had several purposes. They responded immediately to needs of neighbors. They developed communities' capacities for public work. Some pushed national reform to address the widespread social and industrial problems brought about by rapid urbanization. Finally, like Liberty Bailey's land-grant universities, settlements served as models for research and theory building far different than that of the detached academic or scientist. For settlements, vigorous investigation of conditions and social circumstances was vitally important, but problems needed to be seen in a comprehensive way, in relationship to each other. In addition, research needed to be closely tied to strategies for action.

Founders of early settlements like Jane Addams, who established Hull House in Chicago, articulated democratic philosophies that called forth a multitude of people and their many talents—educated men and women of middle and upper classes, working-class immigrants, local politicians and philanthropists, as well as national leaders. In her paper, "The Subjective Necessity for Social Settlements," Addams wrote, "Young men and women, longing to socialize their democracy, are animated by certain hopes which may be thus loosely formulated; that if in a democratic country nothing can be permanently achieved save through the masses of the people, it will be impossible to establish a higher political life than the people themselves crave."[11]

Settlement houses created seedbeds for experimentation and training grounds for reformers of the early twentieth century, especially for women. With a passion for improving the lives of women and children, settlement workers and the neighbors of Hull House organized playgrounds for children; they ran kindergartens and a variety of adult education classes; they sponsored vocational education programs and health programs; they worked to reform working conditions for wage earners, with attention to women; they provided nutrition centers and pushed for improved housing conditions.

Jane Addams's elemental love of beauty, art, and literature infused settlements with the idea that working people should also have access to important ideas. Like the free thinkers organizations of the nineteenth century, settlement houses themselves were spaces where people gathered to debate, learn, organize, and discuss important issues of the day. "A settlement soon discovers," said Addams "that simple people are interested in large and vital subjects. Simple people do not want to hear about simple things; they want to hear about great things simply told."[12]

Hull House built a library, an art gallery, a labor museum. Yet Addams's understanding of art, unlike the Chicago English professor's, did not see it as something brought to culturally deprived victims. Rather, she had a remarkable and deep appreciation for the richness of culture, history, and creativity that was embedded in each immigrant culture.

Addams, out of her belief that learning happens through life experiences as well as through formal education, promoted settlement work among college-educated people as a means to expand and use their education in public work. "We have in America a fast-growing number of cultivated young people who have no recognized outlet for their active faculties. They hear constantly of the great social maladjustment, but no way is provided for them to change it, and their uselessness hangs about them heavily." [13] The strength of the settlement approach to education was that it taught young people to put theory into action applied to practical problems. Settlement workers learned to work with immigrants in a reciprocal fashion. In this sense, settlement houses were a sort of citizenship school that created multiple opportunities for public work.

Educational programs of many kinds from day care to Montessori kindergartens, to cooking classes and vocational programs, all provided a context to practice active citizenship. Settlement houses were public spaces where residents and neighbors learned together and worked to solve local problems, often to affect change at municipal, state, and national levels.

If settlement workers had liberal arts education, neighbors, many of them immigrants, had other kinds of knowledge necessary for understanding the problems and resources. Work was a central theme within the settlement movement. Believing that human labor was a source of dignity, Addams established the Hull House Labor Museum. Her intent was to, "interest the young people working in the neighboring factories, in [sic] older forms of industry, so that, through their own parents and grandparents, they would find a dramatic representation of the inherited resources of their daily occupation. If these young people could actually see that the complicated machinery of the factory had been evolved from simple tools, they might at least make a beginning towards that education which Dr. Dewey defines as 'a continuing reconstruction of experience.' "[14]

Immigrants were hired to demonstrate and teach their craft, thus showing first- and second-generation factory workers that work is a product of human thought and manual skill, not simply dependent on machinery.

By 1910, hundreds of thousands of working people were using more than 400 settlement houses, located primarily in eastern and midwestern industrial cities. Settlements were often the hub of public work in cities. Neighborhood House, founded in 1897 as a Jewish settlement and located in the Flats area of St. Paul, suggests the public dimension of settlements. Neighborhood House was called "the center of the community," or simply, "the meeting ground." As a Jewish settlement, it was sponsored by more affluent Jews who worried that poor immigrants escaping the wave of European prosecution might lose their cultures. The settlement drew inspiration from similar centers around the country, like Hull House in Chicago and Henry Street in New York.

Neighborhood House

"Texas Street was the street. Like Basin Street in New Orleans, Texas Street." Helen Turner recalled the scene in the Flats area of St. Paul, Minnesota, also called the West Side. Turner grew up in the teens and

twenties. "You couldn't take a step down the street without saying 'Hi.'
Everybody knew what was cooking in everybody's pot. People had a
sense of community." Texas Street was called with a mixture of affec-
tion and disgust, "the Texas bullyards." Mudholes remained after
every rain. Cows and horses walked down the road, making matters
worse.

The Mississippi River shaped the calendar and the rhythms of life
in the Flats. Every spring around Passover, people prepared for "high
water," when melting waters from northern tributaries poured the
river over its banks. In Helen's house, all the furniture was made to be
disassembled. "Every spring we'd move all our stuff upstairs." Beds, tables, and even the stove, which could be attached to a chimney on the
second story, were made for such a purpose. "We'd live there for two
or three weeks during high water."

Down from Turner's house was the corner with State Street, "crossroads of the Flats" in the years between 1900 and 1940, when the Jewish immigrant population gave a distinctive style and character to the
community. On one corner lived Burstein, a Jewish butcher. On another was Betty Agranoff, who taught at Roosevelt Junior High
School. Next door was a synagogue, and kitty-corner across the street
was Makarofsky's fish store. Helen Turner would stop off at Makarofsky's to get fish for her mother on the way home from school. He was
"very old and venerable," she remembered, a deeply religious and ob-
servant Jew much beloved by his neighbors.

A block away was Gershon Abramovitz's hardware store, which
served as an informal town hall. "All the men used to stand around
and settle the woes of the West Side and the world in Gershon's,"
Turner recalled. On the right of the store were reins, collars, and other
gear for horses; on the left, barrels of nails and other housewares.
Straight ahead through the entrance was the long counter behind
which Gershon Abramovitz sat. A short man with a mustache, usually
wearing a vest, Abramovitz had "a full head of hair" and "a beautiful
smile," said Turner. "Anything to be settled, people would go to see
him. I call him 'the Bürgermeister' of the West Side." The store was
where one could find out about the latest rumors of political intrigue
or war in Europe. Abramovitz spoke and wrote fluently in seven languages, and was the main link between the Flats and Europe. Syrians,

German Catholics, and Irish as well as Jews, would come to him to have letters written. He was the man, often, who arranged passage for one's family.

Helen Turner's father had come to the Flats after escaping from the Russian army, which conscripted Jewish males. A glazier, or glass cutter by trade, he found scant work of that sort in St. Paul. But like many Jewish immigrants, he was determined to remain independent. America's old traditions of self-directed work resonated powerfully with such men. A community loan association advanced him $25 for a horse. He became a peddler. When he had enough money, he took it to Abramovitz, who bought tickets to America for his wife and her brother. Helen Turner was born several years later on the Flats.[15]

The Flats was full of peddlers. Peddling might be considered (without much of the civic overtones) a kind of "public work." Peddling gave the area a distinctive, busy, public quality all hours of the day. More than one-third of the first graders in Lafayette School listed their father's work as "peddler" or related occupations, like "peddler supplier," in the early years of the century. Fruit, vegetables, scrap iron, junk, clothes, fish—almost anything that could be sold from carts or collected and taken somewhere else to be sold became the basis for peddling. Businessmen who did not peddle themselves bought from peddlers. There was constant flow between peddlers and feed stores, secondhand dealers, and grocery stores.[16]

Jewish immigrants were not the only settlers of the Flats. It was a polyglot, working-class community. French Canadians were followed by Germans, Irish, Scandinavians, and the first Jewish settlers. Later, the area was also the site for the first Mexican immigrants, settling out from the stream of migrant laborers. Ralph Stacker, who grew up in the Flats in the teens and twenties, remembers the ethos of mutual aid. "For the Jews, you had to help. You are your brother's keeper." This was a common sentiment among most ethnic groups. "The Catholics, the Italians down along the river; they all helped themselves." "Nobody on the West Side—Irish, Germans, Mexicans—nobody closed the house. Nobody had keys. Women were safe to walk the streets at night."

This was the community in which Neighborhood House was founded. As with other settlements, it soon decided not to limit itself to Jewish populations. In 1903, Neighborhood House reorganized on a nonsectarian basis "to serve the residents of 'the Flats' through helping the individual, through fostering family and neighborly friendliness, and through cultivating human relationships across lines of race and language, party and creed."

Neighborhood House taught English, gave regular "citizenship classes" to immigrants, held sessions on cooking, sewing, health care, and other subjects, and served as the launching pad for a variety of community projects. "Neighborhood House was the nucleus of the whole community," said Mat Moreno. Moreno, a workingman, was born on the Flats in 1924, one of the earliest Mexican families. He described the clubs of Mexican men that met there: "Anahuac Society, an Indian name. It was a business society of the elders. If there was a community problem, these gentlemen would gather and decide what to do." A Mothers' Club was organized by Mexican women. The Aztec Club sponsored dances and other social gatherings. On the fifth of May, a parade would gather outside to celebrate the Mexican defeat of the French in 1862. At Christmas, Anahuac held a pageant with costumes and presents for children. "We had Easter parties, summer camp, classes to learn English, mothers' clubs, exercise classes. If there was a dance on the West Side, Neighborhood House was where it was held. You'd have to see it to appreciate it."[17]

Constance Currie became the director of Neighborhood House in 1918 and for more than three decades presided over the center. Known for her fierce opposition to language of prejudice of any kind, she combined strict discipline and warmth as she assumed leadership in the community. In 1923, the settlement opened a new building on Robertson Street. Rooms in the four-story building all had fireplaces. Classes were held upstairs. In 1928, a large gym was added. On the third and fourth floors were apartments for part-time instructors or interns from the University of Minnesota, as well as transients who had no place to go.

The public space created at Neighborhood House served as a model for debate and conversation that rippled across the Flats. One golden gloves boxing match at Neighborhood House attracted 1,200 fans. "It was like a United Nations meeting," said Bill Kuehn.[18]

Not only did Neighborhood House provide important local functions. The public culture of Neighborhood House, in turn, nourished wide networks of reform across the Twin Cities area in the 1930s.

These ranged from academics at the University of Minnesota (graduate students from the university lived on the top floors) to labor activists and educators in the mushrooming union movement, and the political reformers who created the Farmer Labor Party.

Activists from these decades recall a connection between the settlements and the larger public stage, generating a sense of public work that transcended any particular institution, job, workplace, or occupation. Nellie Stone Johnson, a leading black labor organizer of the Minnesota Farmer Labor movement of the 1930s, worked closely with settlements like Neighborhood House and Phyllis Wheatley, an associated settlement house in the section of Minneapolis where blacks lived, called the North Side. She was also active in a variety of other reform efforts, all of which interacted in fluid ways.

Settlements, unions, popular educational institutes, and many other groups and institutions created wide public spaces across the area, with local roots and larger patterns of interaction. Noting her own union, she said "the union was connected to the community." She continued: "Membership in the Hotel and Restaurant Workers was made up of a lot of community people, black and white, Mexicans, and some Asians." It had local roots. "We had a storefront office on the North Side that had orange crates and a potbelly stove. If people had a grievance, they would come in and argue things out, because they believed they had a say." But the union spirit was not simply local or "communal."

Johnson's accounts from the thirties show the connections between settlements, store front offices, labor education classes, and broad political movements like the Farmer Labor Party. These were for Johnson broadly symbolized by the movement's overall vision of a "cooperative commonwealth." The interconnections also generated a sense of public purpose that informed her efforts wherever she was. "Whatever I was doing on my job, my real work was public work," she explains. Johnson has a simple definition of public work: "Whenever you're dealing with the community 'politically,' helping out regardless of what the issue is, it's public work. All my life I've been involved in it."[19]

Public work was, in Johnson's opinion, undermined by a rising "credentialism" in labor and other activist groups that stressed the need for expert credentials and specialized knowledge. "It began to get to the point where teachers in the labor schools had to have certain degrees. But that degree had nothing to do with whether you get out there and organize." What Johnson observed in the labor schools was a wave that affected every institution in the middle decades of the twentieth century.

The history of settlement houses forms a powerful example of the forces that advocates of democratic knowledge had to contend with. Settlements had originally been vital centers for research about community conditions that strongly influenced the research being done at academic institutions like the University of Minnesota and the University of Chicago. Their approach bore resemblance to that of Liberty Hyde Bailey and other leaders who sought to bring a democratic spirit to land-grant education.

As the historian Ellen Lagemann has observed, settlements engaged in what they considered social science "as a combination of study and action that addressed problems holistically. They did not separate out what would later be seen as the economic aspects of a problem like unemployment from sociological or political or even anthropological aspects. Their focus was on the comprehensive problems faced by an individual or group or community. They collected statistics not in connection with an abstract question, like the extent of national income, but rather as part of an effort to document malnutrition or track the whereabouts of out-of-school youths."

Yet this view of legitimate and worthwhile research came under fierce assault. Powerful institutions like the Carnegie Corporation, a large grant-making New York foundation, sought to undermine settlements as research centers. Henry Pritchett and the Carnegie trustees favored what they considered the more detached, objective model of research conducted by scientists and research institutes which had no ties to local communities and which professed value neutrality in their policy recommendations. In 1921, the Carnegie Trustees passed a resolution refusing to accept any proposals or applications for funding from settlements, preferring instead to "seek out those forces in the social order that promise to be significant and fruitful."[20]

Thus, efforts to sustain and build vital public cultures and spaces in both rural and urban America faced enormous forces moving in the opposite direction, toward the domination of public affairs by experts. This dynamic would form a context for the way in which the nation struggled to deal with the Great Depression. Remarkably, despite the attacks on the intelligence and civic capacities of ordinary people, the vast movement collectively called "the New Deal" nonetheless emerged that renewed for a time the idea that democratic government is government *of* the people and *by* the people, as well as *for* the people.

People's public spaces constantly interacted with government, especially in the years of the New Deal. Thus public spaces became vehicles for millions of people to gain some sense of power, authority, and standing in the corridors of policy making and politics, otherwise a universe removed from the local neighborhood.

CHAPTER 5

Making a New Deal

In the Civilian Conservation Corps there was a sense of high expectation. We worked hard and we were expected to do it right. We used our muscles . . . we built barracks, dams, fought forest fires, reclaimed streams, and planted forests. Even though the CCC was one of President Roosevelt's jobs programs, I never felt I was on welfare.

James Ronning, Civilian Conservation Corps[1]

*T*he Depression convulsed the nation. "I come home from the hill every night filled with gloom," said one Washington reporter. "I see on streets filthy, ragged, desperate-looking men, such as I have never seen before." By the election of 1932, more than 15 million workers had lost their jobs. In 1929, U.S. Steel had employed 225,000 full-time workers; by April 1, 1933, the full-time workforce was zero. "Yes, we could smell the depression in the air," said one writer, "that historically cruel winter of 1932–1933, which chilled so many of us like a world's end. . . . It was like a raw wind; the very houses we lived in seemed to be shrinking." Rexford Tugwell, soon to be one of the architects of the New Deal in the Roosevelt administration, reflected in his journal, "No one can live and work in New York this winter without a profound sense of uneasiness. Never in modern times, I should think, has there been so widespread unemployment and such moving distress from sheer hunger and cold."[2]

By the time Franklin Roosevelt delivered his second inaugural address on January 20, 1937, flush with "the blizzard of '36," the mood of the country had changed. Roosevelt swept the electoral college by 523 to 8, bringing with him 331 Democrats to the House to face 89 hapless Republicans.

Throughout the campaign, Roosevelt portrayed Alfred Landon, his Republican opponent, as the servant of "the old enemies of peace"— business and financial monopoly, sectionalism, and war profiteering. Roosevelt's belief that government is the agency of the people was the key to his victory.

In his second inaugural address, Roosevelt continued this argument. Painting the portrait of a nation where millions were "denied education, recreation, and the opportunity to better their lot . . . one-third of a nation ill-housed, ill-clad, ill-nourished," he proposed that such problems were challenges, not obstacles. They were reasons for "hope" not "despair." The nation, he declared, had the means to act. He called upon the citizenry to find through "government the instrument of our common united purpose to solve . . . the ever-rising problems of a complex civilization."[3]

Roosevelt's view of government as the people's instrument recalled the older formulation of Abraham Lincoln: government *of* the people and *by* the people, as well as government *for* the people. But it had far different content and political meaning in the urbanized, industrial world of the 1930s. Far larger and more diverse citizen-based organizations were essential, to give ordinary people a sense of power in the corridors of decision making.

Roosevelt's 1936 election had been intimately tied to a huge movement of workers called the Congress of Industrial Organizations, or CIO. The CIO sought to unionize America's basic industries like steel, automobiles, transportation, and others, on a nationwide basis. This represented the organization of many millions of new workers into unions. It also represented a shift in organizational form from the previously dominant labor group, the AFL (American Federation of Labor), which had been largely based in crafts and local unions.

Roosevelt's challenge to "the old enemies of peace" found strong parallels in the language of the political arm of the CIO, the Labor Non-Partisan League. During the 1936 election the League attacked "the manipulators of other people's money and the exploiters of other people's labor"; it called for a "battle of the people against the economic royalists."[4]

In the 1930s, the labor movement formed a central strand among a myriad of far-ranging movements for reform and change, from farm policy to old-age security, from education to child welfare. These brought into partnership with government farmers and professionals, artists, Hollywood producers, actors and actresses, and many others. Like Nellie Stone Johnson, the union organizer in Minneapolis, almost all had local settings and groups in which they worked day to day. They also felt themselves part of the enormous process of reform called "the New Deal." The New Deal involved literally tens of millions of citizens. The interaction among everyday settings, local organizations, and larger networks of reform created public spaces for political action and a democratic culture of public work. This generated the powerful sense that government was "the instrument of our collective will."

The 1936 election reflected the strength of the New Deal movement. It also gave it new impetus, leading to the pivotal victories of unions in auto making, steel industry, meatpacking, rubber processing, electrical production, transportation, and other sectors of the economy. The story of union organizing, in particular, illustrates the efforts of Americans to adapt older ideas of the worker as producer to the changed environment of the twentieth century.

Union successes were outgrowths of an effort many decades in the making. A sprawling, strikingly diverse coalition had developed that set about to push the idea of "industrial democracy." It included trade union leaders like Sidney Hillman, economists like Leo Wolman, jurists such as Felix Frankfurter, and future cabinet officers like Frances Perkins and Henry Wallace. It involved, as well, important new sections of business like the Lehman Brothers and Goldman Sachs, consumer-oriented industries like home construction, and mass merchandisers like Filene's and Macy's.[5]

Depending on the group, the call to bring industrial democracy to the shop floors and the factories had many different and sometimes contradictory meanings. But overall it was unified by several ideas that lent it continuity with older producer themes: the need for large-scale unionization of workers in core industries; the need for more dignity, independence, and voice for workers themselves; and the need to humanize America's workplaces.

What was called the labor question had been central to the broad progressive movement since before the beginning of Roosevelt's career. President Woodrow Wilson, for instance, reiterated this theme in a cable to Congress from Versailles, after World War I, as he met with leaders of Europe. "The question which stands at the front of all others amidst the present great awakening is the question of labor. How are the men and women who do the daily labor of the world to obtain progressive improvement in the conditions of their labor, to be made happier, and to be served better by the communities and the industries which their labor sustains and advances?"

In the 1920s, a wide coalition had formed around the idea of industrial democracy. All had different interests. Yet they shared in the attempt to translate traditions of the independent producer inherited from nineteenth-century America to a new and radically different age of factories, cities, and mass consumption. One of the most striking voices in this effort was that of Morris Cooke, president of the Taylor Society. The Taylor Society itself had evolved considerably after Frederick Taylor's death in 1915 from its narrow focus on maximizing output by rigid control over workers. In Cooke's 1928 presidential address, he argued for labor groups strong enough to create some measure of cooperative action "ready to grapple with any group of employers guilty either of cupidity or industrial illiteracy." Workers needed not simply "a full dinner pail" and a "full garage," but more importantly "a share in the world's highest culture."[6]

The industrial democracy movement contained within it the seeds of its own transformation to a far more centralized government, whose policies focused much less on catalyzing citizen effort than on generating consumer demand. But for a time in the 1930s, this industrial democracy movement also created institutional and political space for a massive stirring of ordinary working people. Thus in response to potent social forces, workers forged their own forms of public space, appropriate for a new age.

Three ingredients were essential to the new labor movement's success in the 1930s and to the democratic culture of public work that Nellie Stone Johnson remembers. In the first instance, labor organizers and democratic activists fused local cultural themes and traditions with a new democratic vocabulary of change that recalled older American traditions. Secondly, labor organizers built on networks of community and workplace relationships that had developed over decades, often invisibly. These formed the basis for public spaces that crossed community and ethnic lines. Such public spaces opened possibilities for civic education and interaction among diverse groups often with histories of former antagonism. Third, on such foundations a larger popular culture reflected themes of public work in movies, radio, art, and education.

Democratic Language

At both national and local levels, key organizers of the CIO had learned to combine imaginative organizing with a process of listening to the cultures of groups with which they worked. "We made every effort to make the councils part of their neighborhoods," explained Steve Nelson, a leading activist. Nelson described the accumulated organizing lessons that organizers of all political stripes applied to organizing of neighborhood groups that worked on neighborhood issues and problems affecting the unemployed. "For fund-raising we tried to stage events that fit into the cultural life of the community. Most [neighborhood] councils relied on bingo, raffles, picnics, and block parties. [In Chicago] since the Catholic church was always sponsoring such affairs, they were part of the natural way of life." Harlem council meetings organized by radicals began with a prayer, in deference to the black community's strong religious orientation. Council events in the heavily Catholic anthracite coal areas of Pennsylvania included "Hail Marys and Our Fathers."

Ethnic languages were melded together by a broad language of citizenship and democracy connected to the producer identities of workers. Progressive political groups with names like Thomas Paine and Abraham Lincoln appeared across the country. Thomas Jefferson was described as the ancestor of all those "Americans who are fighting against the tyranny of Big Business with the revolutionary spirit and boldness with which he fought the Tories of that day." "We used to celebrate every holiday and use all our events as ways of educating people about their heritage as Americans," recalled Terry Pettus, a leader in the political movement called the Washington Commonwealth Federation of the 1930s and 1940s. "Later I used to argue with the activists of the Sixties. Why give away symbols like the flag and the Fourth of July?"[7]

The language of labor as the foundation of American democracy itself gave authority and credibility to organizing efforts. Recalling the great ideals and the living legacy of democratic insurgency from the past gave legitimacy and a mainstream character to actions that otherwise would be dismissed as deviant. Further, a democratic language helped position the labor movement as the very embodiment of the American spirit and its quest for freedom.

Organizing Strategies

Organizers used two essential principles. They learned to find and build on the existing, often informal ties among people. Through these associations they created larger public spaces that crossed communal and ethnic differences.

In factories, despite the industrial changes that regimented workers and fragmented many tasks, workers created their own forms of socialization and contact, often out of sight of management. Small work groups were able to impose some degree of collective control over the process of work. These workplace groups were buttressed by social networks that extended outside of factories into ethnic communities.

Unions created public spaces for people from different ethnic groups to work together and achieve a new sense of power and visibility, sometimes in dramatic fashion. In 1936 and 1937, a wave of what were called "sit-down strikes" occurred, in which workers simply stayed in the factories, refusing to move until management granted union recognition. Louis Adamic, a journalist, described how workers experienced a new awareness of common ties. "'Why, my God, man,' one Goodyear gum-miner told me, 'during the sit-downs last spring I found out that the guy who works next to me is the same as I am, even if I was born in West Virginia and he is from Poland. His grievances are the same. Why shouldn't we stick?" In Flint, Michigan, the famous sit-down strike against General Motors management resulted in a striking new sense of visibility. "When Mr. Knudsen put his name to a piece of paper and said that General Motors recognizes the UAW-CIO—until that moment we were nonpeople," one worker told Studs Terkel decades later. "We didn't even exist. That was the big one."[8]

Workplace action was given support and context, especially on local levels, by new forms of public space and collective action that extended across previous ethnic divisions. Whole communities mobilized to support sit-down strikes against the industry giants. In Steelton, Pennsylvania, the historian John Bodnar found an evolution over time toward more public, diverse spaces that created the groundwork for the steelworkers union success by the 1930s. Ethnic groups had developed before 1930, partly in an attempt to create a haven from the larger American culture which they experienced as often hostile. In the process, broader "national" identities replaced village identities. One member of the Croatian St. Lawrence Society described their lodge as "a place to express themselves where they 'felt safe from the American class of people.'" While ethnic ties often divided workers before 1930, the experiences in ethnic groups also taught workers "the value of confronting social problems and economic difficulties with large, formalized institutions and organizations rather than with isolated kin groups," according to Bodnar. Thus such organization "was actually laying the basis for the type of cooperation that would be necessary for the eventual triumph of the CIO."[9]

Sometimes public spaces developed which formally recognized the importance of cultural, political, and economic diversity and democratic vision. This pattern developed as a key part of the process of organizing the meatpacking industry in Chicago, where a former social worker and trade union activist, Saul Alinsky, pioneered in shaping a group called the Back of the Yards Neighborhood Council. Like Liberty Bailey and Jane Addams, Alinsky made explicit a broad philosophy of democratic action that focused especially on developing the capacities of ordinary people themselves.

After attending the University of Chicago, where he became interested in welfare issues, Alinsky worked for the Chicago Area Project, a service agency concerned with problems of juvenile delinquency begun by Clifford Shaw, a leading social scientist. Shaw's model of "problem solving" differed notably from the conventional approach to professional service work. Professional social work in those years increasingly focused on the professional as the most important actor, since his or her knowledge derived from a "scientific" methodology detached from communal experience. In contrast, Shaw believed that communities held within themselves the resources and capacities to solve problems like juvenile delinquency: The professional's appropriate role was more catalyst and facilitator than "problem solver." Theorizing from Hull House's practical respect for community capacity, Shaw developed a model of public work that shaped Alinsky's thinking.

Alinsky began to do volunteer organizing with the Congress of Industrial Organizations where he was influenced by the labor leader John L. Lewis, "one of the most outstanding figures of our time," as he put it. At the CIO, Alinsky saw first hand the tactics of ridicule, confrontation, and irreverency that organizers had practiced for decades.

Late in 1938, Clifford Shaw assigned Alinsky to the community called "Back of the Yards" in Chicago, the area of 90,000 impoverished immigrants in the shadow of the meatpacking companies. The CIO was beginning another round of union organizing in Back of the

Yards, seeking to revive a tradition of unionism that had been crushed with the defeat of an Amalgamated Meat Cutters' strike in 1922.

It was a complicated task. Despite academic observers' view of the community as chaotic and unorganized, in fact it was a highly elaborated but sharply divided maze of interests and groups, based largely around national identities.[10]

Working closely with Joe Meegan, a young Irish resident who had already sought to build an area-wide community group, Alinsky helped organize a remarkably diverse array of interests in the Back of the Yards Neighborhood Council (BYNC) around a campaign to support the Packinghouse Workers' Union. The Council brought together priests, small businesses, housewives, youth, communist organizers, the American Legion and labor rank and file in an unlikely, freewheeling mix.

The first "community congress" of the organization was held with 50 organizations represented on July 14, 1939, Bastille Day, two days before a scheduled strike by the packinghouse union. The BYNC's founding statement expressed its aspiration to become a new sort of public space: "This organization is founded for the purpose of uniting all of the organizations within that community known as 'Back of the Yards' in order to promote the welfare of all residents of that community regardless of their race, color or creed, so that they may have the opportunity to find health, happiness and security through the democratic way of life." Community support allowed the union to achieve a significant victory over the packinghouse industry.

The broad base of BYNC allowed it to fight effectively for a range of community issues throughout the 1940s, from hot lunch programs to recreational projects that involved teenagers directly in their planning and implementation. A by-product was a sharp decline in juvenile delinquency rates. Because the community culture changed, young people had a new sense of stake and possibility, and the whole neighborhood developed greater hope for its future.[11] Before "Back of the Yards," community organizing consisted mostly of councils of social service agencies rhetorically dedicated to "uplifting the poor." BYNC represented a distinctively different approach, that initiated a vibrant tradition of community organizing as public work.

Thus, the key to successful popular action during the union organizing efforts across the nation proved to be organizing methods that respected the uniqueness of each community and tied local roots to larger arenas. These activities in turn fed into a much larger popular culture of reform, spreading far beyond the specific activities of unions.

The New Deal's Public Culture

Democratic culture in the 1930s and 1940s was redolent with images, themes, and language of public work. Such images appeared in Hollywood movies, in the humor of popular cultural figures like Will Rogers, in music, in art like the Regionalists' movement, and in new media like photo journalism. Film critic and historian Lary May observes that a common theme in movies, for instance, was the creation of new political activist relationships across lines of class or cultural division. A common movie plot involved a struggle of ordinary citizens against threatening interests like corporations or organized crime. By the end of the movie, the characters would succeed in taming unaccountable power. Often these plots had explicit democratic themes. Sometimes the outcome would be symbolized; a young man of working-class background, for instance, would marry a young woman of great affluence.

In his "Freedom's Plow," the African American poet Langston Hughes vividly combined ideas of the citizen as producer with the unfinished quest for freedom.

> Free hands, and slave hands
> Indentured hands, adventurous hands
> White hands and black hands
> Held the plow handles
> Ax handles, hammer handles
> Launched the boats and whipped the horses
> That fed and housed and moved America
> Thus together through labor
> All these hands made America.

"Ballad For Americans" was a song sung by Paul Robeson from the industrial union organizing campaigns that was popular enough to be played at both Communist Party and the Republican conventions in 1940. The song conveyed the cultural pluralism that was part of this public culture, radically democratizing the definition of "citizen." To the rhetorical question, "Am I an American?" comes the answer: "I'm just an Irish, Negro, Jewish, Italian, French and English, Spanish, Russian, Chinese, Polish, Scotch, Hungarian, Litvak, Swedish, Finnish, Canadian, Greek and Turk and Czech and double-check American." This kind of public imagery upheld a cultural mosaic radically at odds with the homogenized, melting-pot image of citizenship of the early twentieth century in which the ideal was the White Anglo-Saxon Protestant.

Government agencies reflected this public culture and also played important roles in catalyzing it. For instance, the Post Office Art Project of the 1930s frequently depicted the public nature of work literally—with art featuring everyday working people, in different settings. Its process of creation often prompted vigorous community discussions since the protocols of the Treasury Department, which sponsored the project, required that art designs receive the approval of local residents. Franklin Roosevelt and other architects of the New Deal believed that popular art of this sort was an essential element of national renewal. They sought to democratize culture by reworking the relation between artist and community and by sponsoring a wide range of artistic products. As Edward Bruce, head of the Treasury Department's Section of Fine Arts, put it, "Our objective should be to enrich the lives of all our people by making things of the spirit, the creation of beauty, part of their daily lives." Across the range of federal arts projects, the government employed and commissioned over 10,000 mostly unknown artists. In ten years, they produced 100,000 paintings, 18,000 sculptures, over 13,000 prints, and more than 4,000 murals, in addition to countless photos and other works. "In the process they created a public art expressing the ideals, fulfilled and unfulfilled of that era," write historians Marlene Park and Gerald E. Markowitz in their *Democratic Vistas: Post Offices and Public Art in the New Deal.*[12]

New Deal cultural programs not only created public art depicting the work and aspirations of ordinary people, they also expanded the definitions of who produces art. These efforts shifted thinking about artistic production as a creative act of individual genius to the idea that creative potential resides in the general population. The New Deal sponsored many community arts programs that taught art, music, and writing skills. Moreover, popular cultural artifacts themselves became defined and understood as forms of art. For instance, the Federal Writers' Project chronicled slave narratives. It also recorded important cultural forms like slave music and folktales. The New Deal art in its many forms illustrated that public work involves the creation of social as well as material culture.

Roosevelt's Tree Army

The programs of the New Deal also helped to reinforce the sense of government as "the instrument of our collective will," as Franklin Roosevelt had put it. Together, the interplay between the activity of tens of millions of citizens and government agencies and initiatives generated a sense of powerful partnership, and the feeling that the nation was gaining control over its collective destiny.

Government explicitly promoted public work in the New Deal. Roosevelt's plan for economic recovery aimed at providing immediate and widespread relief by putting people to work on public projects that built or repaired the nation's infrastructure and promoted conservation. The Civilian Conservation Corps formed a striking example.

The Civilian Conservation Corps (CCC), established in the first few days of Roosevelt's presidency, employed 3 million young men in conservation efforts throughout the nation between 1933 and 1942. Roosevelt, himself a long-time conservationist, had experimented with smaller scale conservation efforts while governor of New York. He believed there were important character-building benefits to be gained through disciplined, public work. In his message to the Seventy-third Congress calling for the CCC, he wrote, "I propose to create a Civilian Conservation Corps to be used in simple work, not interfering with normal employment, and confining itself to forestry, the prevention of soil erosion, flood control, and similar projects. More important, however, than the material gains will be the moral and spiritual value of such work. The overwhelming majority of unemployed Americans, who are now walking the streets and receiving private or public relief would infinitely prefer to work."[13]

Authorized quickly by Congress, the CCC was implemented in little more than one month. Four federal departments managed the program in a cooperative effort that was unprecedented. The Departments of Agriculture and the Interior planned and organized the work which spread to every state in the country, as well as Alaska, Hawaii, Puerto Rico, and the Virgin Islands. By the end of 1935, 2,650 camps were in full operation.[14]

The Labor Department was responsible for recruitment and enrollment. The army managed the logistical problems. Mobilization of thousands of unemployed men living primarily in the East to work in other areas of the country required resources that only the army had available. Army officers supervised construction and running of the camps themselves, while the conservation work was supervised by foresters.

The CCC had an extraordinary impact on the country. At that time, America had no conservation policy and was faced with severe erosion of its natural resources and the effects of natural disasters as well. It was also gripped with a crisis in confidence and morale. An account of the work accomplished by the CCC over its nine-year existence is staggering. Two billion, 300 million trees were planted, hence the term "tree army;" 3,470 fire towers were erected; 97,000 miles of truck roads were built; 4,135,500 man-days in fighting fires were logged. Soil erosion was stopped on more than 20 million acres of land. The CCC also built beautiful recreational facilities in parks throughout the country, still appreciated today. Slowly, CCC participants realized that they were helping to create a substantial national treasure of fine, beautiful and enduring quality.[15]

The benefit to individual participants was no less remarkable. Education and work training were among the most important advantages of the CCC. Although education and job training were not explicitly included as outcomes of the program when it began, training later was officially authorized and educational advisors assigned to each camp. Over the history of the Corps, more than 40,000 men learned to read and write. Many earned high school diplomas.

Public work was the primary focus, and the expectations for self-discipline and good work were high. "We knew our work was important because we were told this by the supervisor every day—how important it was to have healthy trees. If somebody was careless or not planting trees right, the supervisor would explain why it had to be done a particular way and insist that they be replanted."[16] William

Cleveland of camp number 613 recalls the job training opportunities. "We learned how to use tools, how plants grew, and we learned about conservation. The camp had a botanist who had an enormous collection of specimens. He taught us to recognize trees and leaves. Part of the lodge had displays up. The forester would tell us about poison ivy and poison sumac, what berries to eat and not to eat, and how to orient yourself in the forest so as not to get lost. When men left the CCC, they had work skills they could use. For the fellows who came in with no work training, if they stayed a year, they would leave much better off than when they arrived."[17]

Discipline was central to camp culture. "The bugle was at six o'-clock. We had to be cleaned up, presentable, and ready for breakfast at 7:00, no questions asked. If you weren't, there were two CCC boys, one on each side of the entry to the mess hall to look you over when you came in. If you didn't have your hair combed or were dressed sloppy, they sent you back to the barracks. If you weren't back in ten minutes, you didn't get breakfast. Some tested it, but they soon learned it didn't pay because they'd get KP duty for the weekend. We didn't have many problems."[18]

Self-discipline was an important part of what young men learned, recounts James Ronning, a past enrollee now actively trying to revive the Civilian Conservation Corps. "We lived like a family. . . . We learned how to work together and play together. We even learned how to eat together—when they passed the food around, we took a fair share so that everybody got enough."

Although several racially integrated camps existed, most blacks served in segregated camps. Francis Crowdus was a member of one such camp located in Corydon, Indiana. "In 1933, I was going to high school. We didn't have anything, because it was the height of the Depression. My mother was a widow making $5 a week and I had two brothers going to school." Pay for CCC enrollees was $30 a month; $25 from each check was sent to the family. Members were given a pair of boots, clothing, food, and lodging for their work.

Crowdus remembers the discrimination. "We had to go to Louisville to go to a movie. The theater had a room upstairs which seated ten blacks. I remember in Corydon there was a baseball league and our team won the championship, but we couldn't go to the tournament because it was segregated. When we threatened to boycott Corydon business, we got permission to go to the tournament in Evansville. After we won the tournament, they hired our pitcher.

"I have never been in a place where I admired men as much. We maintained a moral standard in our camp. You also had to be articulate to get around. You'd be questioned on things. Every one would talk about things like politics. We studied history and broad subjects. If you didn't know how to read, you'd learn. Most of the guys were readers; people had inquisitive minds."[19]

Like settlement houses, cooperative extension services, and the freethinkers movement of the nineteenth century, some CCC camps like Crowdus's in Harrison County also created citizenship schools alive with intellectual energy and larger democratic vision. Here people learned to relate their everyday work to large public issues.

The Corps was not simply a jobs program. Rather it represented a national response to urgent public needs through the mobilization of the amateur, hardworking labor of ordinary citizens. It enrolled almost 3 million young men over nine years. Perhaps most striking was the pride and dignity that "the boys," mostly poor, from small towns and farms, gained from the sense that their work mattered to the country. Work was hard and exhausting. Men lived in barracks. But participants felt they made a national contribution. "We have this park," Robert Ritchit, a CCC veteran from Hansell, Iowa, said. "It was a wilderness before, and now it's a nice place to go. I had something to do with that. I was part of the country and of history."[20]

During the 1930s, the nation sought to deal with the cataclysms of the Great Depression. Through a partnership between citizens and government, people developed the sense that they could regain control over their lives. This process both emerged from and reinvigorated a rich culture of public work.

After World War II, several factors contributed to the erosion of public work and public life. The centralizing tendencies of the war reinforced hierarchical structures, especially in government. The fears and turbulence of the Cold War fed a flight toward the private realm. Business, academic, and policy leaders who helped to shape the New Deal developed a far different understanding of the economy, labor's role, and government action. By the 1950s, government economic and labor policy focused almost entirely on questions of consumption, not production. Thus productive and public identities largely disappeared.

In this context, a "new gentry" of professionals and experts, long in formation, came into their own. Institutions that had sustained vibrant cultures of public life and public work increasingly took on the character of service providers in which experts sought to fix people and solve problems for clients. Consumer culture, itself manipulated by experts, replaced public cultures. These dynamics were to regenerate new hierarchies of deference.

CHAPTER 6

The New Gentry and the Loss of Public Space

Everywhere in American life, the professions are triumphant. . . . We already devote an impressive percentage of the gross national product to the training of professionals . . . and the day is coming when the 'knowledge industry' will occupy the same key role in the American economy that the railroad industry did a hundred years ago. . . . Thorsten Veblen's sixty-year-old dream of a professionally run society has never been closer to realization.

Editors of *Daedalus* magazine, 1963[1]

A joyous and patriotic public wel-
comed home soldiers from World
War II. The war effort had enlisted not only soldiers but a vast army
on the home front: women worked in war production industries;
families saved coupons, rationed meat and fuel, and contributed volunteer efforts in their neighborhoods. Yet it was a paradoxical time,
both frightening and exhilarating. The evils of war and fear of losing
freedom to tyrannical rule mixed with a great optimism about the future of America. After the arduous experience of war and depression,
it was as if America took a break.

For the first time since before the Great Depression, millions of
Americans believed it was possible to have part of the dream of American abundance. The trauma and international news that were daily
experiences of the war years allowed Americans to compare their lives
firsthand with people in other countries where conditions were far
more difficult and where everyday goods were scarce. In the war's aftermath, Americans came to equate the ideals of a democratic society
with the successes of modern capitalism. Capitalism became the very
embodiment of the triumphs of modern life itself. For many with
vivid memories of economic hardship wrought by the depression and
the stresses of war, freedom meant the ability to share in the nation's
abundance.[2] Abundance, as we shall see, was defined primarily in economic terms, inextricably tied to purchase of consumer goods. Work
became increasingly a means to an end, not an end in itself.

A few dissented from this understanding of American society. For
instance, Lewis Mumford, a well-known educator, warned about the
rise of a bureaucratic, narrowly technical civilization and the loss of
an ethos of citizenship based on public work. In *The Conduct of Life,*
what he called the "culmination" of his career, Mumford argued that

"our present civilization lacks the capacity for self-direction because it has committed itself to mass organizations and has built its structures from the top down, on the principle of all dictatorships and absolutism, rather than from the bottom up." Mumford believed technological civilization was "efficient in giving orders and compelling obedience and providing one-way communication; but it is . . . inept in everything that involves reciprocity, mutual aid, two-way communication, give and take."

To counter such trends, Mumford proposed a "public work corps" that would put each young man and woman to work "doing a thousand things that need to be done, from planting forests and roadside strips, supervision of school children in nurseries and playgrounds to the active companionship of the aged, the blind, the crippled, from auxiliary work in harvesting to fire fighting." Broad education was essential to his plan. Education for citizenship through public work was, for Mumford, even more important than the particular tasks themselves.[3]

Yet overall, Mumford's voice was the rare exception. The social, political, and economic forces of the time became intertwined in a way that constricted public life and eroded both the explicit language and the everyday experiences of public work.

The 1950s witnessed a culmination of powerful trends which began at the turn of the century: an increasing reliance on scientific knowledge and on those who employed it to solve all major public problems; a growing emphasis on consumerism; and changing work patterns for both men and women that led to specialization of tasks. Such trends changed the lens through which people saw themselves and the world. All these changes contributed to the loss of a sense of larger public significance and meaning.

In the 1950s, Americans returned to the household as the locus of production. Family life offered stability in an unsettling public world that now encompassed the entire globe. The Cold War and nuclear threat conjured up terrifying specters of a world on the brink of annihilation. Increasingly the large institutions of government, education, and business seemed far beyond the reach of ordinary citizens who wished to make a difference. Although involvement in churches, synagogues, and other community activities continued and even expanded during the 1950s, the scope of people's public work through these associations also narrowed dramatically. Simply, people lost both the civic confidence and civic muscle with which to act on the public stage.

Suburbia

In the 1950s, owning a home—one's "dream house"—now came in reach of the American middle class. The 1950s marked a dramatic movement of people from cities to suburban areas and from eastern and midwestern cities to the West. These vast streams of population were fed by federally sponsored low-interest loans through the Veterans Administration and the Federal Home Mortgage Association. Accessible financing combined with government-supported highway construction and a perceived abundance of inexpensive energy for transportation promoted the migration from cities to the suburbs. Within the decade, the American dream of home ownership became reality for 31 million of the nation's 44 million families.[4]

History repeats itself in curious fashion. The postwar possibility of individually owned plots of farmland-turned-suburb recalled a nineteenth-century democratic ideal that Thomas Jefferson had sketched in his National Survey for land acquisition west of the Alleghenies. Jefferson's scheme linked concepts of life, liberty, and the pursuit of happiness to an agrarian landscape of individually owned small farms. He connected in visual terms the principles of democracy with widespread land ownership by many independent farmers. His specific plan turned out differently than he wished—when land sales actually began, large areas were acquired by land speculators rather than by small farmers. But the ethos and imagery of agrarian democracy continued well into the twentieth century. It flowed powerfully through the writings of Liberty Bailey and the country life movement.[5]

The American dream included "the right to own a home," a right which to this day is an essential staple of public rhetoric. But it was often justified in ways that privatized the meaning of homeownership. "Get [workers] to invest their savings in homes and own them. Then they won't leave and they won't strike. It ties them down so they have a stake in our prosperity," commented one corporate official describing his philosophy about the relationship between good business and satisfied workers.[6]

Imagery around home ownership changed from the associations of independent "freehold"—the concept rooted in agrarian democracy of a place that was the citizen's own base, from which to participate in a larger public world. A generation before, Progressives like Mary Baker Follett had argued that in urban society the new form of freehold should be the individually owned home, from which citizens could go out to deal with a diverse public environment of different races and cultures. But in the 1950s, home ownership almost entirely lost its civic and public overtones. It came to mean "a man's castle." Unlike freeholds on what Liberty Bailey had called "the open countryside," castles conjure up images of moats, enclosing walls, and drawbridges that in many ways convey dramatically the culture of the fifties. Restrictive racial covenants, homeowner associations that discriminated against Jews, and a variety of other measures were employed to create isolated and homogeneous enclaves.

An emphasis on homeownership meshed closely with postwar industrialists' eagerness to increase consumers' capacity to purchase manufactured goods. It was also spurred by the federal government. In 1938 and 1939, federal economic policies had begun to shift dramatically from an emphasis on production to management of consumer demand to fuel an ever-expanding growth machine.[7]

Suburban exodus from cities or in-migration from rural areas sometimes had a pastoral edge. People sought out living environments that were closer to nature, places to escape the harried pace of urban life. "We wanted to move to a place that was more rustic," explained a woman who moved from Atlanta with her family to Sandy Springs, a growing suburb. She didn't like the commute into the city for her job, but she liked the setting. "Where we lived we still had woods, a creek, a ravine in back."[8]

More generally, however, suburban development took place in large tracts. William J. Levitt helped shape this story. A developer who adapted Henry Ford's production line method to housing construction, Levitt mass-produced inexpensive, single-family suburban homes practically overnight, beginning in the late 1940s. For $6,999, a government-financed, no-money-down, 25-by-32-foot home could be purchased. Levitt's large-scale construction process was a model of efficiency. Broken into twenty-six separate steps, the prefabricated homes were built by teams of workers, each carrying out specific tasks—pouring concrete, installing electrical wires, plumbing, roofing, and siding, or planting trees. The technique allowed one hundred houses to be built at one time. The first phase of Levittown offered some 17,000 homes for 82,000 people. In later, more upscale housing developments appealing to more affluent buyers, Levitt offered three higher-grade models—a Cape Cod style, a three-bedroom "Rancher," and a two-story Colonial costing between $11,500 and $14,500.[9]

Some critics raised objections. Lewis Mumford criticized modern technological civilization with a sustained attack on Levittown. Others echoed his warnings. They expressed reservations about the consequences of a uniform, suburban life. Urban planners, for instance, argued that rapid, uncontrolled expansion created neighborhoods without adequate parks, community spaces, churches or schools. They predicted hidden costs—a destructive competition for limited resources between cities and new developments; growing segregation of races from all-white housing tracts; and environmental stress through excessive consumption of nonrenewable resources. Sociologists also worried that city exodus would create an uprootedness and further isolate generations from each other. Some predicted that conformity to a homogenized living environment also threatened dire psychological problems. Many architects despaired over the repetitive, banal design of mass-produced single family homes, which took no account of individual preferences or community contexts. Mass production eclipses the importance of aesthetics and even the very ideas of public spaces and convivial places, they argued. Obviously, such objections had a self-interested quality: Professional interests were threatened by Levitt's style of massive development. But they raised concerns that would become widespread in the latter years of the 1960s.[10]

Yet for millions of citizens, Levittown and its successors provided welcome solutions to many postwar problems. Because of the depression and World War II, a tremendous pent-up demand for housing had accumulated. During the war, building materials were costly and difficult to come by, and most construction went into the war effort. Extended families lived together but very often not by choice; people felt crowded and cramped in their lifestyles.

Suburban developments like Levittown created affordable housing for first-time home buyers, particularly young families who wanted to move out of apartments or shared living arrangements with parents. They also established a home-building industry that became central to American economic success over the last half century. Perhaps equally as important, suburban home ownership created a new social space, where definitions of productive activity were radically reworked.

The Domestic Ideal

In his 1955 graduation address at Smith College, Adlai Stevenson, Democratic Party candidate for president in 1952 and 1956, described to women graduates what they could look forward to. In Stevenson's view, their important roles in life would be to "influence us, man and boy," to "restore valid, meaningful purpose to life in your home," and to keep husbands "truly purposeful."[11]

Stevenson's opinions were widely shared at the time. Popular culture and civic leaders of both sexes proclaimed that building a strong, secure family and home life for children and husband and running a modern household should be the main, full-time work for married women. Large numbers of women had joined the paid labor force during World War II. Immediately after the war, millions returned home to traditional roles; only 7 percent of all middle-class wives were in the paid labor force. Expectations about the life path of middle-class women changed dramatically.

During the early fifties, fewer women pursued careers requiring advanced degrees. Two out of three women who entered college withdrew before graduation. In one study, 60 percent of those who left college did so in order to marry or because they believed their college education would not help their chances for marriage.[12]

Demographic data captured these patterns. People married younger. In the fifties, the average marrying age dropped to 22 for men and 20 for women, departing sharply from rates over the century before, when women tended to marry in their early to mid twenties, and men in their mid- to late twenties. Marriage rates climbed higher than any previous time in the twentieth century. In 1940, for example, 42 percent of women were married by age 24. In 1950, 50 percent of all women aged 24 were married. By the end of the 1950s, 70 percent of women in the same age group were married—an all-time high.

Women in the fifties had more children. They also had them more quickly than before. The fertility rate rose 50 percent between 1940 and 1957. Almost one-third of all women had their first child before they were twenty years old. At the same time, the rate of divorce was slower than any time before or after that decade. From a statistical point of view, family stability seemed a defining characteristic of the time.[13]

After the tremendous strains on family life brought about by the Great Depression and on the heels of prolonged separations imposed by World War II, family togetherness became a central value for millions of Americans. Popular media, however, made togetherness a kind of national ideal defined by a model of nuclear families (married couple and children, without other generations or relatives). The ideal was purified of the messy complexities, tensions, and actual work of any substantial relationships. Throughout the 1950s, images of happy families playing and working together in their modern homes filled women's magazines and television as backdrops for advertisement. Television sitcoms like *Ozzie and Harriet, Leave it to Beaver,* and *Father Knows Best* dominated popular culture. Although family life was far more diverse than media images and opinion shapers implied, the stereotypes depicted in these sitcoms shaped middle-class expectations and reinforced prescribed social roles of the time.

In these scenarios family life was pleasant and secure, shielded from the larger world of politics and fears of the Cold War. Nastiness vanished. Troubles were minor and often comical. Well-meaning dad bumbled around at home trying to fix a mechanical emergency. Mom managed the household with exceptional proficiency, but became befuddled in the public world only a few blocks from home. Above all else, family members were relentlessly fond of each other. Their relationships endured. They tolerated individual peculiarities. Harsher realities such as financial problems, divorce, drug use, and violence were not visible. Failure was unthinkable. Moms were not employed outside the home. The most popular depictions of dads' work, though rarely described in any detail, was assumed to be a white-collar, respectable position that afforded the good family life.[14]

Such weekly installments, though recognized as entertainment, became the yardsticks with which many families measured their own normalcy. In recalling life in the 1950s, television images of life portrayed by the Cleavers, the Nelsons, or the Andersons often first come to mind.

Such ideals and expectations also came with costs. Suburban life separated people from their extended families and older neighborhoods. The new mobility associated with growing affluence and corporate job expectations meant that communal associations were often fleeting. In Levittown, for example, one out of every six families moved each year. In the New York area, less than 6 percent of suburban residents lived in the same home in 1960 as they did five years earlier in 1955.[15] This transient quality of suburban life meant that building and sustaining communities was more difficult. The lack of diversity in race, class, income, or even age groups (though often the reason people preferred suburban life) also constrained resources for public work.

The separation of home life from the public world produced gender roles more rigid and narrowly defined.[16] As Stevenson implied in his graduation address, women's authentic and satisfying work was defined in traditional ways, in the private sphere as nurturers and creators of stable family life. Men were to negotiate the public world as decision makers and family providers. But even men's work roles and work identities were changing. No longer did workers readily imagine themselves as independent producers, building a commonwealth, but now the purpose of work became far more instrumental: to achieve and maintain the "American standard of living," defined as acquisition of material goods.

Popular culture in the 1930s—movies, songs, and art—had commonly portrayed a vigorous and active public life. Life pursuits in the 1950s came to focus on private pleasures. The goal of creating healthy, stable family life had dimensions that required new learning. For many this meant a more up-to-date way of looking at the world–one which broke from older practices handed down over generations, methods based on experience and common sense. More and more ordinary people came to rely on "expert" advice to help them create their lives. Popular culture and advice stressed new child-rearing practices based on psychological theory and the latest family health advances. Successful homemaking, it was thought, required a home with up-to-date conveniences. Household management itself became infused with scientific information and organizational techniques used in businesses to increase efficiency. Family recreation also carried modern expectations.

People worked hard to create safe, healthy, physical and emotional environments for children. And in this way, to some degree, they sustained their producer identities. "I always felt my work at home with my children was important work," recalls a housewife raising two children in the fifties. "In our family, we weren't flag wavers, but we were patriotic. We believed that raising children who would become responsible citizens was an important contribution all of us could make for the country."[17]

The domestic ideal was not devoid of expectations for the public realm, but public life was now narrower in scope and was generally pursued in relationship to the family. Women continued their involvement in civic and community groups, but these activities were more social in nature than political or public. They assumed leadership roles in scouting or 4-H, for example; they were active in their churches, or involved in their children's school. Such civic activities were often described in terms of their contributions to the family.

"PTA was a common form of civic involvement in those days," remembers Betty Newland, "but the issues we tackled weren't defined as broadly as they are today. We only dealt with issues affecting the school our children attended, like fund-raising projects . . . nothing outside the immediate school. We had no power to solve larger problems."[18] Newland's comment conveys the loss of public spaces that brought a diversity of people together, willing to work for a larger common goal despite their differences. Sustaining these public spaces was difficult when large portions of the population lived and worked with others like themselves. The societal norm was to conform. "Being ordinary is being better," writes David Halberstam about the television families who became role models for middle class Americans. "They were to be as much like their fellow citizens as possible and certainly not better than them."[19] Life was more complicated, however, than the message conveys.

Some people's lives, even in middle-class white America, formed exceptions to the dominant message. Janet Ferguson, a woman originally from the Midwest, married to a Red Cross executive in Atlanta, felt caught up by the turbulence surrounding impending desegregation in the South. "People would say to me, 'You don't understand, you're not from the South.' But from the moment I came to Atlanta, there were many opportunities to get involved. We had a knock-down-drag-out fight in the League of Women Voters about whether to admit black women. The Human Relation Council worked to integrate the libraries. In the late fifties, after the Supreme Court ruling outlawing segregated schools, there developed a real threat to close down public schools in all of Georgia, so we worked with people across the state who wanted to keep the schools open."[20]

Yet Ferguson was the exception. Most people had few tools and lacked ways to imagine acting on public issues like race relations or the Cold War. When 1950s images of a secure home life are contrasted with the terrors of nuclear war, it is no wonder people withdrew from public life.

In contrast to the happy, care-free images created by the media, a climate of political fear threatened public expression. In response to the perceived communist threat at home, for instance, some political leaders like Senator Joseph McCarthy from Wisconsin, sought to rout out all those activities he viewed as subversive. These ranged from efforts to achieve racial integration in the South to union organizing in northern factories.[21] The atmosphere of fear and suspicion created by the McCarthy hearings reinforced the dominant cultural norm of conformity. But the ironies of such dynamics were also vivid. Thus, for instance, anticommunist evangelists from conservative, rock-ribbed Republican areas of the Midwest or South, staunch supporters of McCarthy that they were, often focused on the threats posed by experts, consumerism, the "Great State," and the loss of small business and worker autonomy.[22] Many liberal critics of McCarthyism, in contrast, unabashedly endorsed science and the technocratic culture.

Meanwhile, however, the popular culture of consumerism reached new heights. Advertising, mass marketing, new shopping opportunities, and the new mass media all converged to drive out images of "producers" as the central American icon and replace it with the consumer.

Consumerism

The rise of consumer culture changed the very meaning of America's core ideals in dramatic fashion. This was vividly apparent in an exchange which made world headlines in 1959. In a 1950s model of a modern America kitchen, full of the latest appliances, Vice President Richard Nixon argued with Nikita Khrushchev about the meaning of freedom. In what was to be known as the "kitchen debate," Nixon proclaimed that American freedom emanated from a high technology growth machine whose penultimate achievement was the democratic right of ordinary citizens to choose among many varieties of consumer products. These declarations reformed the language of politics in America. Consumer choice became the touchstone of the public good.[23]

In framing the international debate in such ways, Nixon proposed that by embracing modern life with its family-centered values and a healthy investment in a consumer culture, the nation would gain superiority over the "Red Menace." His image of the American "model home" represented more than simply a physical structure. It implied a full-time homemaker surrounded by an array of the latest conveniences and a male breadwinner, the products of whose labor allowed the family to maintain a lifestyle characterized by a never-ending purchase of new and improved products. Superiority in the Cold War, Nixon argued, depended not so much on weapons as it did on an abundant, flourishing family life typically played out in modern homes in suburban neighborhoods.

"Houses became almost sacred structures," writes the historian Elaine Tyler May, "adorned and worshiped by their inhabitants." In them, women could find visibility and dignity. Men could parade their successes as a breadwinner. In such ways, the images and lures of consumer culture transcended class, suggesting "an ideal of individuality, leisure, and upward mobility."[24]

Nixon returned to the United States a political hero. Americans responded positively to his "standing up to Communism." The American lifestyle he portrayed was indeed the life many postwar Americans wanted. Although he exaggerated the widespread prosperity in the United States, the domestic life Nixon described was, in fact, one that many were able to achieve.[25]

Thus consumerism understood as an abundant domestic life became inextricably linked to American security and freedom. In a convoluted way, to build the country now meant to purchase and use goods. The school of thought called "neoclassical economics" encouraged and justified such changes, but in ways that had an unreal, almost magical quality. In their terms the consumer was sovereign. Independent, rational individuals "chose" what they would buy on the open marketplace. Their imagery had an eerie kinship with the ideals of civic autonomy invoked by leaders of the earlier agrarian democracy. Such economic theorists imagined a world as it existed in the time of Adam Smith in the eighteenth century. The property mainly took the form of individual farms, businesses were owned by individuals, and things produced were evaluated in terms of their usefulness to persons and to the community.

In the twentieth century, many dynamics have transformed a world of small businesses and entrepreneurs into full-scale capitalism. Scientific management and organization of the workplace, giant corporations, the mass media, the growth of advertising, and the modern large government, all have combined to render older concepts and language increasingly anachronistic. The consumer culture of today is a very different context in which to live out democratic ideals.

Consumerism had deep effects on peoples' behavior, their identities and their collective lives. In 1930, Waldo Frank, a leading progressive intellectual, observed that a consumer culture feeds on a frenzy for the new, the different, and the exotic. Social critic Christopher Lasch retrieved Frank's observation in the early 1990s—that possession replaces use in consumer capitalism. "A fresh plaything renews the child's opportunity to say: this is mine," Frank argued. Yet if "toys become more frequent, value is gradually transferred from the toy to the toy's novelty. The arrival of the toy, not the toy itself, becomes the event." Lasch extends this analysis by observing that consumer shopping takes on an addictive quality, fueled by mass advertising. "It hardly matters what I buy, I just get a kick out of buying," explained one shopper. "It's like that first whiff of cocaine. It's euphoric and I just get higher and higher as I buy." Surveys of those who are "compulsive shoppers" report that shopping becomes a means to "alleviate loneliness," "dispel boredom," and "relieve depression."[26]

These patterns of behavior help create the dynamics that lead people increasingly to see their work in instrumental terms—as means to an end. The accumulation of enough money for purchase of consumer products supersedes producing things of use and larger value.

Concepts of work as a "calling" in older religious terms—work that has value in itself, work that generates a larger commonwealth of values—sharply eroded.

Contributing to the allure of consumer culture were changes in patterns of power in everyday lives that weakened people's sense of efficacy and authority. Increasingly, in many settings people ceded decision making to a new class of experts.

Science: The New Religion

Richard Hofstadter, dean of American historians in the 1950s, former Marxist champion of the working class in the 1930s, illustrated a dramatic shift in American letters and academic discussion in his description of "the common man."

> He cannot even make his breakfast without using devices, more or less mysterious to him, which expertise has put at his disposal, and when he sits down to breakfast and looks at his morning newspaper he reads about a whole range of vital and intricate issues and acknowledges, if he is candid with himself, that he has not acquired competence to judge most of them.[27]

Hoftstadter's views were commonplace in mainstream political discussion in the 1950s and early 1960s. In the 1950s, a culture of professionalism permeated work and home life. It emphasized rationality, methodical processes, and an objectivity that suggested, to an anxious middle class, ways of reimposing order on a fast-changing, turbulent environment.[28]

Even in domestic life professional expertise played a central role. Parenting, for instance, took on new dimensions for mothers, particularly, as women tried to fulfill the growing gender expectations in building a satisfying family life. Many women now lived apart from extended families with their traditional sources of support and knowledge. Lacking technical knowledge of child rearing, mothers came more and more to rely on professional expertise, now readily available through women's magazines and a plethora of manuals. Meanwhile, experts sometimes displayed an overweening arrogance. "Old functions of child welfare and training have passed over into the hands of sociologists, psychiatrists, physicians, home economists and other scientists dealing with problems of human welfare," wrote two child guidance experts. "Through parent education the sum of their experiments and knowledge is given back to parents in response to the demands for help."[29]

In popular culture, expert advice often had a benevolent, even fatherly face that hid the power relationships. Dr. Spock, the famous author of child care books and an expert in children's health and development, was a household "counselor" for mothers. Spock's psychoanalytic philosophy taught parents that their own behaviors had enormous consequences in their children's lives. Putting special emphasis on the importance of the mother–child bond, he argued that the most creative people developed their talents through "the inspiration they received from a particularly strong relationship with a mother who had especially high aspirations for her children."[30]

Reflecting the current theories, Spock's approach moved away from parent as strict disciplinarian to a more child-centered approach. Quality interaction with parents, separate rooms, educational toys, and lessons were all part of the formula. But despite the reassuring, caring language used in parenting manuals written during the 1950s, an undercurrent of anxiety appeared in experts' expression of grave concern over children's health, safety, and happiness. Child development professionals became preoccupied with the role of parenting in the child's emotional adjustment, and many psychoanalysts associated maladjustment and psychological disorders in children with mother's "over anxious permissiveness" or "maternal hostility."[31]

Child rearing was only one domestic area dominated by experts. Scientific knowledge offered techniques for greater efficiency in household management. Housewives were inundated with advice about the latest equipment, interior design schemes, food preparation, even the latest technique on how to achieve satisfying sex lives. This "professionalizing" of women's domestic life promised to bring greater satisfaction and expressiveness. In fact, the opposite occurred.

A study which examined the habits and attitudes of more than 4,000 adults in 1957 discovered that reliance on outside expertise was among the most striking characteristics of the postwar era. The researchers concluded:

> Experts took over the role of psychic healer, but they also assumed a much broader and more important role in directing the behavior, goals, and ideals of normal people. They became the teachers and

> norm setters who would tell people how to approach and live life. .
> . . They would provide advice and counsel about raising and re-
> sponding to children, how to behave in marriage, and what to see
> in that relationship. . . . . Science moved in because people needed
> and wanted guidance.[32]

People probably looked to experts less out of an actual need for
guidance than from a loss of confidence in their own skills and common sense. The view of the professional as the problem-solver infused
every dimension of society, including American and European politics. In the 1950s, Gunnar Myrdal, a hero of American liberalism for
his studies of race relations in the South, argued that "increasing political harmony . . . [is emerging] between all citizens in the advanced
welfare state. The internal political debate in those countries is becoming increasingly technical in character." Social policy in countries
like his native Sweden—long a model for progressively inclined
Americans—was if anything, even further advanced toward a technical view of politics. Myrdal, drawing on the experiences of Sweden,
depicted welfare state populations as simple consumers of government—"like domesticated animals . . . with no conception of the wild
life."[33] In such a view, ordinary citizens no longer resembled the "sovereign actors" so vivid in the 1930s. The rise of expert knowledge and
the reorganization of society according to scientific and technical
principles impacted not only social policy. These trends also transformed the structure of workplaces and the nature of work itself.

A pervasive technical approach to management of workers and to
the organization of their work created striking institutional similari-
ties, even across diverse political systems like communism, social
democracy, and capitalism. "From the standpoint of the employee,"
remarked the historian Arnold Toynbee, "it is coming to make less
and less practical difference to him what his country's official ideology is and whether he happens to be employed by a government or
commercial corporation." State-owned businesses in social democratic nations produced patterns of hierarchy and efficiency-minded approaches that were found in the most capitalist of American firms.[34]

The irony of the new class of professionals was that they reintroduced an earlier pose of disinterested, altruistic public service not
seen since the old aristocracy of the eighteenth century. For the new
gentry, possession of scientific knowledge acquired authority analo-

gous to that which allegedly superior breeding had once commanded. Moreover the authority allowed the new gentry to stand outside. "We are only here to help you," became a mantra in professional fields.

The Experience of Work

Conventional wisdom holds that the artisan and his craft largely disappeared by the first decades of the twentieth century. Yet the sustenance of craft in a number of occupations, including many manual jobs and emerging professions, allowed citizens to continue to see themselves as productive contributors up until the 1950s. For example, many auto mechanics remember fondly when there was more art in their work. "I can tell you the moment when being a mechanic was no longer work with craft," says William Myers, one-time auto mechanic who now is a professor of philosophy at the College of St. Catherine in St. Paul. "It was when Volkswagens were mass produced in the United States. Mechanics became parts exchangers. All that was needed was a manual and the part. The 'art' was gone when the intellect was no longer needed."[35]

People voice similar sentiments about a variety of other kinds of work. Pat Borich, recently retired dean of the Minnesota Extension Service, says his respect for cooperative extension came from his father's experiences in the 1930s where his work as a county agent was a craft. "Over the years, Extension turned into a technology and information service, that brought the 'good news' from research labs and academic studies out from the university, and then tried to seduce people into paying attention." As a result the work became far more technical and narrowed.[36] Paul Light, a distinguished analyst of government civil service observes, "It was only in the fifties that an administrative view, descending from scientific management, completely took hold. Civil servants lost their flexibility. In government a notion was that narrow spans of control are the only way to organize human endeavor."[37] These memories not only recall experiences of craft from the past but signal the sea change developing after World War II.

Over the last generation, the reliance on scientifically based techniques for workplace efficiency and for professional practice radically accelerated the erosion of craft. It changed the experience of work. A technical approach that became a culture weakened workplace social networks, fragmented work roles, and stripped many jobs of more complex skills combining intellectual with manual tasks.

Craft weds imagination with manual effort. In professional settings, craft integrates techniques with a way of thinking that includes judgment. It is an artful capacity to appreciate context, timing, patterns of human relationships, and multiple points of view. Craft entails public dimensions—the art of work combined with a consciousness of the beauty or usefulness of the product itself in the larger environment. Craft, in this sense, generates the kind of power and authority in the world accorded those who create things of great value. "Things must be right in themselves, and good for use," wrote Eric Gill, an English philosopher of craftsmanship earlier in the twentieth century.[38] This sense of dignity, power, and visibility has vanished from a myriad of workplace settings.

" 'I'm just a clerical' is a sentiment that almost every office worker has felt and at different times accepted, hated, fought against, humbled before," observed Liz McPike. McPike was on the staff of "9 to 5", a group organizing women workers for more voice and power made famous in the Dolly Parton film *9 to 5*.

Darlene Stille, a clerical worker who became a leader in a similar group, Women Employed, described the isolation and loss of social networks in the glass and steel world of the downtown Chicago Loop. "We're all split into little departments. We walk through the hallways and we nod, but we don't know each others' names, even after five or six years." In her own office before her involvement in Women Employed, Stille, the first woman in her family to go to college, felt at a dead end in her life, overwhelmed by despair. "I worked in a great bullpen. It was noisy. It was uncomfortable. It was gloomy. It was depressing. I just couldn't believe that after all those years of effort, this is what it had come to."[39]

New technologies and broad changes in work have also led to growing levels of unemployment, underemployment, and dislocation, dramatic by the 1990s. "As 'third wave' technologies fragment the old mass production system, millions who used to work in or around factories need help just staying afloat," writes Robert Reich, Secretary of Labor in the Clinton administration.

Such changes, beginning in the 1950s, have had increasing social and economic impact over the last 40 years. They produced growing social and economic divisions. In *The Work of Nations* (1992), Reich describes the small class of those who handle information and concepts in their work, such as media professionals, ad executives, college professors, symbolic analysts, and scientists. These benefit greatly from economic reorganization, but they are also "seceding" from society— distanced from the income levels, civic life, and even physical spaces of their fellow citizens.

The changing nature of work ultimately has eclipsed its larger meaning and significance for many millions of Americans. "Most of us are looking for a calling, not a job," Nora Watson told Studs Terkel. "Most of us have jobs that are too small for our spirits. Jobs are not big enough for people." Terkel's book, *Working,* is a vivid illustration of such sentiments across a huge range of settings in contemporary America.[40]

Thus, in homes, communities, and workplaces the experience of work constricted in the 1950s. Private places replaced public spaces— often in even the most "public" of settings, like large offices, government agencies, and forums where public policy was debated. Yet a vast subterranean ferment, a desire for richer and more powerful public roles, was building across the nation.

The civil rights movement especially reintroduced a language of freedom understood as collective self-determination. It found powerful resonance among those young people who were the direct heirs of technocracy and who simultaneously felt its constrictions. In the 1970s a community-organizing movement began to develop important practical strategies for furthering this work. This is the legacy we have today as we continue America's experiment in democracy.

CHAPTER 7

Citizenship Schools

The world is deluged with panaceas, formulas, proposed laws, machineries, ways out, and myriads of solutions. It is significant and tragic that almost everyone of these proposed plans and alleged solutions deals with the structure of society, but none concerns the substance itself—the people. This, despite the eternal truth of the democratic faith that the solution always lies with the people.

Saul Alinsky, 1946[1]

*T*he decade of the 1960s burst on the nation's consciousness with a kaleidoscope of democratic energy and social experiment. New music and new lifestyles, the civil rights movement, anti-war protests, women's liberation, the environmental movement, the gay movement, Black Power, self-help groups, rural communes—all tumbled across the social and political landscape. It was as if suddenly a river had burst its boundaries. The catalyst that had unleashed this force was the black freedom movement, developing in the American South.

Ferment had been apparent in the 1950s among middle-class young people who seemed the apparent heirs of technocracy, yet felt themselves to be its victims. Millions began to declare a cultural independence from their elders. They embraced rock and roll, music strongly influenced by African American culture. In a more openly critical vein, they responded to Beat poetry, the sardonic commentary of *Mad Magazine,* and the restless, angry writings of Allen Ginsberg and Jack Kerouac. All challenged middle-class, suburban, white-collar society—supposedly the very embodiment of the "American Dream," and they did so in ways directly inspired by African American culture.

Cultural critics labeled American culture hollow, fraudulent, and dehumanized. In 1955, Ginsberg after reading his poem, "Howl," to an overflowing audience of college students, responded to a question about what he was rebelling against with an impassioned statement:

Moloch! Moloch!
Nightmare of Moloch!
Moloch the loveless! . . .
Moloch! whose soul is electricity and banks!
Moloch whose poverty is the specter of genius!
Moloch whose fate is a cloud of sexless hydrogen!
Moloch whose name is the Mind!

Mingled with estrangement that implicitly contrasted middle-class culture with the earthy, sexual images associated with blacks was an often open; direct identification with blacks on the part of middle-class youth. "At lilac evening I walked with every muscle aching," wrote Kerouac in *On the Road*, "in the Denver colored section, wishing I were a Negro, feeling that the best the white world had offered was not enough ecstasy for me, not enough life, joy, kicks, darkness, music, not enough night."[2]

As the civil rights movement swelled across the South in the early sixties, young people from every region of the country found in its themes, language, and vision ways to articulate their feelings of often inchoate discontent. In particular, the southern movement's call to "make democracy real" resonated with young people. They adapted its meaning to their own situation.

The strengths as well as the weaknesses of student hopes for a more active, direct democracy were articulated in 1962 in a manifesto of youthful revolt known as *The Port Huron Statement*, largely written by Tom Hayden, a former student leader at the University of Michigan with strong ties to the civil rights movement. The manifesto sought a radical democratic alternative to the dominant ideologies in the world like liberal democracy and communism. It invoked the specters of nuclear war, loneliness and materialism. All were embodied in a technocracy without passion or purpose. "Our generation is plagued by program without vision," it declared. It pointed not only to politics but to higher education, suburbs, unions, and corporate bureaucracies. The *Statement* sketched its alternative:

> We would replace power rooted in possession, privilege, or circumstance by power and uniqueness rooted in love, reflectiveness, reason and creativity. As a *social system* we seek the establishment of a democracy of individual participation, governed by two central aims: that the individual share in those decisions determining the quality and direction of his life; that society be organized to encourage independence in men and provide the media for their common participation.[3]

In such passages, students conveyed urgency. Yet they took the stance of detached *social critics*, outside of American culture and institutions. In the *Statement* there was virtually no reference to American *antecedents* of its quest for "participatory democracy," no recitation of prior movements, no mention of the aspirations of those who had preceded them. Rather, the document expressed disillusionment, mingled with arrogance. "We are people of this generation, bred in at least modest comfort, housed now in universities, looking uncomfortably at the world we inherit," it began. It posed students themselves as the enlightened force for change: "We ourselves are imbued with urgency, yet ... Americans [generally exhibit what] might be called a glaze."[4]

The Port Huron Statement was an insightful critique of the bureaucratic state. Yet it also condemned virtually every American institution. It can be vividly contrasted with Martin Luther King's "Letter from a Birmingham Jail." King's "Letter" written in 1963, also raised themes of democratization, but it was grounded in rich cultures of work and religion in the black community.

Youthful activists focused on criticisms and rhetorical calls for an alternative culture and institutions rather than practical strategies to implement their ideals within the settings most people lived and worked. Even worse, their arrogance toward other Americans reflected their own privileged position. Finally, student discussion of active democracy subtly reflected elements of Nixon's redefinition of American ideals. Children of the consumer culture, they reinforced the shift from a work-centered democracy to a democracy based on personal fulfillment articulated in values like personal independence and self-realization.

For millions of hard-hats, ethnics, and other blue-collar workers, students seemed to have opportunities for learning and advancement that most could only dream about. College activists of earlier generations once shared a common focus on work with working-class people. By the 1960s this had disappeared. These dynamics created fuel for sharp political polarization.

The youthful revolt of the 1960s raised critical questions and had important outcomes that remain with us in the 1990s. Opposition to the war in Vietnam has profoundly shaped America's role in the world ever since. But it was less visible efforts—the citizenship and freedom schools of the civil rights movement, and the low-income community groups of the 1970s and 1980s—that provided lessons of especially enduring importance for those who would revive public life and public work in America.

Cochran Gardens

Cochran Gardens, a public housing project in St. Louis, Missouri, is one of the most dramatic examples of inner-city renewal in our lifetimes. It was not a quick process; it has taken more than twenty years. But at its heart is the powerful story of how people in even the most desperate circumstances can reclaim power over their lives through the public work of rebuilding a community.

For Cochran residents, freedom began at the most elemental level—venturing outside their private walls. It included, as an essential ingredient, reclaiming authority from a variety of expert-dominated systems that had systematically defined and named poor people as deficient and incompetent.

Bertha Gilkey lives in Cochran Gardens, a complex of apartments that has now been purchased by the tenants. Flower-lined paths, trees, grass, and play equipment for children frame a beautiful, clean, and racially integrated apartment complex. Gilkey grew up in Cochran Gardens when it was far different: a place of broken windows, rubbish, shootings in broad daylight, and angry, fearful people, many of whom were afraid to leave their apartments.

In the late 1960s, the Housing Authority in St. Louis envisioned the demolition of Cochran Gardens; it was "too far gone," in the administrators' view. A nearby complex, Pruitt Iago, had been blown up not long before. Like Pruitt Iago, Cochran resembled a colonized nation, where virtually all authority and power resided outside. Downtown housing officials made management decisions. The local school's teachers knew little about the community. "There was a little module of a white house with a picket fence and a two car garage," Gilkey recalls. That was the image of a "nice neighborhood," one with little relevance to children's lives. A nearby church had many well-intentioned white liberals, but they, too, saw tenants only in terms of their deficiencies. "They held meetings where they invited tenants," says Gilkey. "But they would set the agenda, and talk about what we should do."

Bertha Gilkey, a teenage mother, was asked by her social worker what she wanted for the neighborhood. "I said, I want Cochran Gardens to be a good place to live. We, the tenants, were going to make it happen." The social worker replied, "you can't do that because you don't have the expertise. You aren't experts." For Gilkey, this was a turning point. "I thought a minute and then said, 'experts got us in trouble in the first place. We'll be just fine.' "

Bertha Gilkey had been encouraged to join community work in civil rights activities by a woman she calls her "mentor," an older woman named Mabel Cohen. Gilkey had developed skills and political confidence through these activities, and she was a teenager of remarkable leadership talent and drive. She knew things could change. "I had a long-term strategy and a short-term strategy. In the long run, I knew we would change Cochran Gardens. But I knew no one would really believe that. So we started with small things." When she was 20, in 1969, Cochran Gardens residents elected her to chair their struggling tenant association.

She asked what people wanted. Everyone wanted a laundromat, since existing ones had been vandalized. Gilkey and other tenants organized their neighbors around simple, clear goals. These aimed at slowly building confidence and relationships among people in the projects. They worked in one building at a time. "Let's get our laundromat locked," people said. There were no locks. "There were no doors on the buildings, for that matter!" says Gilkey. "They had all been taken down."

Tenants organized a fundraiser for a lock. Then they held another for paint for the hallway walls. They moved floor by floor, but insisted "everyone who lived on a floor was responsible for painting that floor. If they didn't organize and get the paint it didn't happen." Kids who lived on a floor that hadn't been painted would come and look at the painted hallways and then go back and hassle their parents. The elderly who couldn't paint prepared lunch, so they participated in the work as well.

The Housing Authority had abandoned any screening process for selecting new tenants. "Cochran had become a dumping ground," Gilkey remembers. So tenants organized their own after-the-fact screening, setting rules of behavior, electing monitors on each floor. There were to be no fights, no garbage out the windows, no loud disruptions. In 1976, seven years later, a formal screening process began; Cochran tenants officially won control over Cochran Garden's management—one of the first tenant management contracts in the country. Slowly people got the message; they became involved; behaviors changed, as people became accountable.

Large-scale renovations of buildings at Cochran Gardens began in the 1970s. The first redone building was named for Martin Luther King. Symbols and public occasions were central. "Everything we did we had a recognition ceremony," Gilkey says. "We put up plaques. We honored people. We had parties. There would be a dedication for everything." The new laundromat had a ribbon cutting. As with the houseboaters on Seattle's Lake Union, Bertha Gilkey and the tenants sought to make visible their work and their vision to each other and to the larger public world.

A central focus was on reaching young people. "Kids had seen so much death many didn't know what life was about. We got kids to start growing things outside, so they would know the value of life, how it takes time to grow things." Teens were put to work doing renovations on the building, and in the process they gained pride and skills.

Overall, the tenants reclaimed authority from experts, not by doing away with expert and professional knowledge (Gilkey herself went on to get a master's degree) but by putting expert knowledge at the service of the community, after the fashion of Hull House and co-operative extension. Tenants worked with the local school; they had many meetings between teachers and parents. The art class constructed a model of what Cochran Gardens would look like when it was a lovely complex, and it was placed at the school's front. Tenants organized a health clinic, a day care and other services and businesses—and most employees lived in the projects.

Finally, Cochran Gardens helped to create a larger stage, on which its work became visible. They organized other tenants in St. Louis, and Bertha Gilkey became a major figure in the national movement for empowerment of public housing tenants. During the Reagan administration, she worked closely with Jack Kemp, Secretary of the Department of Housing and Urban Development—interestingly, conservative populists like Kemp proved much more sympathetic to tenant initiatives than did most liberals.[5]

Stories like Cochran Gardens form a larger tapestry consisting of thousands of neighborhood groups, community-based economic development corporations, self-help groups, community housing projects (some catalyzed by government initiatives like VISTA), the federal poverty program, and many other independent groups. These developed out of sight of the political mainstream in the 1970s, 1980s, and into the 1990s. They have involved perhaps a quarter of the adult population in the substantial work of community regeneration and problem solving. In the process, they have renewed public cultures where ordinary people's energies are valued and visible. As *The Christian Science Monitor* observed, grassroots community activism was arguably the "invisible story of the decade" during the 1970s.[6]

At the heart of all these efforts has been a renewal of productive citizenship and the experience of freedom associated with it. In countless community efforts, people have come to believe that the solution to the challenges they face can rarely be found in programs, government bureaucracies, and expert systems by themselves—though partnerships with government and professionals often are essential. This learning process involved breaking apart narrow definitions and limitations, often imposed on people by well-meaning professionals. This impulse toward freedom and self-definition became the animating spirit of the massive civil rights movement among African Americans in the Deep South of the 1950s and 1960s.

The Freedom Movement

"Old woman, what is this freedom you love so well?" asks Ralph Ellison's protagonist in the great American novel, *Invisible Man*. "I guess now it ain't nothing but knowing how to say what I got up in my head," she replies. "But it's a hard job, son. Too much is done happen to me in too short a time. Hit's like I have a fever. Ever' time I starts to walk my head gits to swirling and I falls down."[7] The black grandmother, speaking from experiences of years of invisibility and oppression, also identifies both the critical importance of self-naming and the difficulties that that entails.

"Freedom" was the structuring theme of the civil rights movement of the late 1950s and the early 1960s in ways that have been little explored. In civil rights, freedom meant escape *from* repressive conditions or restraint, release from the degradation of segregation. Today, we understand freedom in similar ways, freedom *from* control. This often translates into the ability to do whatever one likes, regardless of what authorities dictate.

But in the civil rights movement, freedom had expanded meanings. It also embodied the positive capacity *to* participate and contribute as full, independent, and powerful citizens in public affairs: to engage in the substantial work of citizenship. It was precisely this public participation—in rallies, sit-ins, demonstrations, voter registration drives, and public problem solving—that generated the movement spirit, despite violent opposition and great danger. Freedom's most powerful resonances came from its public dimensions.[8]

The civil rights movement as its first act challenged the very *definition* of being "Negro" in southern society, the profound alienation that stemmed from being named and dismissed by white society. Constraints were both psychological and physical—built into language and structured into the segregated lunch counters, swimming pools, schools, and other places from which blacks were barred. "People were talking about becoming free, free of mind, and free in spirit," remembered Annie Devine, a leader in the movement in Canton, Mississippi. John Hulett of the Lowndes County Freedom Party argued that through the movement "people began to take on a new life and they see themselves as being men and women." This was possible because people understood themselves as part of a much larger movement.[9]

Freedom meant a refusal to accept a naming by "the other." It required acts of individual and collective self-discovery and self-definition. Freedom also involved new experiences of collective power in communities—what current community organizing understands as "organizing for power," or empowerment. A central lesson of successful community organizing grounds democratic action in the places within daily life where people can surface their own issues and interests and define the world in their own terms. Especially, a reclaiming of authority from experts and professionals has proven critical, as the Gilkey story illustrates.

This struggle required public work. Blacks took the main leadership, but the movement also involved work by myriad of Americans in many settings from many backgrounds in order to overcome pervasive fear and entrenched practices that prevented change in the racial status quo. In turn, locally collective action depended on free spaces. Free spaces are sites in communities that have an important measure of autonomy, where people can design and determine their own agendas. They also have important public dimensions. They are places of relatively free exchange of ideas, debate, information, and sites connected to larger networks of communication and action outside the local area.[10]

Barber shops and beauty parlors, for instance, proved a central distribution center for literature in the movement's early days. "We ran special workshops for black beauticians. We used the shops all over the South as a center for literature and discussions because the beauticians didn't care what white people thought about them," recounted Myles Horton, director of Highlander Folk School. The movement also built on the legacy of the African American church as a setting where blacks could define who they were and what they wanted. Such settings during these years were full of energy and ideas, with a kind of public electricity that often seemed overwhelming to outside visitors.[11]

The history of the movement began with the Montgomery Bus Boycott sparked by Rosa Parks's refusal to give up her seat for a white man on Friday, December 2, 1955. Montgomery became the crucible in which the themes of the civil rights movement developed and first came to nation-wide attention. "When Momma Parks Sat Down, the Whole World Stood Up," ran the words to the civil rights song commemorating the event. When the quickly formed Montgomery Improvement Association held its first mass meeting the next Monday night, the black community turned to the young, dynamic minister of Dexter Avenue Baptist Church, Martin Luther King, Jr., to give the major speech. His arguments set the stage for ten years of struggle.[12]

King grew up in a professional family in Atlanta, Georgia, home of the largest and most prosperous black middle class in the South. At divinity school and graduate school, he developed a distinctive philosophy that drew on popular African American religious traditions, the perspectives of the religious philosophy known as personalism, and Gandhi's belief in *Satyagraha,* or the idea that love and truth and anger can be joined in a force for nonviolent social change.

King's genius was his capacity to wed this personal religious philosophy to the broad democratic tradition in America. He rejected Marxism for its depersonalization of the individual and its doctrine of class conflict. And he dissented from the customary left-wing focus on government as the metaphor for the future, opposing any system which reduced the individual "to a depersonalized cog in the ever-turning wheel of the state." Rather, King held to a tradition of the "Christian commonwealth" that drew on older themes of biblical ideals and productive citizenship.[13]

Martin Luther King used this distinctive philosophy to frame the struggle in Montgomery. "We're here," he declared, "because first and foremost we are American citizens, and we are determined to acquire our citizenship to the fullness of its meaning." King challenged blacks to discover in themselves a new "sense of somebodyness" that would transform the relations between whites and blacks. And he grounded his call in American traditions and religious faith. "If we are wrong," he said, "the Supreme Court of this nation is wrong. If we are wrong, God Almighty is wrong." Such themes continued to structure King's philosophy throughout his years as a civil rights leader. "One day the South will know that when these disinherited children of God sat down at lunch counters they were in reality standing up for the best in the American dream and the most sacred values in our Judeo-Christian heritage," King wrote in his central philosophical statement, "Letter from a Birmingham Jail." He portrayed the movement as "carrying our whole nation back to the great wells of democracy which were dug deep by the founding fathers." In turn, his language created a scaffolding for the grassroots effort crafted by leaders like Ella Baker and Dorothy Cotton.[14]

The Southern Christian Leadership Conference (SCLC), the organization which King headed, was formed in early 1957 out of discussions among King, Ella Baker, Ralph Abernathy, Fred Shuttlesworth, Bayard Rustin, and others as an effort to spread "the Montgomery way" across the South. Its base was the black church. Baker, using her own earlier experiences of labor union and co-op organizing, argued that a large-scale organizing program was needed to train laity. "Instead of 'the leader,'" she said, expressing skepticism of over-reliance on black clergy, "you would develop individuals who were bound together by a concept that provided an opportunity for them to grow." Baker sought to develop SCLC's first program, called the "Crusade for Citizenship," into such an organizing effort.

Her work helped young people organize in their own group, the Student Nonviolent Coordinating Committee. Meanwhile, SCLC itself undertook an enormous program called the Citizenship Education Program, which was adopted from a smaller program at Highlander. The Citizenship Education Program, or CEP, sponsored "citizenship schools" in small southern communities.

Citizenship and the related freedom schools formed a little- known foundation for the entire civil rights movement in the Deep South. The CEP taught blacks, many of whom were illiterate especially in rural areas, to read and write in order to pass arduous literacy tests that authorities used to disenfranchise poorer citizens of both races. But from its beginnings at Highlander Folk School, the strategy of citizenship schools stressed the importance of connecting voting and literacy to a dynamic conception of citizenship itself. To that end, organizers of the schools avoided normal academic approaches and treated "students" as adults who could come and go as they pleased, bring sewing to classes, or chew tobacco. Most important, there was a constant interaction and reciprocal process between teachers and learners. Students' roles as coproducers of the learning were conveyed through a number of means. The curriculum built on people's own culture and stories. It featured participatory discussions in which people helped develop definitions of key concepts. Even the "texts" were familiar documents like the Constitution of the United States, the Declaration of Independence, and scripture. Through their entire process, such schools also lifted up the dignity of ordinary people and their labor— as factory workers, farm hands, teachers, domestics, or students. This focus on dignity of work helped to show the linkages between democracy and labor.

SCLC developed a training center called Dorchester for people in rural Georgia, and also sometimes held trainings in Atlanta and at the Penn Center in South Carolina. In these, thousands of community activists, ranging from preachers to illiterate sharecroppers, came from across the South for a five-day training session on the meaning and skills of citizenship. The curriculum included much more than the mechanics of registering and voting. Students learned how to conduct voter registration campaigns, combat illiteracy, and work on community problems like poverty or roads.

The CEP model taught an elemental, demanding concept of citizenship that recalled Jane Addams's observation: "Simple people are interested in large and vital subjects, [they] do not want to hear about simple things." As Dorothy Cotton, the Director of the Citizenship Education Program put it, they taught "a whole new way of life and functioning."

The CEP included a key session on "What is a citizen?" "I'd begin by asking the group 'What is a citizen?'" Cotton recounts. "People would say things like 'it's somebody who is a good Christian,' or 'if you don't break the laws you are a good citizen.' Then the conversation would evolve, as people raised new topics. We'd talk about the constitution, as guaranteeing rights but demanding responsibilities as well. We'd move from immediate ideas to larger issues. In these discussions people started to get a new awareness of their power. There's the First Amendment—the idea that people have a right to assemble, to petition the government for redress of grievances, to act in their own behalf. 'What does that really mean in the context of our lives?' people would ask. People learned what owning these documents could mean."

The CEP experience also conveyed the larger public stage on which people acted. "It was important that they could be connected to this larger movement group, the Southern Christian Leadership Conference—they needed to know where to go when they needed help. They also learned about politics, how government is put together, the difference between mayor or city council government, for instance. How laws might be made. How they themselves could take other actions on community problems."

Finally, the CEP experience taught people how to set up citizenship schools back in their own communities. "We'd always point out that we were trying to model teaching styles that they could use to engage ordinary people of many backgrounds," Cotton recounts. "We'd tell people to pay attention not just to what we're talking about but how we do it. We had people coming in who didn't know anything about what is called 'group dynamics' these days. They needed simple rules and ideas, like what to do if somebody dominates the discussion."

Most important, the citizenship school experience recalled the dramatic lesson of the country life movement, the settlement houses, and the CCC. Ordinary people, even people who were poor and uneducated in a formal sense and who suffered from long histories of abuse and oppression, learned that they could develop intellectual and civic self-confidence.

"The citizenship program was about teaching people to free themselves," says Cotton. "People learned new ways of functioning as they learned to think in different ways about themselves and each other.

For instance, they began to own the statement that "it's supposed to be 'government' of the people, by the people, for the people"—but it's true *only if you make it so.* They could no longer sit back and wait for someone else to do it."

This meant a stance toward oppression far different than the victim consciousness that seems to paralyze many groups in the 1990s. In citizenship schools, people expressed anger and grievance out of ancient brutal experiences of segregation. But they dealt with these through strength, framed by possibilities for action. "People would get anger out and understand that they could create something out of that energy," explains Cotton. "People had lived in this malaise, this brainwashing, in a sense. People had been taught to think they were less than other people by subtle and not so subtle means. But people moved from that to a feeling that if change was going to come, they had to do it themselves. What the citizenship schools did was create a space in which to develop self-confidence and the belief that people can act. One woman said, 'the cobwebs come just a moving from my brain.' "[15]

By the end of the CEP era in 1968, poor whites had begun to appear in the classes as well. "One guy named Preacher Red asked to meet us in Atlanta," Cotton recalls. "He said he had hated Dr. King at one point. But he realized that the reason he didn't like King was his feeling that his folks, poor whites, were being left out. They saw blacks as making progress and they knew they needed a movement too."[16] A number of poor and working-class whites came to Dorchester sessions, according to Cotton.

Citizenship schools were key elements of a broad movement through which people learned new ways to define themselves and claim their power and authority in the larger society. The freedom movement had limits as well. The movement reflected its overt objectives. Despite the enlarged democratic vision of leaders like King and Baker and many others, the movement was explicitly defined as an effort to end the bitter legacy of legal segregation. Like the suffrage movement a half century before, it used a language that explicitly stressed formal rights, not the transformation of power relations. It succeeded in its own terms, abolishing the segregated statutes, registering millions of new black voters and reviving a language of "democracy" that had wide resonance. It represented only one stage in democratic renewal, however.

The freedom movement's themes found lasting expressions in a powerful drama played out across the country by the late 1960s and early 1970s. Although much of the civil rights movement and the northern student movement on campuses evaporated in angry and sometimes violent rhetoric, new community groups sought to put their ideals into everyday practice. Community groups have remained to this day instruments of public work.

Schools for Public Life

In American cities in the 1960s, 1970s, and 1980s, enormous racial conflicts erupted. Yet working relationships also formed across racial divides, not by exhortation or abstract appeals to good will. Rather, concrete self-interests tied to effective, skillful organizing provided the glue for solving public problems. In the process, common work helped to overcome histories of mutual antagonism. Such interracial connections multiplied despite all the difficulties. In Chicago, for instance, plans for a crosstown highway coalesced black and white homeowners on the southside in opposition. "White people joined with a black group not because they loved each other but because they wanted to stop the highway," explained Heather Booth, founder of a training school for community leaders called the Midwest Academy. "One leading racist guy made his slogan, 'blacks and whites united against the crosstown.'" In Boston, Massachusetts, communities inflamed over the busing issue were brought together by a community organizing group called Massachusetts Fair Share around issues like redlining by banks (practices which ruled out home mortgages for low-income and working-class areas). "I don't know how much melding together is going on," explained Bill Thompson, a former civil rights leader who went on the Fair Share staff. "But people learn from each other. And the issues predominate." In Oakland, Waymer Thomas observed that community organizing brought many opportunities for interracial discussion and he saw develop over time a new spirit of respect. "We've been able to sit down and discuss things because of the issues in common," Thomas recounted, "without saying 'you're white, you're black, you're Mexican.' "[17]

In the 1970s and 1980s, a large community movement spread across the country. On this base, but also moving beyond it, the network that Saul Alinsky began added important dimensions to community organizing tradition. It created larger citizen organizations bridging many divisions of income, class, and race. Most importantly, the network further developed the idea of "schools for public life" through which ordinary people cultivated public capacities.

After Saul Alinsky's death in 1972, the Industrial Areas Foundation (IAF), his network of community organizations that had begun with the Back of the Yards Council, went back to older democratic traditions and fleshed them out. It began to build "people's organizations" that were larger than local communities, wedding the struggle for power to a democratic vision. The result has been a wealth of lessons for democratic renewal.

The IAF has reinvigorated an understanding of citizenship and public action by taking advantage of the multiple resources and new ways of understanding power in the modern world. The network groups developed larger impact and reach over the years. For instance, the highly successful citizen group known as COPS, or Communities Organized for Public Service, based largely on the Catholic churches in the barrios of San Antonio, redirected the entire development patterns of the city. Since its founding in 1973, it has secured more than $1 billion of infrastructure improvement in once decimated areas—new roads, schools, drainage systems, businesses, and communications.

At the heart of their success are "schools for public life," a concept that integrates learning with doing developed by Ed Chambers, the director of IAF, and Ernesto Cortes, first organizer of the COPS group. "Schools of public life" are self-funded citizen organizations where people learn the arts and skills of everyday politics, politics far more multi-dimensional than voting.[18]

The IAF network forges a thoughtful, constantly evaluated political practice out of the tension between the "world as it is" and the "world as it should be." It teaches people not only specific political information about legislation, issues, and the skills to cooperate and act together effectively. It also adds a dynamic intellectual life involving a practical *theory* of action, employing and constantly developing concepts like power, mediating institution, public life, the meaning and management of time, judgment, imagination, and self-interest. Such concepts, in turn, are tied to discussion of the democratic and religious values and traditions that inform and frame their efforts—justice, concern for the poor, the dignity of the person, diversity, participation, heritage. IAF workshops in inner-city New York or among Mexicans in the barrios of San Antonio commonly have discussions like debates about the meaning of Madison's concept of "self-interest" in the *Federalist Papers* or current theories of poverty in works by scholars such as William Julius Wilson. To see them in action is to feel once again the spirit of democratic intellect and conversation that flowed through nineteenth-century America, or the settlement houses, country life discussions, and CCC camps like Francis Crowdus' in the twentieth century.[19]

In these public-life schools, discussion of key ideas tied to action form the most important learning. For instance, IAF teaches a rediscovered idea of the public arena itself, akin to the kinds of public spaces that mushroomed in the 1930s. Focusing on the idea of the public arena, different than private life, in which certain behaviors are far more effective than the ways one is with friends or family, has worked dramatic changes in local groups' practices over the last fifteen years.

Public spaces are places for accountable, productive work with people whom one might well not like or agree with on many issues. Public space is a distinctive, vital arena in its own right, where citizens exchange ideas and power, achieve visibility, engage in conflict and collaboration. IAF organizations have also reworked the practical theory of public life and its relationship to private life. The theory of public life highlights the distinctiveness and interrelationships between public and private life.

A basic workshop given in every national training session and reproduced countless times in local groups is what IAF calls "the public and private workshop." In their typical pedagogical approach, making a distinction to be discussed, the trainer divides the board and makes a series of paired contrasts.

Private	*Public*
family/friends/self	church/school/work
sameness/commonality	difference
fidelity/loyalty	accountability
giveness	choice
intimacy/closed	fluid/open
vulnerability	dramatic role
the need to be liked	the desire for respect
self-giving	quid pro quo/self-interest

It was the most meaningful experience I ever had, more important than seminary or college," said the Reverend Doug Miles, a dynamic minister who heads one of Baltimore's largest black churches, Brown Memorial Baptist Church. "It altered my view of the ministry," Miles continued. "The church had been functioning so that if the pastor was not involved, the program did not go. I began to see the fallacy of that. The ministry was not something *I* was responsible for; it was something the church was responsible for. I began to see the need to share responsibility, not to be afraid of training people to become leaders." After the 10-day training session, Miles instituted a program of leadership development in his church, tying 10-day principles to scriptural and theological reflection. By 1987, the church had grown many-fold.[20]

In sum, IAF schools for public life, like the citizenship schools a generation ago, model the kind of intellectual vitality tied to practical and constructive results that needs to become common throughout all of American society. For instance, teaching this concept of the public arena and putting it into practice has led to the resurrection of the vital commonwealth idea from American history. As groups worked with a variety of players in their environments, they also shifted from simply *protest* organizations to the assumption of some *responsibility* for policy initiation and what they call "governance." IAF groups believe that it is not sufficient to simply protest. To "move into power" in the modern world, citizens must also assume a role in creating and sustaining the basic public goods of their areas, especially its infrastructure like roads and communications, schools and housing stock.

This shift toward governance has generated examples of how large partnerships can combine difference with discovered commonalties, conflict with cooperation, across a remarkable array of racial and economic divisions. All are illustrated by the efforts of the Baltimore BUILD organization in the late 1980s and early 1990s to achieve what they called the Baltimore Commonwealth, described in Chapter 8.

CHAPTER 8

A Nation Divided

So here we stand among thoughts of human unity, even through conquest and slavery; the inferiority of black men, even if forced by fraud; a shriek in the night for the freedom of men who themselves are not yet sure of their right to demand it. This is the tangle of thought and afterthought wherein we are called to solve the problem of training men for life.

W. E. B. Du Bois, *The Souls of Black Folk*, 1905[1]

*O*ur age witnesses bitter and corrosive divisions along economic and especially racial lines. Battles over affirmative action, school desegregation, congressional districting, housing patterns, and issues with more thinly veiled racial overtones like crime and drugs transfix America's public affairs.

In such a context, a vast number of proposals have been advanced based on strategies for enhancing understanding of the other: multicultural workshops, prejudice reduction programs, conflict resolution efforts, initiatives to celebrate diversity. In schools, multicultural curricula have become commonplace. Yet these make little difference. More broadly, for all the rhetoric of good will, American race relations continue to deteriorate.

In the late 1980s and early 1990s, Baltimoreans United In Leadership Development, or BUILD—the largest mainly black local organization in the country—tried a different approach. The group crafted an ambitious plan for revitalizing public schools called the Baltimore Commonwealth. The plan combined a set of strong incentives for high school graduation with strategies for improvement of schools and devolution of power and responsibility.

The Baltimore Commonwealth also generated a broader lesson. Public spaces formed around a project like this can create settings for diverse interests and viewpoints to work together across racial lines. In the process, people learn skills of public work that can produce relationships of respect and productivity in many other arenas. In Baltimore, collaborative work on schools by BUILD, the business community, city officials, unions, and others created a mechanism for an ongoing conversation about the city and its future, after a period of extreme polarization. The BUILD initiative conveyed Du Bois's point:

Education itself, in all its forms, should prepare people for the work of public life.

The Baltimore Commonwealth

> Moses said to the Lord, 'Why hast thou dealt ill with thy servant? . . . Where am I to get meat to give to all this people? . . . I am not able to carry all this people alone, the burden is too heavy for me.
>
> . . .
>
> And the Lord said to Moses, 'Gather for me seventy men of the elders of Israel . . . and I will take some of the spirit which is upon you and put it upon them; and they shall bear the burden of the people with you, that you may not bear it yourself alone.'
>
> Numbers 11: 10–18

In 1981, the Black Caucus of the Industrial Areas Foundation network of organizations produced a new document, *The Tent of the Presence*, based on the passage from Numbers where Moses gathered a carefully selected group of elders at the "tent of meeting," the center of the Jewish community. There, Moses shared with them power and responsibility for leadership during the travels to the promised land.[2]

Tent of the Presence argued that the black community in America— and the black church in particular—stood at a crossroads. African Americans faced a dangerous movement "to the right" in American politics. But in such an environment a simple politics "of the left" would not work. Sixties-style "movement leaders," dependent on charismatic appeals and moral exhortation, were simply ineffective. For the black community to avoid an increasingly dangerous isolation and marginality, a new style of leadership would be needed along with new organizational forms. Like Moses, the black clergy had to choose individuals with promising talents and abilities and "share some of the spirit" with them. A new form of collaborative leadership should emerge, spreading leadership, power, and responsibility more widely. And new broad-based citizen organizations were needed, owned by the members, funded with their own money, aimed at gathering durable power over time. Baltimore, Maryland, was an ideal test case for the new approach.

Baltimore's African American community had a rich history to draw on. The city had always had something of a mixed regional character, "caught midstream between the freedom of the North and the tradition of the South," as a Baltimore Urban Coalition report in 1934 put it. "The Negro rides the street cars in Baltimore as he does in New York, sitting where he finds a vacant seat. Yet . . . Negroes and whites attend separate schools and separate motion picture houses." Gerald Taylor, raised in Harlem and organizing in the New York area for years before he came to the city in 1984, immediately felt the contrast. "There's still respect for property—you don't see a lot of graffiti in Baltimore," he observed. "Because it was a segregated city, there were a limited number of places that blacks could go. But you also see a lot of overlaps, friendship networks, a density of community ties to build on."[3]

Through the nineteenth century, the city was famous as a center of cultural and political strength: Bethel AME church was a founder of the African Methodist Episcopal denomination. The city had been home of famous abolitionists like Frederick Douglass and William Lloyd Garrison. As early as 1890, African Americans gained representation on the city council. The black school tradition dated back to famous institutions like Sharp Street, established in the eighteenth century; African School, founded in 1812 by Daniel Coker; and black girls' schools like St. Francis Academy, begun in 1828. In the decades of segregation, institutions like Frederick Douglass High School and Morgan State College were seen as beacons of black education, turning out national leaders like Lillian Jackson of the NAACP, Clarence Mitchell, the lawyer, and Congressman Parren Mitchell.[4]

A long tradition of civic action and protest had emerged from the dense network of community institutions in black Baltimore as well. Abolitionists like Elisha Tyson had been prominent figures in Baltimore as early as the Revolutionary War. In the 1880s the state supreme court, prodded by the African American legal organization called Brotherhood of Liberty, admitted blacks before the bar. During the Great Depression of the 1930s, activist organizations like the Young People's Forum, the People's Unemployed League, the Fellowship of Reconciliation, and the Women's International League for Peace and Freedom combined protests against economic hardship with challenge to segregated educational and employment patterns. Every Friday night in the early 1930s, the Young People's Forum drew hundreds of people to its meetings on controversial public issues, held at Bethel AME church. It led a widespread boycott to demand the hiring of black clerks in downtown stores, and petitioned the city and state for an upgrading of black schools. During the civil rights movement of the 1960s, leading ministers like Vernon Dobson often consulted with Martin Luther King, Jr., and his staff, and helped spark a wide-ranging series of successful protests for desegregation of public facilities in Baltimore.[5]

By the latter years of the 1970s, however, the civil rights movement had largely run out of steam. "I was becoming an old, disillusioned preacher," remembered Dobson. "The last demonstration we called, we had had a press conference where we announced we'd have 300 people. Ten came." For the Reverend Doug Miles, the memory of those years was more painful yet. Miles had led a group of ministers to meet with Alan Hoblitzel, president of Maryland National Bank, to protest the institution's plans for an increase in interest charges on credit cards. "Out of the ten who said they would come, four showed up. Hoblitzel escorted us to a classroom. Then he told us what he was not going to do—what we didn't have the power to make him do. I sat there and my blood boiled but I realized that was the truth. We didn't have enough clout." The credit card fees were increased.[6]

Politically it was a time of retreat. "For the first time I heard middle-class black people talking about 'those people in the ghetto.' It was a mental dissociation from the pain that none of us are more than a step away from." Miles himself prepared to pull his congregation back from social commitments and cut back his involvement with groups like the Black Ministerial Alliance.[7] Leaders like Dobson and Miles, discouraged as they were, understood the perils of public apathy. Indeed, the same period marked a growing perception throughout the city of "two Baltimores"—with a prosperous, middle class increasingly distanced from a growing, largely black underclass. The division took many forms.

William Donald Schaefer, elected mayor in 1971, led Baltimore to national prominence with a vigorous promotion of a downtown "renaissance" that took Norman Vincent Peale's philosophy of positive thinking to new heights. Occasioned by a large-scale development along the harbor called Harbor Place, Schaefer sponsored flamboyant public events. On "Sunny Sundays" at the Harbor he led crowds in clapping for the sunshine. Playing on the saying "think positive," on "Pink Positive Days" he organized rallies to applaud the harbor. Schaefer's exuberance undeniably aided corporate development. But he also fashioned a political machine built directly around his personality. He tolerated no opposition. "Schaefer didn't want anybody to challenge him at all, especially in a public way," said Michael Fletcher, who covered city politics for the *Baltimore Sun*. When he encountered resistance, reaction was swift. "Schaefer could act like a vindictive bully," added another newspaper writer. According to critics, the mayor combined a quick temper with a marked tendency toward a politics of denial. "Anything that raised negatives about Baltimore, he just did not want to hear," said Miles. "He didn't even acknowledge that there were homeless in the city."[8]

Problems mounted below the surface celebration. Housing for low-income city residents became scarce. Seventy percent of the officially unemployed 20,000 Baltimoreans were African Americans— and the actual numbers of unemployed ran much higher. Eighty percent of the school system was black. Increasingly the system divided into a few special programs for gifted students in magnet schools and neighborhood schools, called "zone" or comprehensive schools, which were overcrowded and scandalously short in supplies of basic materials like textbooks.

"For the first ten years I worked here, the system was excellent," remembered Irene Dandridge, president of the Baltimore Teachers Union, or BTU. The next ten years [the middle 1960s], the community lost its commitment to schools. It was discouraging. Teachers began a mass exodus to the county and we couldn't recruit new teachers." The mayor's appointment of Alice Pinderhughes as superintendent of schools echoed such diagnosis. "We had developed a few city-wide schools with high-achieving students," she described. "But the majority are not. White exodus started. Then middle-class blacks began sending their children to private schools. The comprehensives lost their image of being community schools. There was a major morale problem there; they felt like second-class citizens."[9]

The erosion of city schools as well as decent job possibilities for many young people fed more subtle social decay. When Carl Stokes grew up in the fifties and sixties in a public housing project in the poorer black area of Baltimore, it was a safe, intact community. "We had no drugs—we didn't know drugs. The project was safe. The project was a stepping stone for a lot of families who would move out when they could; it was public housing as it was supposed to be." But just as he was leaving, the neighborhood went through marked changes. Drugs appeared on the scene. Shoot-outs between dealers and police occurred in the middle of the day. Desperate unwed mothers and children populated the deteriorating apartments.

Perceptions about a growing crisis under the surface were shared by other parts of the community as well. Robert Keller, city and then metropolitan editor for the *Evening Sun,* took a position as the executive director of the main business group, the Greater Baltimore Committee, out of the sense that the city had reached a crucial turning point. "There were major fundamental problems in jobs, education, the cultural infrastructure," he recalled. "I felt this was a community that was either going to be on the edge, on a new forefront of civic cooperation, or we were going to disappear into the bay." It was against this background that BUILD began shakily in the late 1970s. It took on the problems of the public schools in 1984, and then crafted a wide-ranging alliance and strategy for school transformation and democratization, known as the Baltimore Commonwealth.[10]

BUILD began in 1977 with a sponsoring committee led by an ecumenical group of ministers. For three years, it worked on local neighborhood issues like police protection, arson control, and rat eradication, while a coalition of black and white churches raised an initial funding base. But the early years were not easy. Some pointed to mistakes by an abrasive IAF organizer, no longer with the network. "The first organizer here really screwed some things up, alienated people and congregations who still haven't come back in," according to one priest at St. Ann's, an inner-city congregation who sought for several years to get his congregation to join. The organization did not cohere into a promising project until Arnie Graf came in the spring of 1980. By that time, the *need* for a new and powerful citizen organization in Baltimore's black community had become widely apparent. The question was whether it could succeed.[11]

Arnie Graf, white, Jewish, soft-spoken, presents a considerably different figure than the image of the traditional, "tough-guy" Alinsky organizer. But Graf demonstrated keen intuition into what motivates people, and toughness under a gentle humor. When he came to Baltimore early in 1980, Graf already had years of experience behind him.[12]

The IAF approach that Graf taught included a careful analysis of targets for action, potential victories, and appropriate strategies. All these practical themes had been missing in the failed efforts by black leaders in the late 1970s. In particular, Graf knew that Baltimore banks and savings and loan associations could be pressured under existing federal and state legislation to reveal where they were making loans. Disclosure of such information would give the organization tools to use in reaching agreements for more mortgage loans in black communities. BUILD members were taught to do the research on banks and legislation. They discovered that most banks lent only a small portion of their mortgage funds in inner-city and mainly black areas. Provident Bank, for instance, despite its self-description as a "community bank," lent $660,000 out of more than $50 million, less than one percent.[13]

In the spring of 1981, the organization launched a major campaign with a dramatic, colorful action. "Sixty or seventy of us went to Provident Bank and asked for a meeting with the vice president," remembered Gary Rodwell, a former Eagle Scout who had long waged his own private wars against discrimination he felt in Baltimore. "We wanted to ask them to become a participating member of the Maryland Housing Investment Fund," a state program that insured mortgages in lower-income areas without cost to the lender.[14]

The bank officer refused. So the group formed long lines at the windows and asked for change into pennies. Police came. Officials panicked. And the president of the bank asked to meet with a delegation. Several meetings later, Provident agreed to invest several million dollars in low-income neighborhoods.[15]

Rodwell, who became treasurer of BUILD in 1981, felt the action was the sort of effective effort he had been waiting for all his life. "I said to myself, 'this is it. I'm finally doing something that can have impact.'" Doug Miles, whom Arnie Graf had finally enticed to the demonstration after repeated rebuffs, was similarly deeply affected. "I hadn't been involved in anything where you could get sixty people there since the anti-war movement," said Miles. "It was a magnificent feeling of excitement." He soon joined the Strategy Team, the key group of leaders who make day to day organizational decisions in BUILD, and saw a dramatic difference in its approach. "In the late seventies, we really never thought we would win," said Miles. "Winning was just being able to say you were on the right side; it was a moral victory. Nothing substantive came out of it."[16]

When he began going to BUILD meetings, Miles was struck by written agendas, meetings that began and ended on time, and most of all, the focus on actual accomplishment. "There was a constant teaching role about what leadership is, what power is—how power isn't a dirty word. The need for accountability. The difference between the world as it is and as it should be. The stuff was a mind-boggling change." All of this conveyed the idea of public life as serious *work,* in sharp contrast to the protest styles inherited from the 1960s.[17]

Involvement in BUILD and other IAF groups seems regularly to create considerable personal change. The late Marian Dixon, president of the BUILD organization in 1982, had been a teacher for many decades. Dixon conveyed a calm indomitability. The stories of her encounters with city officials and other members of the power structure form a major part of the folklore of the organization—she was well known, in particular, for insisting on respect and proper etiquette from elected politicians, not allowing them to call her by her first name in a public setting or allowing them to "get away" with evasive rhetoric. Dixon credited assertiveness to her experiences in BUILD and in a ten-day IAF training session. "BUILD taught me to demand what was right," Dixon described. A devout church member and lay leader, Dixon thought certain facets of Christianity had previously taught her and others the wrong lessons. "You're not supposed to have self-interest. You're not supposed to want power. You're supposed to be meek and humble and be trampled on! But we learned."

In contrast, experience taught Doug Miles a certain humility—he realized *he* alone was not responsible for his church. He learned a willingness to bend and compromise where appropriate. "Back in the seventies, we didn't believe in compromise," he explained. "So when we couldn't get everything we wanted, we'd go off with a nice quiet whimper into the darkness of the night."[18]

In John Gwaltney's insightful work *Drylongso,* a study of "core black culture," one of the key figures, Hannah Nelson, recounted the pervasive feeling of powerlessness felt by blacks in urban areas. "The most important thing about black people is that they don't think they can control anything except their own persons," she argued. "So everything is very personal." Dixon agreed that blacks historically felt considerable powerlessness, but she pointed to the *public* consequences. "Black people generally don't understand the power and self-interest of whites. It doesn't mean you're dumb. You've just never thought about it." When people feel completely powerless, she continued, there is a hopelessness which simply precludes attention to the other. "There's just no need to focus on it." IAF taught careful attention to others' self-interests. And BUILD began to accumulate the successes which made the lessons come to life.[19]

Such practical lessons and experiences formed the background for the campaign around revitalization of Baltimore public schools. By the early 1980s, IAF groups across the country had begun to take leading roles in policy initiation, especially around key questions of infrastructure. "The classic approach in the seventies was to pressure government for X, Y, or Z," said Mike Gecan, regional IAF director in New York. "But now governments can't or won't do it. Nehemiah never would have happened if we hadn't taken on responsibility." In New York, the infrastructure crisis had become acute. "Nobody else is taking on the big things like streets or corruption or bridges, whatever. There's a great vacuum. The political leaders don't really deal with these issues. They see themselves as captives of the bureaucracy. The whole productive side of government has begun to collapse."[20]

Gecan, like other IAF leaders and staff, saw pitfalls in assumption of responsibility for infrastructure programs—"if we take on the role of government, part of the danger is they'll just do less and less." IAF groups' goal is to revitalize the older understanding of government and elected officials as public "servants," neither saviors nor enemies. In the meantime, however, there were also benefits in taking on such questions: an education for members in the intricacies of policy issues; a sense of ownership and "stake" in key elements of community life; and perhaps more intangible but crucial to the organizations' self-defined mission of recreating "public life," the creation of important occasions to work with diverse elements of the larger community in a collaborative, ongoing way.[21]

In Baltimore in 1983 BUILD began to investigate the shortages and disparities in school supplies, especially in the zone schools. They discovered that such schools were short not only in paper products— writing materials, toilet paper, paper towels—but also textbooks, film projectors, typewriters, and an array of other basic resources. By that time, with victories in hand around bank loans, auto insurance, and utility rates, the organization had accumulated a notable reputation in the city. BUILD's third convention in October the next year drew over 1,500 delegates. Unlike the convention two years before where not one elected official appeared, the audience this time included a congressman, two candidates for governor, a half-dozen members of the General Assembly, the state's attorney, and a number of city council members—though then-mayor Schaefer continued to boycott the group, after a confrontation with Dixon and others the year before. The question was what to do with such power.[22]

Graf saw continuing weaknesses in the organization. "We could turn people out. But I knew we were still not deep. You don't do house meetings. You don't train people carefully enough. But it can't last." Graf himself had been deeply affected by the civil rights movement and saw the same prophetic spirit in BUILD. But the civil rights movement had faded, with an incomplete legacy. The challenge for BUILD was how to sustain such transformative energy. "So we stopped for a while," Graf described. "We did a series of retreats about what our purposes were. We did house meetings. And we talked about what to do about the schools."[23]

The new superintendent of schools, Alice Pinderhughes, was vulnerable to pressure, they knew. A Schaefer appointee, Pinderhughes lacked a graduate education and, despite her race, was viewed with considerable skepticism in the black community. When they first approached her about supply shortages, she was doubtful about the accuracy of the charge. A simple confrontation might well have forced the issue into the open in a way that would have won. But BUILD leaders, doing a careful analysis of Pinderhughes' "self-interests," concluded that whatever the precariousness of her position, she did indeed care about the schools. She needed some new and positive visibility. She could use allies. And a "public relationship" with

Pinderhughes was important if they were to take on the broader crisis of the school system as a whole. So a delegation of BUILD leaders approached her, and together they broke the story about school shortages. It was the beginning of a new stage for BUILD.[24]

BUILD used this method of "public relationship building" throughout its campaign around the schools over the next several years. In BUILD's analysis, locally owned and rooted businesses—from local industry to insurance, banks, and other service providers—all had what they called "institutional self-interests" in seeing that the school system did not disintegrate. From the point of view of key business leaders as well, schools provided a perfect "neutral issue" around which to repair a badly fractured city. "BUILD had first approached us on unemployment," remembered Alan Hoblitzel. Hoblitzel took on the presidency of the main business organization in the city in 1984. "I was initially skeptical. I had read about their adversarial nature, their confrontations, things like that. The question was whether you could sit down in a cooperative vein to deal with problems that are common." Hoblitzel knew he would have difficulty selling anything to other business leaders that smacked of "quotas, track programs, things that seemed to invade the way people ran their businesses." But he felt there had to be some other way to get businesses "to be aware of and sensitive to the needs of minority groups." Thus, when BUILD leaders told him about the Boston Compact, an incentive program begun by Boston businesses to help secure jobs for college graduates, he was interested. "I told them this may be something we can both rally around. This would help convince youth that something was out there for them, that there would be a job. And it would assist the business community to be responsive to people's needs."[25]

The unfolding series of discussions had moments of drama. Miles, Graf, Hoblitzel, and Bob Keller all remember a crucial meeting in the fall of 1984, just before the BUILD convention, that was a turning point—though their accounts vary somewhat. Hoblitzel recalls it as the meeting he went to with an intention to reach a serious agreement. Miles has a different story. "We had had several meetings without reaching agreement," said Miles. "Hoblitzel kept looking at his watch, saying 'I have to catch a plane. I really don't have time to pin anything down.' He said a final 'no.' Then I looked at him and said, 'Mr. Hoblitzel, you and I stand at a very unique position, a crossroads in the life of this community. We can take the leadership of building one community, or become perpetual enemies. Wouldn't the history of Baltimore read better if a black preacher and a white businessman helped save the city rather than further divide it?' He sat there a minute. He headed for the door, put his hand on the doorknob. Then he turned around and said, 'we can work this out. Put together some ideas. When I get back from this trip we'll get together more people and sit down and see what we can do.' " Miles said "it was nothing but the spirit of the Lord that saved that day." The power of BUILD likely also had a hand.[26]

Soon after the convention, Gerald Taylor replaced Graf as executive director of BUILD. Taylor had already acquired a remarkable reputation as an organizer: During the civil rights movement, as head of the New York Youth Division of the NAACP, he had been the brash challenger to the organization's old guard, which joined civil rights demonstrations only with reluctance. In the 1970s, Taylor acquired a national reputation in community organizing circles for successfully building a large community group in Williamsberg-Greenpoint, a white ethnic area of Brooklyn. Taylor also worked for a time as a teacher in the famous Harlem Prep storefront schools, through which many black teenage drop-outs acquired a high school education.

Taylor combined organizing talents, an indefatigable interest in ideas, and a sense of the careful craft involved in building public relations. Taylor also suggested the word, "commonwealth," as the description of the new agreement. "I was intrigued by the word and the idea, commonwealth," said Taylor. "That's what we were about. About the wealth of the city that was created and produced by the people being commonly dealt with." Taylor had also been influenced by the economist Joan Robinson, who often used the term. Others saw the utility of the label. "I thought it was wonderful, but not for the reasons that I've come to understand," remembered Keller. "We thought, 'we've got to market this thing.' It was a way to describe the 'neutral' issues that a lot of people can rally around—education, community stability, good jobs."[27]

For the next four years, the Commonwealth Agreement, later the Baltimore Commonwealth, went on two tracks: The development of the program for high school graduates soon became a national model. Meanwhile, less visibly, BUILD sought to use the incentive plan as a scaffolding around which to open discussions with the Greater Baltimore Committee (GBC) around a range of other issues, like adult unemployment and housing.

In the first instance, the incentive plan for high school graduates continually expanded, but it was a slow process. "We had hundreds of hours of meetings, negotiations," remembers Taylor. "To put this kind of project together on a serious scale is very hard work."[28] By June 1989, city high school graduates with attendance records of 95 percent in their last two years were guaranteed three job interviews at one of the 150 members of GBC, and additional help in securing employment. If the interviews themselves did not produce a job, the city Office of Employment Training evaluated the young person and provided additional training. At the end of April 1988, BUILD, GBC, the new mayor Kurt Schmoke, and a coalition of area colleges and universities announced a further element: A $25 million fund guaranteed financial aid through college for any graduate from Baltimore schools with good attendance and a B average.

Even in the first couple of years, when the school aid packages were not as extensive, the program was not widely known, and patterns of juniors and seniors had been shaped by years of school experience, teachers and counselors in zone schools noted a considerable impact. "Traditionally we had two or three students go on from here to the University of Maryland," said Charlotte Brown, guidance counselor at Patterson High School. "Last year, with the Commonwealth Agreement we had between twelve and fifteen, and two students went to Loyola." When Steve Johnson, a Patterson student, got word he was accepted to Johns Hopkins—the first student to go there from any of the zone schools, in anyone's memory—the news was broadcast over the public address system again and again, all day long.[29]

In the 1990s the Baltimore Commonwealth itself has created a series of striking incentives that make education meaningful to low-income, working-class, and minority students.

Moreover, like earlier public spaces in American history, the Commonwealth created a new forum, citywide and in the tangible, localized spaces of particular schools alike, through which diverse elements of Baltimore could meet, identify problems, disagree, find areas of agreement, and plan and work on programs together. Gerald Taylor described the creation of such forums as the move from simple protest to governance: "The first struggle for the black community, coming out of a segregated history, is the fight to be recognized. When you've been out of power so long, there's a tendency to not want to be responsible or to be held accountable. But to participate in creating history, one must move into power," he said. "Moving into power," in Taylor's view, meant being prepared "to negotiate, compromise, understand others have power and ways of viewing the world other than your own." It involved agreement "to engage with others" that eliminated violence or alienated protest as a strategy. Perhaps most notably, it served as a declaration of independence by the black community that recalls Frances Harper's Reconstruction Era image of the "commonwealth of freedom." BUILD members took a leading role for Baltimore as a whole, signaling that they would no longer simply be "objects" of forces beyond their control. The Commonwealth Agreement—like the "Nehemiah Project" in New York and similar efforts elsewhere—was a language of human agency that taught the most important of lessons, that things like school systems are human artifacts.[30]

The Commonwealth Agreement, in sum, served as a public space that reknit and created relationships that were badly frayed in some cases, virtually nonexistent in others. "The Commonwealth created a vehicle by which we could continue to have a dialogue about the school system and other issues in a way that I never would have expected," explained Alan Hoblitzel, chief executive of Maryland National Bank. "It's changed the thinking of a lot of businesses in the city. And it's been a way to learn about people. It's just not my normal experience to sit down with a black minister and talk about the issues we do." Kurt Schmoke, mayor of Baltimore, echoes the views of other political leaders like Henry Cisneros in San Antonio, whose contacts with IAF groups have given them a different view of the role and meaning of the citizenry. "As an elected official, I can't solve all the problems," explained Schmoke. "It's a gamble because if you have powerful organizations out there, when it comes to disagreements, they have influence. They can battle you. But the benefits outweigh the risks." The Baltimore Commonwealth around schools subsequently led to a series of other initiatives around adult unemployment and other issues.[31]

The sort of collaboration pioneered by BUILD furnishes a powerful example of public space and public work. For BUILD, public life is a contested, turbulent arena that mixes values, interests, and differences with common purposes.

America today is in urgent need of models such as these. We need examples that show that despite enormous divisions and hostilities people do have common concerns and, moreover, that they can develop the public capacities for working together on such concerns. The challenge is to translate BUILD's kind of public work into worlds far removed from inner-city communities and inner-city schools. Stories like the Commonwealth Agreement raise the question, how narrow jobs in many environments might be transformed into public work.

CHAPTER 9

Turning Our Jobs into Public Work

It is time for those of us in the world's freest press to become activists, not on behalf of a particular party or politician but on behalf of the process of self-government.

David Broder[1]

*I*n the climate of America in the mid-nineties, dominated by soundbite politics and Calvin Klein ads that exploit the sexuality of young adolescents, it is easy to miss emerging cultures of public work. But projects like the Baltimore Commonwealth and organizations like BUILD are far from unique in communities. They are also paralleled by widespread if still inchoate changes in workplaces.

Despite the facile rhetoric about "empowerment" of workers, here and there power dynamics have begun to shift in workplaces. The practice of what the IAF Black Caucus calls relational power is evident in settings other than community organizations. In some places, work roles have expanded to add more interactive, public dimensions. In many arenas today—including places as diverse as newspapers, K-12 schools, health settings, higher education, and government agencies—renewed attention is given to the quality of products and the craft of work. These changes prompt public discussions of questions such as: What is produced? What does it matter? What is the collective accountability for outcomes?

When work and its meanings become topics for discussion, work cultures begin to change. Work roles often expand and become more fluid. People's sense of stake in the organization and its work deepen. Thus the meaning of accountability also shifts. These changes can also regenerate civic meanings of work. They can rebuild the civic muscle of organizations through which ordinary people can act in the world on pressing public concerns.

Public Journalism

As much as any occupation today, journalism illustrates both the weakening of the tie between work and democracy and also new possibilities for renewing that tie. Many journalists share the view of most of the public that news coverage of politics and elections contributes to cynicism and public disillusionment. As a result, by the mid-nineties a noteworthy movement called "civic" or "public" journalism has begun to ask exactly the question, how might the work of journalists contribute to democracy's revival?

David Broder, nationally known columnist, blames the press for part of the problem with American politics. "A very large percentage of the information that the American people get about politics comes from people who disclaim any responsibility for the consequences," like political consultants and journalists themselves. Broder urges journalists to remember that their primary commitment is to democracy.[2]

Journalists as recently as the fifties and sixties felt they were at the center of democracy. "We didn't articulate a detailed theory about it; we just knew it," recalls Davis Merritt, Editor of the *Wichita Eagle* in Kansas. Journalists saw themselves as champions of the people against the rich and powerful. They brought to public attention secrets that the public needed to know. They highlighted hidden injustices. They monitored official behavior. They revealed patterns of government lying like the Pentagon Papers on the Vietnam War or Nixon's deceptions about Watergate.[3]

Newspapers are private businesses with strong public aspects. They illustrate what the Massachusetts Supreme Court Justice Lemuel Shaw in the nineteenth century was getting at: "Private" businesses may have "public" qualities. Ideally what advertisers "purchase" when they buy ad space is the credibility of the newspaper among the general public, a credibility that rests on giving an important degree of independence to reporters and editors.[4]

A powerful public dynamic has always been part of the profession's practice. Journalists interact with a diverse public in a variety of ways. By necessity they need to talk plain English to large audiences rather than rely on technical jargon. They see themselves bringing information of use to the public. Many see journalism as a public craft. Jay Rosen, a leading theorist and scholar of journalism's role, puts it this way: "When I interview journalists, almost inevitably they say they want to have an impact on the world. They want a public life."[5]

Against this backdrop the collapse of public confidence in politics, public affairs, and major institutions has had stunning impact on newspapers. A Times Mirror Company poll in 1994 found that 71 percent of Americans believe the press "gets in the way of society solving its problems." Readership of papers has suffered. In 1965, 71 percent of adults said they read a daily paper the day before; by 1995, the figure stood at 45 percent. In 1971, 49 percent of journalists polled said they were very satisfied with their jobs; by 1992 that figure had dropped to 27 percent. One study found that one in five journalists planned to leave the field in five years—twice as many as a decade before.[6]

These trends generate a variety of responses in journalism. Some simply argue that public hostility comes with the job. "We're not here to be loved," says Cokie Roberts of ABC News and National Public Radio. Leslie Stahl, Washington correspondent for CBS, argues that "we are going to be loathed and despised for one reason or another no matter what we do. That's the goal; that's our job." Others voice a fatalism, suggesting that perhaps journalism might disappear into an amorphous thing called "the media," focused on attracting customers through entertainment. Signs of such patterns are certainly in evidence. Many papers scramble to mimic the sensationalism and gossip of tabloids. "Where once newspapers embodied cultural values, they now seem mired in a tabloid culture that gorges itself on sex and sleaze," writes the press critic of the *Washington Post*.[7]

In this context, public journalism emerges as an alternative that believes, simply, in asking new questions about the profession's accountability to the public. What ends should journalism serve? Does it have any responsibility for the state of democracy itself? What is the relationship of journalists to the public, beyond simply reporting from a supposedly objective and unbiased perspective? If journalists give up their supposed role as completely "objective" and "unbiased," what is the source of their authority and power?

The Project on Public Life and the Press is an example of a new activism that addresses such questions in a constantly evolving, open-ended practice and discussion. The Project argues the importance of journalists reknitting a tie with "the public" is based not only on advocacy but also on concern for the health of the civic enterprise as a whole. Its leaders are Jay Rosen and Buzz Merritt, editor of the *Wichita Eagle*. Many small- and medium-size papers across the country have responded enthusiastically.[8]

The first major projects of public journalism focused on the 1992 elections. Instead of posing as outside observers of elections and public affairs, public journalists refocused election coverage on issues of direct concern to citizens, not candidates. They also tried to improve public conversation about key issues. The *Wichita Eagle* and the *Charlotte Observer* (N.C.) organized surveys and sponsored citizen discussion groups in order to develop questions for their election campaign coverage. This forced candidates to respond more directly to citizens themselves.

In Madison, Wisconsin, the *State Journal,* public television, WISC-TV, a commercial station, and the Pew Center for Civic Journalism created "We the People." The effort included extensive citizen education and public forums held over a period of time in which citizens talked through questions and issues of importance. These showcased the idea that ordinary people have capacity and intelligence for serious public deliberation. The *Star Tribune* in Minnesota, public television, public radio and a partnership of news media in New Hampshire, all laid out plans for large initiatives to seek a stronger citizen presence in 1996.

At the center of public journalism is the realization that journalists are themselves citizens. This raises the important discussion about the craft of reporting: What are the possibilities for newspapers to become public spaces? How might papers cover public work in many different settings? Such questions are driven not by partisan viewpoint (journalists with a strong sense of the craft adhere strongly to the value of listening to a variety of views, across the range of perspectives in a community). Rather, public journalists at their best ask what is the civic health of the whole community?

At the *Virginian-Pilot* in Norfolk, for instance, the paper began a major feature called "Democracy and Citizenship: Creating New Conversations." In its front-page announcement in April, 1995, the paper told its readers:

> More and more Americans hate politics, seeing it mostly as mudslinging and manipulation. Many see government moving further away from citizens. The media often seem to focus on the sensational instead of things that matter in everyday life. The Virginian-Pilot would like to play a role in turning around that trend . . . we

want to create a conversation about how to make public life better in Hampton Roads.

Cole Campbell, editor of the *Pilot,* challenged readers to think of themselves as actors, "people who have a stake in the news, not clients receiving a professional service." At the same time, Campbell believes reporters need to recognize their roles as citizens, both to the community and to the newspaper.

For the *Pilot,* public journalism involves changes in coverage and changes in the way the paper is run that suggest new patterns of accountability, in which citizens, as well as officials, are seen as responsible agents. The paper sponsored citizen forums across the state. It began to look for complexity and nuance in its coverage of controversial issues like abortion and gun control, getting views from moderates on the issues, exploring different aspects of opinion even among the staunchest partisans. The paper also began to rethink the journalists' roles. It organized a "public life" team of reporters to rework its coverage on a range of subjects, and held a weekend retreat to begin a serious intellectual examination of current ideas about democracy. It decentralized decision making, creating largely self-directed teams in the newsroom. To reinforce the idea that many employees have a role in this effort, Campbell instituted a "building block award" to highlight the often invisible work that goes on in the newsroom by people behind the scenes.[9]

Tom Warhover, the editor of the public life team, described the changes. "We have had to do a whole lot of soul searching. We have to ask basic questions: What is our journalistic purpose in life? Not only what are we against. What are we for!?"

Warhover says that "the crux of it has been to move from a narrow focus on politicians, news that is essentially about politicians and for politicians. We've tried to start covering public life." Public life requires a much wider range of sources. "Traditionally in journalism, when we pick out the sources, the good quotes, they're usually on the extremes. So we've had to learn to listen beyond the quotes. Listen for internal tensions. Where are you torn on an issue? What would the people that are least like you have to agree with you about? Where is there agreement as well as disagreement?" A public-life focus also means a shift that sees experts "on tap, not on top." "It doesn't mean ignoring experts," Warhover argues. "Experts often have critical pieces of the information people need. But we have come to see experts as part of the mix, not the source of truth."

This has led to improvement in morale at the paper. Warhover recounts a recent conversation with a colleague. "Before we had to generate our own excitement," she said. "The old style of journalism doesn't make for many who call up and say, 'What a great idea. I want to get involved.' It makes for people who call up and say, 'Hey, asshole. What are you doing?'" But recently, she had seen striking change. "In the last six months I've had more people excited about my stories, including people in government," she said. "I'm not used to that."

Change has proven to be a complex and slow process. It involves building new relationships, changing old patterns of coverage, and taking more time to do stories. "Five or ten years ago, there was a move to get more people in the paper," Warhover recalls. "But what that meant was, run out on the street and get a quote from 'Joe Six Pack.' Then we'd stick it in the story. It was a marginal inclusion that basically portrayed people as victims who had a right to have their complaints heard. What we're doing now means looking at people in much more complicated ways, in terms of a whole range of citizen roles. It is much richer."[10] When reporting is recast in these ways, citizens help define what problems are important and what needs to be done to address them. But this process also cultivates new forms of influence and productive outcome, in which journalists are partners with diverse community, in the determination of what is the work of the public.

The concept of public work was first introduced to a group of editors and reporters from across the country at the American Press Institute in 1995. Many thought the concept of public work could help expand the public journalism project. The concept opens new questions for wide discussion: What is the public work to be done by the whole community? What are the roles of various groups in accomplishing it? The following chart was constructed by the group as it sought to explore these issues, using the approaches to citizenship outlined in Chapter 1 ("civics," "community," and "public work").

APPROACHES TO CITIZENSHIP

	Civics	Community	Public Work
End of Politics	Distribution of goods	Community, consensus	Public works, commonwealth
Definition of Citizenship	Voter, consumer	Deliberator	Producer
Politician Role	Deliver goods	Convene discussion	Call people to work; provide tools, resources, for work
Power	Zero-sum; tied to scarce resources	Based on information	Relational; can be generated, catalyzed
Self-Interests	Clear, narrow	Embedded in community	Clear, expansive
Journalist's Role	"Watch dog": inform public	"Guide dog": create forums, amplify public voice	"Sled dog": hold citizens accountable for public work claimed; create public spaces

None of these approaches are "wrong," most believed. But the concepts associated with public work expand the repertoire of roles and possibilities for journalists who wish to become, in Broder's words, "activists for self-government."

In Jay Rosen's view, many journalists are weary of simply building relationships with public officials. And they worry about idealizing "the citizen." "The concept of public work gives journalists a way to have serious expectations of citizens as well as officials. It communicates the idea that citizens should not be thought about in 'warm and fuzzy ways.' Before the concept of public work, we hadn't been able to give citizenship a muscular quality that went much beyond voluntarism or participating in community life. Public work creates a far more interesting and complicated identity for citizens. You are called upon to give your capacity, not simply your time and caring." Public work also expands expectations for the press, according to Rosen. "Journalists can help identify the common work in the community and then continue to report on what is being done."[11]

Journalism is a striking example of rethinking work in more public ways, whose significant lessons stem in part from the fact that journalists are employed by profit-making businesses. Recent studies suggest that highly successful companies are never simply driven by profit making alone, despite the dogmas of free market economics. For these businesses, making money is part of a complex of values and larger purposes. The story of public journalism is a story that holds many implications for the American economy.[12]

The news media is not the only setting in which concerns for the public meanings of work have begun to reemerge. Developing the civic implications of work is a primary focus of the Center for Democracy and Citizenship, based at the University of Minnesota's Humphrey Institute.

Since 1987, the Center has collaborated with a network of partners to develop a framework for citizenship education and action. The framework is organized around the overall theme of public work. The Center sought originally to explore how the lessons of the citizenship schools of the civil rights movement as well as citizen action groups could be translated to work settings. It investigated how professional practices and work identities could be liberated into more productive public work.

The Center's strategy is to develop democratic theory strongly enriched by practice. To this end it engages with groups across many different work and institutional cultures to compare lessons from an array of experiments in civic renewal. Settings have ranged from cooperative extension service to a black hospital, schools, youth groups, a large nursing home, a Catholic women's college, a Korean youth center, a public health teen project, local government, and the Corporation for National Service. The Center also organized a national "New Citizenship" effort. In 1994, the New Citizenship and the White House Domestic Policy Council completed a bipartisan study which analyzed successful citizen-government partnerships. The Center's work has concentrated in overlapping fields of youth development; health; higher education; and citizen–government partnership. These have been the seedbed for developing a theory and practice of public work.[13]

Youth Development

The sense of usefulness is the severest shock which the human system can sustain, and that if persistently sustained, it results in atrophy of function.

Jane Addams, *Twenty Years at Hull-House*[14]

Today the uselessness that Jane Addams noted in the early twentieth century among youth is writ large. America's youth culture in the 1990s is characterized by pervasive passivity in the form of consumerism and the never-ending search for personal fulfillment. Jobs are seen as essential by many, but the meaning of work experiences has atrophied. Work on the farm, or in apprenticeships, or in unpaid but serious tasks in a variety of school and community activities once was the normal pattern. Such experiences gave young people the feeling they were making contributions to something of significance. They taught important skills and developed intergenerational relationships. Today jobs for most young people are means to the end of having enough money to buy things. "The youth market" is a key pillar of the economy. Researchers, discovering the impact even small children can have on their parents' buying patterns, spend enormous energy to develop targeted marketing strategies aimed at the young. Public spaces have become shopping centers where young people "hang out," surrounded by enticements and fantasies that consumers in the age of the Wizard of Oz could not have imagined. And though jobs today of any sort can teach elemental skills—punctuality, self-discipline, minimal responsibility—few young people get the experience of making things of social and civic value.

Today, most adults in the youth development field—including teachers, youth workers, counselors, clergy and others—see young people as clients to be served or as consumers of the knowledge they "need to know." Although their intentions are far different than simply marketing to young people, their practices can unwittingly reinforce the patterns which see youth as passive recipients, not active creators.

According to conventional wisdom, teenagers and young adults are disengaged from public issues. Times Mirror Center reports that for the first time since World War II, young people show less interest in public affairs than their elders. Only one in five follows major issues "very closely."[15]

In fact, youth today have a more complex set of attitudes about the world than polling suggests. More detailed probing finds a generation not so much apathetic as furious at adults' apparent inaction on mounting social problems. Young people are angry at what they perceive as adults' labeling of them as "problems." They are jaded by sixties-style protest. They worry about future work prospects and are uncertain about how to respond to the problems they see all around them. Senior trips to Washington, D.C., or exhortations to be "good citizens"—the stuff of earlier generations' civic education—do not address such problems.[16]

Since the middle of the 1980s, a movement for community service has been proposed as the answer to the dilemmas of youth disengagement. Its advocates claim that community service infuses a self-centered generation with a civic ethos. Thus, for instance, the Grant Commission's report *Youth and America's Future* stated that "if the service commitment begins early enough and continues into adulthood, participatory citizenship would become ... traditions of local political participation that sustain a person, a community and a nation."[17]

Using this rationale, community service initiatives expanded rapidly in the late 1980s and the 1990s. Detroit schools now require 200 hours of community service for graduation. Atlanta adopted a 75-hour minimum requirement to increase "understanding of the obligations of a good citizen." Minnesota and Pennsylvania have developed statewide financing for service learning.[18]

Community service mainly refers to a variety of individual voluntary efforts, from work in food banks to homeless shelters, from helping in nursing homes or hospitals to tutoring projects and literacy campaigns. Service involvements can make a number of educational contributions—connection with other cultures, experiential learning, and personal growth. But from a public-work perspective, the limitation is that service programs do little to develop young people's confidence and skills for creative production. In high schools even sophisticated service programs stress personal growth. Educational objectives reflect this emphasis: "self-esteem," "a sense of personal worth," "self-understanding," "belief in the ability to make a difference," "consciousness about one's personal values." Absent is the conceptual understanding that for young people to fully develop, they need experiences in making things of use that are visible to the whole community.[19]

The Center for Democracy and Citizenship has found that teens and younger kids have great interest in work through which they can become producers of things of importance to themselves and the larger community. The main vehicle for experimenting with this work-centered approach has been Public Achievement, an initiative spearheaded in 1990 by the Center, Minnesota 4-H, and past St. Paul Mayor, Jim Scheibel.[20]

Public Achievement has involved between six and seven hundred young people ranging in age from 7 to 18. Its design grew from extensive discussions with several hundred teens about how they might best learn about citizenship. The results were interesting and important: Though young people dislike the term "politics" intensely, they have positive reactions to the word, "public." They have a range of associations with the term—public parks, bathrooms, rock concerts, and "ordinary people" like themselves. They identify a multitude of problems in which they see a direct and personal concern.

Public Achievement is a 1990s model of citizenship schools. It provides opportunities for teams of youngsters as well as for the young adult coaches from community organizations and local college campuses who work with them. It cultivates capacities for public work and creates spaces for experimentation. Youth design and implement strategies for action. They organize public forums to deal with diverse groups of peers. "It is very interesting to see how kids have to unlearn things they've already picked up from watching adults," says Juan Jackson, a dynamic trainer with Public Achievement. "Teens have learned to largely ignore younger kids, for instance—they'll ask their opinions, but it will be window dressing. Public Achievement pushes kids to take others seriously, even if they haven't had the same experiences or read the same things."[21]

Public Achievement stresses pragmatic public action and relationships with others whom kids may not agree with, but with whom they can work on concrete issues of mutual concern. Many projects, seemingly "small scale" in one sense, have nonetheless taught important lessons in what young people can achieve with serious public work. Teams have organized high school day care centers for unwed mothers. They have created community parks in settings where adults had initially given up, in the face of skepticism by neighbors. They have created curricula and strategies for dealing with issues like racial prejudice and sexual harassment.

In the process, perceptions about self and others change. "This allows me to do something I want, not just something the teachers tell me to do," explained Tracy Veronen, an eighth grader at St. Bernard's Catholic school in St. Paul. Jeff Mauer, a teacher in the school, says the trick is to guide instead of lead. "Adults feel like they have to jump in and fix everything," explained Mauer. "I have developed a new appreciation and respect for my students as I watched them identify issues, devise strategies to deal with them, and evaluate their own progress."

Other adults involved in Public Achievement report major changes in their own work as well. "I felt that we needed to have ways to take kids more seriously. That's why I was interested in Public Achievement," explains Dennis Donovan, principal of St. Bernard's in St. Paul. Donovan wanted young people in his working-class, racially mixed intermediate school to develop what he calls "public talents." These include public speaking, making decisions, and understanding power and diverse interests characteristic of the public world.[22]

For the past two years most kids at St. Bernard's have been involved in Public Achievement projects. "We thought that learning citizenship skills would influence relations in schools, the curriculum, and the way we taught," says Donovan. "It has. Many kids are much better at expressing their interests and negotiating with teachers. Teachers have begun to base their teaching more directly on what kids are interested in."[23]

Jim Farr, a professor of political science at the University of Minnesota, says that involving students in his course as coaches in Public Achievement has changed his teaching and his work. "I went into political science because I liked politics," Farr recounts. "But political theory was about as close as it got. Political science seemed very distant from public life. I felt a great gap between why I went into the field and what I was doing." Public Achievement offered new strategies for teaching. "It gave my students a great opportunity to try out theories of democratic education and citizenship in real-life settings." Matt Musl, one of Farr's students and a coach, said, "I learned from trying to teach politics and political concepts to young kids. I also learned a lot from the politics of St. Bernard's, watching the kids interact with each other and with the school."[24]

Farr says that involvement for several years in Public Achievement taught him a great deal about democratic conversation and practice. "In a university setting, you become used to speaking a language of political theory or social science to undergraduates and colleagues, but you are not challenged to speak in ways that engage the real world. Here, suddenly when you have to speak with teachers, principals, parents, community leaders, and kids, it becomes a whole different thing." In Farr's observation, learning skills of conversation grow most effectively from the work. "Talk follows work. A lot of the focus today is 'learning to communicate, to reach out and express yourself.' But this is much more effective. You learn to communicate with people as you are engaged in projects. Not the other way around."[25]

Young people's experiences in public work of this kind are not unique to Public Achievement. Many of the most striking stories of productive, visible work by young people come from inner-city communities like Cochran Gardens. There, young people's many kinds of involvement in residents' efforts to reclaim the project as "a good place to live" proved indispensable. Hundreds of children and teens developed a sense of their potentials for contribution.

Accounts from young people involved in Children's Express, a project that produces a youth perspectives news service to papers across the country, show the importance that these kinds of experiences can generate. One 10-year-old reporter explained that "It gives me that feeling of importance. For me it is the place that forces me to think, drive harder to succeed and to learn new things."[26]

These examples of public work suggest the elements of a fundamentally different approach to youth development. "Youth development to date has been defined within a human services framework that uses a personal growth language" says Nan Skelton, a leader in the field. "It will require a major shift—a paradigm shift—to see youth as citizens who actually produce things of value. But this shift will also open up many new forms of work, new occupations, and new ways of understanding the social value of young people as co-producers and co-creators."[27]

Health and Public Work

American society in general, and medicine in particular, has need of a profession which has as its unique concern the nurturing of the spirit in man for action. . . . America has said that this spirit must be served and served in a special kind of way when it has been blocked by physical or emotional ills. . . . We should have as a special contribution a profound understanding of the nature of work.

Mary Reilly, 1961[28]

In 1961, Mary Reilly, a well-known leader in the field of occupational therapy, gave the profession's most distinguished annual speech, known as the "Slagle Lecture." The prestigious lectures in those years were running decidedly toward technical and scientific topics, with titles such as "Equipment Design and Occupational Therapy," "Design, Development, and Direction," and "The Development of Perceptual Motor Abilities: A Theoretical Basis for Treatment of Dysfunction." Reilly challenged this whole direction. In her lecture, which she entitled "Occupational Therapy Can Be One of the Great Ideas of Twentieth Century Medicine," she argued that scientific knowledge should be seen as a means, not an end in itself for the field. Occupational therapy needed to remember its central, founding concern with work. After all, occupation—the craft of transforming and building the nation—had always been penultimately American, said Reilly. There was an extraordinary need and opportunity for a profession which took as its central focus "the meaning of work." Like Jane Addams, Reilly called for occupational therapy to become deeply knowledgeable about the history of technology and the personal and societal meanings of work. She also called for the profession to assert with boldness a hypothesis that "man through the use of his hands, can creatively deploy his thinking, feeling and purposes to make himself at home in the world and to make the world his home.[29]

Reilly made an eloquent appeal that also had plausibility in terms of the profession's history. With roots in settlements like Hull House in Chicago, occupational therapy had originated with an appreciation for the healing and recuperative powers of work, and some sense of its larger civic and social meanings. Yet Reilly in the early 1960s was also a prophet ahead of her time. Her effort to recall this heritage went dramatically against the reductionistic trends in medicine and health care in general. It also conflicted with the forces that devalued manual labor. In those years, occupational therapy shared the fascination with scientific discovery and technology that swept over medicine in general. Older, more civic-minded notions of professional practice— which shaped not only earlier generations of occupational therapists but also family doctors, public health workers located in communities, nurses who were civic leaders, and other health practitioners— were disappearing everywhere.

The profession has yet to take fully Reilly's counsel. Medicine is overwhelmingly shaped by the "expert model," in which professionals are conceived of as the major actors with authority and useful knowledge.

Yet there are intimations of change. In recent years, a growing number of critics and leaders within and outside the field of health have argued that it is not enough to name and conceive of people as "consumers" and "clients" of health services. Health is neither a commodity nor a service delivered by experts. Rather, healthy environments and the maintenance of individual health need the productive roles of everyone. Public work recasts our understanding of what is health and who produces it. Against this background, the Center for Democracy and Citizenship has undertaken several health-related projects aimed at regenerating more public, interactive understandings of roles of providers, community residents and individuals. The Reilly tradition of occupational therapy has been an important foundation for the Center's work in this field. It has led, for example, to focus on settings like nursing homes, where questions of the meaning of one's work and life histories are of critical importance.

Nursing homes have dramatized America's inability as a society to deal in a public fashion with issues surrounding infirmity and death, while they also illustrate the removal of older people from productive roles. Nursing homes embody our tendency to cede authority to experts and to institutionalize care giving.

With support from the American Occupational Therapy Foundation for an initial research project, the Center and Augustana Home of

Minneapolis, a long-term care facility, cosponsored the Lazarus Project. This was an effort to develop an alternative to the traditional medical and therapeutic models that typically structure nursing homes. Transformation of the meaning and tasks involved in work roles of staff and residents was at the center of this effort.[30] Augustana is a large, nonprofit Lutheran nursing home associated with a larger campus of 400 apartments in four adjoining high-rise buildings. It employs an administrator, 15 managers, and 500 staff members for its residents.

The Lazarus Project developed an alternative model, called the "public community" model to integrate public work concepts with the everyday jobs that staff and residents do. The Project demonstrated, in often vivid fashion, that even within highly structured, hierarchical environments like nursing homes, staff, family members, and frail elderly residents are willing to take on more substantial roles in decision-making and problem solving. In fact, there is strong desire among staff and residents to shape the environment in which they live and work.

There are immense barriers to establishing public practices within therapeutic cultures of long-term care institutions. Although nursing homes vary according to size, urban and rural location, and affiliation with a community or ethnic or religious tradition, they commonly have an institutional quality that reinforces regimentation and dependency.

Roles are generally categorized in two ways. Care givers' primary function is to provide social and medical services to residents. In contrast, residents (defined these days also as "customers") are the recipients of services; their lot is to express satisfaction or grievance with services provided. Feelings of powerlessness pervade nursing homes. Although facilities typcally provide long-term rehabilitation services for some who will return home, the majority of residents are frail elders, increasingly incapacitated or terminally ill, who live there until they die.

Against such a background, the move to a nursing home is often a traumatic life transition, perceived as a "last stop." For many, this is the first experience in institutional living. "I don't know any other institutions you would be in, other than the army, where you are as regimented as you are in a nursing home," observed Pam Hayle, Director of Therapeutic Activities at Augustana. Government regulations and patterns of care giving constrain residents and staff alike to narrow, scripted roles and ways of interacting.

For staff, a common goal is to "empower clients," but empowerment is conceived typically in individual and psychological terms, a condition one can "give" to another. The paradox is that as caregivers seek to establish nurturing, supportive relationships, their very intensity can reinforce staff control. For instance, decision-making authority for residents is typically claimed by those staff who claim to "care" the most for residents. Staff describe how working with "my residents" fills emotional needs "to be appreciated" and "to make a difference in someone's life." However, the personalized and intimate quality of such relationships, in the absence of more public practices, generates an obligation on the part of the resident who is expected to respond with appreciation.

Staff members themselves express frustration at their inability to meet increasing needs for physical and emotional care. Their own sense of powerlessness, compounded by pressures to avoid all mistakes in their work, limits the staffs' ability to experiment and take risks, or even to imagine change. A regulatory environment emphasizes standardized, unimaginative actions that do not attend to individual context and discourage decision making. Ironically, more than 600 federal and state regulations have been promulgated to insure that homes "create empowering communities."

Against such a background, the Lazarus Project asked, "Can staff, families, and residents learn broader civic identities and assume new roles in helping to create their environments?" At the heart of the Lazarus strategy has been a conceptual approach to leadership development that stresses the importance of ongoing discussion about core ideas of public life. These understandings are deepened and integrated as people apply them in daily work.

Rethinking jobs as public work presents difficulties on many levels, because nursing homes unlike journalism have little if any civic tradition. The focus is on care, nurturance, and rehabilitation, not on building public relationships to solve common problems. Yet the introduction of these ideas can also work dramatic change. However much against the customary grain, we have seen that staff, family, and residents also desire a more open, public process of conversation that surfaces difficult issues instead of suppressing them.

A poignant example occurred early in the project, when a chaplain intern met with a joint committee of residents and staff whose purpose was to give feedback on the interns' performance. She remarked that it was hard for her to see so many people die. Augustana like most nursing home cultures avoided open discussion of death. Staff members were convinced that the subject would unduly upset residents. The committee also was silent about such topics, tending toward platitudes in evaluation of interns such as "you're a fine, caring person; keep up the good work."

Yet in this session an earlier discussion of the concept of public spaces as arenas for addressing difficult problems led to a breaking of the silence. Residents responded, "we know the topic is hard for the staff; that's why *we* don't talk about it. But to us it seems a natural part of the process of moving into a nursing home."

A dynamic conversation about death developed. Some staff thought that discussion of death might threaten the image that Augustana wished to project as a place for living. Some residents talked about wishing to be in charge of the process of how they would die, even if this meant not complying with all the staff expectations or rules. In response, staff spoke of their anxiety when what they thought of as "best possible care" conflicted with resident wishes.

The group recast its mission as a result of these discussions. Instead of imagining their task as limited to support for student chaplains, it took on the toughest questions of nursing home experience: questions of death and spirituality at the end of life, the collective experience of ritual in a nursing home. As a result, participants saw their contributions in far more serious terms, as "important work that could make a difference in the community of Augustana," as one put it, in contrast with regular activities such as music sessions or craft groups. The changed dynamics helped staff members distinguish between therapeutic relationships and public relationships with residents.

The committee convened a large public forum to discuss death and dying with staff, residents, and others connected to the nursing home. Many recommendations emerged for changes in rituals related to death. Perhaps most importantly, the public discussions helped establish a more open process in which residents and staff alike ask questions, share stories, and discuss struggles with dying. This greater openness about dying has encouraged new kinds of interactions among staff, residents, and family. "There's more conversation now," said Kathryn Kading, Director of Nursing at Augustana. "Ways to develop rituals and richer conversations about death and dying are now incorporated into Augustana's strategic planning process."

"These ideas about public work have really added depth to my work," reflects Hayle. "It is more than providing a service. I think about things much differently, and consequently my staff do too." The changes people make in their individual work also contribute toward building a more public culture within the nursing home. Public talk is now commonplace. "In the next year all residents or their families will be interviewed about what makes their lives meaningful." Hayle points out that in contrast to most quality assurance approaches, a public culture encourages discussions about large questions of life's meaning, rather than evaluation of services provided. "Because staff members have a better understanding of public work, they can deal more effectively with conflict. They don't take criticism so personally. In the past when staff would conduct resident surveys, if residents complained of being bored or gave a list of complaints, the staff member would leave feeling bad. Now staff leave with ideas about how to work with the resident to help make life more meaningful. These are big changes."[31]

Health reform that puts citizens at the center of health care also requires a fundamental change in relationship between health institutions and the general public. "Introducing the concept of 'public' created a great change among staff and the community," described Miaisha Mitchell, who served as vice president and strategist for these efforts in Central Medical Center. Central Medical Center (CMC), an African American hospital in St. Louis, used its buildings as public spaces for community problem solving. They brought more than thirty organizations and community programs into the hospital: GED classes; block clubs; women's groups; AA groups; AIDS groups; and church groups. This action opened opportunities for a variety of new collaborative efforts with the community and increased use of the hospital. The police department worked with CMC to create a training program for community patrols and a joint chaplaincy-police project on violence. All these connections illustrate potential for engaging diverse groups in promoting healthier living environments.

Hospitals generally embody the personalized, therapeutic, helping cultures visible in youth work. Thus, the very idea of public life can have major impact. "It allowed people to put aside private grievances and focus on the work." Mitchell recounted. It changed patterns of interaction between doctors and nurses, for instance, with an enhanced ability to focus on the tasks at hand. "The idea of public space meant being able to bring your issues to the table, put them out front as opposed to talking behind somebody's back. If the nurses have issues with the physician, it's much better to relate it to the doctor, in terms of impact on the work." Mitchell says that the concept of public space also reworked relationships between the hospital and the surrounding neighborhood. Community groups of many kinds began to use the hospital and particular spaces like the cafeteria for meetings, programs, and common tasks. Experiences of public work from an institutional standpoint thus allowed community residents to see the institution in new ways, with much more a feeling of local ownership. Meanwhile, health providers changed their understanding of the communities. "We found that the more partnerships we developed, the greater the community involvement with the hospital," says Mitchell. New relationships and practices, in turn, began to generate larger cultural changes.

There are other examples of innovative, reciprocal partnerships between institutions and communities that suggest the reemergence of more public dimensions of work in the health field. At the University of Minnesota, Judy Meath, a director of public health outreach for the student health services, argues that the traditional approach where professionals simply design interventions is ineffective. "In college health, we're very concerned with outcomes, such as lowering alcohol consumption or getting students to quit smoking. But students are in the best position to improve their own health. Rather than intervening in the traditional way, I need to be an organizer more than anything else, working with students to develop their own strategies, being savvy about power. Public health statistics alone don't change behavior. People have to figure out how to act, in their own way and on their own terms."[32]

Health professionals themselves strongly influence the culture of health institutions. Although health professionals' commitment to integrating civic themes with their work is not widespread, there are signs that within some professional groups there is a growing recognition that without a reframing of practice, roles will continue to narrow as resources are reallocated. In health professional education, voices like the Pew Health Professions Commission have called for development of what are essentially civic skills among the workforce. The Commission has argued that to meet society's needs in the immediate future, health workers will need to be collaborative and flexible to address community health problems and their root causes.

The concept of health raises profound issues of our lives and our society: how we individually and collectively deal with aging, chronic illness and disability, the results of accidents or violence, and death itself. In contemporary society, the quality of our collective health depends on an intricate web of cooperation and interdependence. The relational fabric required to sustain individual health and to build healthy environments is rendered virtually invisible by the current political discussions. These focus on quality of care, consumer choice, and financing mechanisms. Conventional discussions fail to integrate concepts of public work, and thus beg the question of who is ultimately responsible.[33]

Recasting health with a public work frame opens up new possibilities to actively engage citizens—both consumers and providers—in tackling health problems and their root causes, as well as developing health policy. Such issues come to the fore especially in the centers of power in an information society: institutions of higher education.

Higher Education

The public is skeptical of the growing costs of higher education and lack of accountability for outcomes. Journals of higher education these days overflow with problems that reflect the erosion of public life. College cultures suffer from growing incivility and balkanization. The craft of teaching has given way to a redefinition of education as an information transfer system, with an increasingly narrow career and disciplinary focus. The dominant response to these pressures in much of higher education has been a market metaphor that sees education as a commodity, students as customers, and securing public support as a challenge of public relations.

Colleges once taught a "hands on" approach to citizenship—professionals working on common tasks with fellow citizens from a wide range of backgrounds. Settlement leaders like Jane Addams, public intellectuals such as John Dewey, and civic-minded trade unionists like Sidney Hillman and the Reuther brothers formed important role models.

Today, such civic-minded understandings of higher education have given way to a far more disciplinary, expert-led model. Thus, in her 1989 "David Dodds Henry Lecture" at the University of Illinois, Donna Shalala, then chancellor of the University of Wisconsin, combined an emphasis on responsibility and service with a starkly expert model. She upheld "the ideal of a disinterested technocratic elite" fired by the moral mission of "society's best and brightest in service to its most needy." The imperative, she said, was "delivering the miracles of social science" to fix society's social problems just as doctors "cured juvenile rickets in the past."

Shalala's perspective reflects the loss of public work in higher education: an approach to teaching and learning which stresses the practical skills, the public identities, and the liberal outlook required if college graduates are to work *with* their fellow citizens, rather than do things for them or to them. Liberal education at its best integrates these aspects. Colleges that educate for public work cultivate people's capacities to imagine and to act beyond given frameworks; they teach a tolerance for different voices and ways of knowing; they tie such intellectual traits to the ability to act effectively on important tasks; and they teach people how to discern the larger meaning of their work.

For this sort of learning to take place requires changes in college cultures. It means interdisciplinary, campus-wide conversation about teaching as a public craft and about the work of the college as a whole. It entails the idea that learning is "coproduced" by students as well as faculty. It creates experiences in shared governance and opens space for many practical projects that make visible impact on the world.

There are intimations of public work again in higher education. Two women's colleges, the College of St. Catherine in St. Paul and Bennett College in Greensboro, N.C., offer lessons.

Today, many colleges are concerned with improvement of learning, but it is often framed in market terms, not in terms of collective work. How can campuses "supply" experienced, prominent teachers in sufficient numbers and quality to meet the demand? The College of St. Catherine is reframing this as a question of public work: How can the craft of teaching and improvement of learning be understood as the charge of the entire college? What are the rewards and structures that can encourage faculty to take leadership in such work?

For several years, St. Catherine's has sought to make teaching more "public." It has created extensive interaction across different disciplines and as a whole college, through interdisciplinary faculty study groups, a new core curriculum and regular public forums about the nature and purpose of teaching.[34] Gil Clary, a professor of psychology, explains that changing the patterns faculty are used to involves a process of hard work. "We have to do it. Knowledge of this kind can't be simply passed along. It's deliberate, self-conscious action that's important. That's how you learn about public life."[35]

In all, this process has begun to create a vibrant public culture around teaching as a craft. Anita Pampusch, the President of the College of St. Catherine says that, "Viewing our joint tasks as one of 'public work' has changed our thinking and our behavior on campus. We have become more constructive in our faculty meetings, more accepting in our community gatherings, and more inclusive in drawing students into discussions of teaching and learning."[36] Driving such issues has been a question of rationale: What does it mean to prepare women as effective and socially conscious citizens of the world they will both help to lead and to create in the twenty-first century?

Colleges that have sustained the tie between their missions and democracy over their entire histories may serve as important exemplars for higher education in the future. Gloria Scott, the President of Bennett College, an historically black college for women, proposes that "Now more than ever Bennett has an important role to play in society. Our goal is to produce not only professionals, but also concerned, participating citizens. We believe this is the very meaning of educating women." Scott sees a crisis of democracy today. "In order to *have* a democracy, we must have a critical mass of people who are educated well enough to sustain it." At Bennett this means many practical experiences in governance. Students serve on the academic council and the board of trustees. It also means that Bennett as an institution is engaged in public work. Bennett students are involved in far more overtly political and public activities than are common for service-learning projects. In the recent Greensboro elections, a critical turning point in local politics, students canvassed many neighborhoods to register voters. At Bennett itself, an astonishing 71 percent of students voted. On the day of the election, despite a downpour, results showed a significant increase in voter turnout among African Americans. At the victory celebration the slogan was "the more rain, the more they came."[37]

These are the kinds of cultures that can be created when educators—those involved in the tasks of higher education—come to think of their work as public work. More broadly, work cultures in youth development, health, and higher education, as different as they are, all present some similar obstacles to renewing public work today. All are structured by patterns of interaction that tend to be private and often personalized; and all have seen the emergence of what the intellectual historian Thomas Bender terms "disciplinary expertise." Professional disciplines of many kinds develop a language, approach, and method for defining what problems are, how they should be addressed, and what appropriate outcomes are. These disciplinary methods are normally applied with little substantial role for others in deciding courses of action.

Cultures with similar obstacles also reveal some common lessons. Public work is nourished by public spaces for discussion and intellectual life. Patterns of action need to see all stakeholders as potential co-producers of people's environments and things of value. Finally, attention to the craft and purposes of work reinvests work with dignity and meaning that most work has lost in America. Until we develop a stronger sense of ourselves as producers we will not find the confidence nor the capacity to address the crisis of government.

CHAPTER 10

A Commonwealth
of Freedom

The true friend of property, the true conservative, is he who insists that property shall be the servant and not the master of the commonwealth. The citizens of the United States must effectively control the mighty commercial forces which they themselves called into being.

Theodore Roosevelt, "New Nationalism" speech, 1908[1]

*T*heodore Roosevelt's understanding of the commonwealth rested on his view of government as issuing from the people. For earlier generations of Americans, government reflected the common work citizens undertook in a myriad of settings. It expressed people's civic identities as "producers" of the nation. And it was the instrument of people's common quest for justice and their aspiration for freedom. The connection of everyday labor with the commonwealth generated a view of government as *of* the people and *by* the people.

Work has been our source of pride and dignity. Most Americans grow up wanting to do something of use in the public world. There once were many ways and settings through which that happened. As people worked, they made a visible place for themselves. We can still see this today—in the lush street front groceries of Korean immigrants in New York and South Central Los Angeles, for instance; or in the exquisite needlework art of Hmong immigrants that have begun to grace public and private spaces in midwestern cities.

The opportunity for public work is the genius of our democracy. Now for many work has become a source of shame and frustration. Both the ends and means of work have lost meaning. People feel jobs slipping away, going overseas, becoming trivial and pointless or even sleazy and degrading. As the *Wall Street Journal* reports, "While American industry reaps the benefits of a new, high-technology era, it has consigned a large class of workers to a Dickensian time warp, laboring not just for meager wages but also under dehumanized and often dangerous conditions . . . [jobs] reduced to limited tasks that are numbingly repetitive, potentially crippling, and stripped of any meaningful skills or the chance to develop them."[2]

As we lose cultures and practices of public work, America's self-understanding shifts in subtle ways. When the crowd outside Constitution Hall in 1789 asked Benjamin Franklin what kind of government the delegates had produced, he gave a reply that became legendary: "A republic. If you can keep it." Many fear for good reason that after more than two hundred years, we will fail the test.

In the 1990s we project onto government, in some ineffable fashion, our own fears and anxieties as a nation. On the deepest level, our anger at government may reflect an anger at ourselves. Government is like a mirror. In the 1990s, Americans don't much like what we see.

During the 1996 presidential election the momentum seems overwhelmingly toward protecting *private* wealth, not building commonwealth.

Theorists of commonwealth government since the Italian Renaissance and early modern England stressed the need for roughly equal distribution of wealth. In America, even elite leaders of the War of Independence often expressed a commonwealth conception of government resting on widespread diffusion of property. John Adams believed the people were free "in proportion to their property" and if "a division of the land into small quantities" allowed many to hold property, "the multitude will take care of the liberty, virtue and interest of the multitude, in all acts of government." He wrote that "Property monopolized or in the Possession of a few is a Curse to Mankind. We should . . . preserve all from extreme Poverty, and all others from extravagant Riches."[3]

American economic trends in the 1990s have gone dramatically in the other direction. "'Survival of the fittest' capitalism is on the march," wrote economist Lester Thurow in *The New York Times,* Labor Day weekend, 1995. "No country without a revolution or a military defeat and subsequent occupation has experienced such a sharp shift in the distribution of earnings as America has in the last generation." Since 1973, the actual per capita gross domestic product rose 29 percent. Meanwhile, the median real wage for full-time male workers fell from $34,048 to $30,407 in 1993. White men's wages fell slightly more quickly than black men's. Young people's wages—men from 25 to 34—were down a stunning 25 percent. Increasingly, American companies are moving production overseas. At the same time, millions of immigrants enter the United States competing for wages. Furthermore, as communism and socialism collapse around the world, capitalists are able to stress profit maximization with little resistance. Over the last decade, only the top 20 percent of the population showed significant increase in income.[4]

Such economic patterns find parallels in other forms of privatization. For instance, nearly 4 million Americans live in gated communities protected by private security guards. Another 24 million live in areas governed by private community associations—a number expected to double in the next decade as increasing numbers of the upper middle class opt out of public spaces and end their support of public goods. "What we're doing is privatizing our public space," said Mary Snyder, a researcher who organized focus groups across the country with people living in such spaces. Residents of gated communities have their own police, parks, schools and other services. "What we heard again and again were people saying they're tired of paying taxes that went to somebody or something else; they just wanted to take care of themselves. In that sense they probably aren't that different than most Americans these days."[5]

Neither opting out nor fury at government will solve the problems we face. No matter how much we seek to remove ourselves—geographically, or by withdrawal into enclaves based on religion, ideology, or lifestyle choices—we share a common fate. We need a new birth of freedom grounded in a commonwealth. In the Bible, Jerusalem is sometimes called "a commonwealth." As the Hebrew people, in the days of Nehemiah, rebuilt the commonwealth of Jerusalem, they also freed themselves from long years of despair, shame, and hopelessness. They restored their proud legacy and took control over their destiny.

Public leadership played an important role. Nehemiah did not moderate or facilitate discussions. He called the people to the common work, grounded in deep cultural memories and resources. He provided inspiration, challenge, and tools. He rolled up his sleeves and joined with the diverse factions of the people. He created public occasions for discussion of the work and for creating the collective accountability necessary to forge unity out of such diversity.

Today, we need a multitude of leaders, inside and outside of government, who remember America's legacy of the commonwealth of freedom, government of the people and by the people. Here and there, public leaders articulate this approach. "Today, people ask who is getting more than they are from government, rather than what they can produce or contribute," said Elizabeth Kautz. Kautz, a businesswoman of mixed Polynesian and Dutch ancestry, is mayor of Burnsville, a suburb of Minneapolis. She ran her election campaign on a slogan that confounded the opposition: "Government doesn't have to be bad!"

What Kautz means is government as the people's instrument. "All of us together need to create a citizenry who is enabled and empowered to do the work of the public. Government can help. It can be a catalyst. I can work with people. But in an era of limited resources and great challenges, I can't pretend to fix things anymore, and neither can anybody in government."[6]

There is evidence of broad popular support for her approach. She won her 1994 election overwhelmingly, sweeping every precinct. On a national level, polling by Stan Greenberg for the centrist Democratic Party group, the Democratic Leadership Council, after the 1994 election suggested wide unhappi-ness with either traditional liberal reliance on government or traditional conservative attacks on government and a public desire for a different framework entirely, much like that Kautz outlines.[7]

Yet these ideas also go against the grain of public discussion today. Kautz says that when she explains her ideas, "at first most people just look at me like I'm crazy." Tony Massengale, a black community organizer in Los Angeles who works with the Drew Child Development Center, says it is quite hard from the community side to imagine entering into partnerships with government. He has organized an Interethnic Children's Council with representatives of many community institutions from African American, Asian Pacific, American Indian, and Latino communities. Even when government agencies show signs of genuine interest in collaborative decision making and work, there is considerable resistance, because it requires a shift in conventional ways of functioning. "Community groups have never been partners with government; government has been the target of complaint and protest for what's not going right. There will have to be mutual accountability if we have a genuine partnership, and that requires change on both sides."[8]

These perspectives recall the older link between government and the work of citizens which is crucial in our time. But it is not an easy matter to renew this link in the 1990s. To repair it will mean challenging the dominant perspective about government today: Government's role is to deliver services and benefits, and the citizens' role is to be a customer and a voter.

Government for the People

Polling indicates that Americans continue to believe that the nation confronts critical issues for which government action will be necessary. Yet most people simultaneously think that government efforts create more problems than they solve. Bill Clinton and Al Gore's "Reinventing Government" initiative to regain support for "smaller, less bureaucratic, more entrepreneurial and flexible government" has been met with a giant public yawn.

Discussion has focused on the wrong thing. The administration's metaphor for reinventing government defines the citizen as customer. This is understandable given pervasive market language, but it is disastrous.

Advocates for reinventing government enthusiastically advance the idea as a way to shatter bureaucracy, create flexibility, and "squeeze ever more bang for the buck." The book *Reinventing Government* (1992), by David Osborn and Ted Gaebler, has become the text of current efforts. They call their approach an "American *Perestroika*." The bottom line, in their view, is to move beyond simply "service" to citizens to "empowerment" of citizens.

Osborn and Gaebler advocate a shift from seeing citizens as *clients* to seeing them as *customers*. In their terms, empowerment largely means market choice. They argue that to adapt to an information age with diverse lifestyles, as well as more highly educated and therefore more demanding consumers, government must not simply produce standardized services; it must get "close to the customer."

Consumer choice is the prevailing notion of empowerment characteristic of our age, a time when consumer language has taken hold in almost every crevice of society. "As a first step, it's useful," Paul Light tells us. But he sees this approach as sharply limited and is convinced that a customer metaphor will ultimately fail. Light, a consultant with Vice President Gore's reinventing government effort, is one of the nation's leading authorities on government bureaucracy.

Government employees, in Light's view, were once motivated by an ethos of public service which stressed their civic identities. But this has largely disappeared. It has been replaced by a focus on specialization and service delivery. However sensitively done, such a focus makes government the center of the action and the public an outside object of action. "Departments and agencies have plenty of advocates for doing things *for* and *to* citizens," Light argues. "But there are almost no voices for seeing government workers as citizens themselves, working with other citizens." Politicians and employees alike have psychologically removed themselves from being *part* of the citizenry. "Citizens are viewed in partial terms—as clients and customers, taxpayers and voters—too rarely as whole actors, capable of judgment and problem solving on their own." Light is convinced that no matter how many bureaucratic layers are pared away, there will be in-exorable pressure to grow them back in what he calls "administrative kudzu," unless we "reinvent citizenship" as a productive activity.[9]

While a consumer-oriented approach may work effectively in private business driven by the demands of the marketplace, with government it produces more whininess than ownership. People end up wanting more for themselves and cutbacks for everyone else.

Government has essential services to provide, but overall service provision cannot be its main function in a vigorous, lively democracy. The messy process of democratic politics will always lose the battle if the goal is simply to meet consumer demand. John Kari, Senior Planner for the Metropolitan Council, a regional planning body in the Twin Cities area of Minnesota, observes that a consumer or customer model simply focuses too much on the immediate short term. "In a consumer model, you want something. When you address issues, everyone bargains for what they want at the moment." Kari focuses on the longer range where groups have to learn how to think of what they need to accomplish together over time. "This can only happen when you can engage in a really tough, honest discussion about what are the priorities, the vision for the future of the whole, and each stakeholder's part."[10] The rationale for democratic politics is not service provision but common work.

Government by the People

As in workplaces outside of the government, within the government there are important signs of change. These changes suggest some of the ways in which government resources and workers can catalyze public work. Existing systems of outreach and delivery such as the cooperative extension system show signs of returning to an older mission of collaborative work with local communities. Some agencies like the Army Corps of Engineers have developed training programs that create much more interactive planning processes in order to address major problems. Finally, new initiatives like the AmeriCorps might have potential to recall the traditions of the Civilian Conservation Corps, catalyzing citizen efforts that build public goods and meet pressing public needs.

The shift from citizen as customer to citizen as producer and the changes that are entailed in work identities and relationships are powerfully illustrated by extension services.

Cooperative extension is a government outreach program based in land grant colleges and supported through federal, state, and local county funds. It was expressly intended by its founding Commission on Country Life to help develop local capacities of citizens to solve problems themselves. Its broad initial mission was "to improve rural and country life." Its diverse activities—helping farmers learn the latest agricultural approaches; educating young people in 4-H clubs; organizing home economics classes for wives, and other projects—all were posed as alternatives to top-down, technical, directive approaches.

Extension services largely lost its "public" dimension in recent decades and also grew far beyond its original agricultural focus. More than 85 percent of children and teens in 4-H, for instance, are from nonfarm families, mainly in small towns and suburbs. Extension, for all its changes, turns out to be an ideal site for revival of an older civic mission. In several states—Minnesota, Wisconsin, Alabama, and North Carolina—cooperative extension has begun to use public work to integrate a "citizenship approach." "We're going to go back to the way Extension started, with citizenship and public work," recounts Pat Borich, recently retired dean of Minnesota Extension Service. Borich oversaw a several year process of "reinventing extension" in civic terms.

Carol Shields, director of Minnesota 4-H, says that a citizenship framework helped people to rethink their identities as well as their work. They changed the nature of the relationships they had with each other and what they did in communities across the state. "The introduction of the concept of 'public' gave people something larger than the immediate situation; it created a broader outlook." Shields said these ideas also created space for more philosophical people in extension to come to the forefront in a new way. "There were some very good thinkers in the system, but it had not been a trait much valued. Beginning to talk about concepts like 'public' and 'citizenship' created a different atmosphere where ideas could come to life."[11]

Other states have also begun to return to the older civic mission that helps citizens develop skills and find resources to solve problems themselves. In Anniston, Alabama, the county extension agent, in most people's minds, had been the guy to call about the sick tree in the yard; or the woman to contact about the local 4-H club. Barbara Mobley, a cooperative extension county agent in Calhoun County for 29 years, tried something different. Instead of providing information and services, she helped people organize their own problem-solving groups. It meant "letting go of previous methods we used in prescribing a 'fix' for a community problem," Mobley explained. "We shared the ownership, and redefined our role to be a catalyst."

As a result, many people are now using extension resources in new ways. An area-wide health council brings together public health nurses, low-income mothers, and teenagers to tackle issues like teen pregnancy. A group called the Women's Empowerment Network provides training in political skills and public speaking for low-income women. A strategic planning and education committee involves both army officials and opponents of a military plan to decommission chemical weapons. "On an issue like this, the military typically will say, 'don't get upset. We have a plan. If anything happens we'll let you know what to do,'" observes Bill Salzer, an Auburn professor who is expert in community conflicts. "This is ripe for panic. But extension brought all the sides together."

Citizens in Louisiana and Florida working with the Army Corps of Engineers illustrate yet another example of public work with government resources "equipping people to solve their own problems." Confronted with permit disputes related to hydrocarbon exploration drilling by oil companies across state boundaries, the Corps used its authority and expertise to bring together rival groups—environmentalists, industry, developers, and local officials—in an innovative process that required collaborative action among the stakeholders themselves. The key was training Army Corps employees to recast their identities, as well as their work: a reminder that they were "citizens," not simply technicians or regulators. "We put the 'civil' back into civil service," says Jerome Delli Priscoli, senior policy analyst for the Institute for Water Resources.

Like the Civilian Conservation Corps, the new AmeriCorps initiative serves as such a catalyst for addressing needs of the nation. AmeriCorps, with 20,000 members nationwide, is still relatively small. It is certainly modest in comparison with the several hundred thousand young men a year in the Civilian Conservation Corps. Yet already the national service initiative illustrates how low-paid amateur effort in a government public works program reminiscent of the CCC can tap a remarkable vein of civic idealism, grassroots energy, and common sense to address critical public needs.

In Bozeman, Montana, a team of young people in AmeriCorps have retrieved 110 miles of wilderness trails, built 8 disability-accessible playgrounds, planted 1,500 trees, restored 4 historical sites, repaired 15 senior citizen homes, and restored streams and repaired cavern tunnels built by the original Civilian Conservation Corps of the 1930s, all in less than a year. "The Civilian Conservation Corps of the 1930s was successful because it sought to address a national emergency," explains Steve Guetterman, of Montana Conservation Corps, part of today's AmeriCorps. Guetterman observes that "our problems today are more pronounced, and embedded in social and environmental structures." The importance of AmeriCorps, however, is precisely that it has begun to create a nationwide network, like the old CCC, which can address critical public challenges.

In another case, in the low-income, crime-ridden Blue Hills neighborhood of Kansas City, AmeriCorps participants, mostly from the community itself, worked with the police to design a community approach to police work. They have closed nearly 20 crack houses and reclaimed a large neighborhood park once abandoned to gang shootings. "We contacted landlords and told them what their tenants were doing; helped landlords devise better screening applications for renters; reported code violations," said LeRon Fields, a young participant, and Steven Bishop, Police Chief, writing a joint editorial response to a recent attack on AmeriCorps by syndicated columnist George Will. "Bit by bit, the drug pushers and users were driven out and working families returned. And [we] found a way to help pull [the] neighborhood back together" in the process.

How we name things matters a great deal. In American history, the basic vocabulary for democratic action has been the idea of people creating our commonwealth through public work. This idea needs retrieval.

A renewed politics of public work offers promise for our time, because it draws on our core resource—people's widespread desire for creative, meaningful work, whether paid or unpaid, that can help shape the world around us. A reinvigorated practice and theory of public work can find grounding in the deepest democratic traditions of the country, while it also creates a new axis for politics. It moves beyond the ideological polarizations based on scarcity. It renews the idea of government of the people—a catalyst and meeting ground for action—rather than simply government as service provider.

Policy in every field—from welfare reform to housing to education—will look far different when contribution through public work becomes the centerpiece. For instance, creating public work opportunities for welfare recipients based on the AmeriCorps infrastructure would fundamentally alter the nature of the welfare debate.

Public work challenges us all to think about how our efforts and institutional practices can develop more public qualities. If we shift the current debate from "what's in it for me" to a more dynamic understanding of what citizens can produce together, we will simultaneously address the most basic questions of a democratic society.

In an information age, ideas matter. Concepts are forms of power. Who possesses them and how they are used shape our decision making on every level, in every institution. A democratic culture for our time demands widespread discussion of large ideas of importance: Who deliberates? Who acts? Who is responsible? Who are the architects of our common fate?

There is a great danger in letting any elite group of people— whether liberals or conservatives, the media or business executives, college professors or religious evangelicals or government officials— answer these questions for us. It is hard work to regenerate democratic practices. America needs to learn again that history matters. Questions of broad philosophy matter. We all need to renew the skills of public work.

No one is innocent in the erosion of democracy. Yet public work provides a medium for every one of us, in every environment, to participate in the great American experiment. Indeed, the fate of our democracy and our commonwealth rests on our efforts.

Public Work

Work: from IndoEuropean base, werg, *to do, act, from which is derived in Greek,* ergon, *action, work; and* organon, *tool or instrument.*

Noun 1. physical or mental effort to do or make something; purposeful activity; labor; toil; . . . something that one is making, doing or acting upon.

Webster's New World Dictionary

*P*ublic work" in *Building America* means patterns of work that have public dimensions (that is, work with public purposes, work by a public, work in public settings), as well as the "works" or products themselves. The term used in this sense appears here and there in American letters—in the rulings of Lemuel Shaw, for instance, in the writings of Liberty Hyde Bailey, in the proposals of Lewis Mumford for citizenship education. Yet on the whole, there is a striking absence of the term *public work* in academic writing. The absence is all the more remarkable in view of the vibrant *experiences* of public work throughout American history. What explains the mysterious omission?

Public work is not normally part of the experience of those who theorize about democracy. Conceptualizations depend strongly on actual experience. The experience of scholars is often highly individual. Also, the received categories of political and social theory keep work and public life separate. Thus the question of the tie between democracy and work is not even posed.

The Greek Ideal

Dominant ways of thinking about politics, democracy, public life, and work descend from the Greeks. Specifically, contemporary political theory continues to reflect the Greek distinction between the public world on the one hand and work on the other.

Democracy means literally political power exercised by the people. Understood in activist terms, democracy is a sphere of public life in which ordinary people exercise power. According to Greek theorists, this public sphere was imagined to be sharply separate from private life, the terrain of practical work and self-interests. "Making history" in the public sphere involved freedom, power, and concern with the largest questions; private life was the mundane world of "making life."[1]

Greeks developed a vivid understanding of public life for the first time. Against the background of an ancient world where radical inequalities of political power were seen as immutable, and concepts like "democracy" or "equality" or "freedom" did not even exist, one can imagine the exhilarating quality of the transformations for those directly involved in them, at least. For the first time in recorded history, ordinary (male) people came to believe that they could be masters of their fate.[2]

Development of democracy occurred over centuries. But in the later decades of the fifth century B.C., a remarkable shift in *identity* developed among the ordinary people of Athens. Even the poorest Athenians came to see politics, or the public sphere, as a vital part of their lives. Family, economics, work, leisure pursuits, all faded into the margins, according to many historians. The Assembly, the body in which citizenry as a whole deliberated, came to be the supreme power. Aeschylus's great play, *Eumenides*, performed for an audience of 15,000 in 458 B.C., conveyed the revolutionary transformations in consciousness as "the political" became the centerpiece of Athenian civic identity.

Strong identities of "the citizen" emerged. "Up to now [people] had been first and foremost nobles, farmers or artisans, or retainers, townsmen or villagers," writes the Greek historian Christian Meier, in his account of how "the Greeks discovered politics." "Their role as citizens, which involved certain political and military rights and duties, had been negligible." Yet as a result of the changes, the citizen role became vital. It was "taken so seriously that one can actually speak of a change in the structure of social affiliations. . . . The citizens were expected to act as citizens, *politai,* that is "politically" (in the Greek sense of the word), and this expectation was now given institutional form."[3]

Athenians democratized the aristocratic ideal. They brought common people into public affairs, an arena in which aristocrats had always been involved. The poorest of citizens, as well as the richest, had the time, recognition, authority, and even financial support to concern themselves with the welfare of the city as a whole. But at least in the ways Greek theorists presented democracy, the public world was also sharply separated from the world of work.[4]

Hannah Arendt and the Public Realm

Contemporary political theory continues this distinction between a public sphere and everyday work. Thus Hannah Arendt, the premier twentieth-century philosopher of public life, followed Greek theorists in viewing work and labor as part of the private world. Manual labor she saw as a necessity without much dignity. Work, on the other hand, was the activity of *homo faber*, or "man the maker of things."

Arendt believed the process of work did not belong in the public arena of "deeds and action." Rather, the worker's "public realm is the exchange market, where he can show the products of his hands and receive the esteem which is due him." Public relationships were created through interactions of exchange among people who remained "private," or isolated: "*Homo faber*, the builder of the world and the producer of things, can find his proper relationship to other people only by exchanging his products with theirs because these products themselves *are always produced in isolation* (italics added)." Indeed, Arendt argues that the combination of thought and manual art which produces craft—the creation of a "model" or idea in one's mind which one then reproduces through shaping materials of the world, requires isolation as its fundamental condition. "This isolation from others is the necessary life condition for every mastership which consists in being alone with the 'idea,' the mental image of the thing to be." Only apprentices and helpers are needed, in relations based on inequality.[5]

In contrast, Arendt saw the public realm as an environment of "innumerable perspectives and aspects in which the common world presents itself and for which no common measurement or denominator can ever be devised." For Arendt, the public world was a world of visibility and disclosure, where people's words and deeds potentially allowed one to achieve immortality. "By their capacity for the immortal deed, by their ability to leave no perishable traces behind, men, their individual mortality notwithstanding, attain an immortality of their own and prove themselves to be of a 'divine' nature."[6]

The source of power in the public world was its plurality, for Arendt. "Being seen and being heard by others derive their significance from the fact that everybody sees and hears from a different position. This is the meaning of public life, compared to which even the richest and most satisfying family life can offer only the prolongation of one's own position with its attending aspects and perspectives." Thus, Arendt argued that public experience had a weight and reality that private life lacked: "The subjectivity of privacy can be prolonged and multiplied in a family . . . but this family 'world' can never replace the reality rising out of the sum total of aspects presented by one object to a multitude of spectators."[7]

Arendt's work, especially her book *The Human Condition,* made a significant contribution in bringing a notion of "public" back into intellectual discussion. By doing so, she retrieves for modern audiences something of the vitality of democracy that Greeks understood. Moreover, Arendt was in many respects a democratic theorist. Her public world was potentially open to all, regardless of race or culture or income or gender.

Yet the separation she created between public life and work also embeds an exclusive quality in her understanding of the public realm. Arendt believed, for example, that public life emerged for ordinary people only at extraordinary moments and times—during the American Revolution, for instance, or the civil rights movement of the late 1950s and early 1960s.

Arendt simply failed to grasp the public, cooperative qualities of much work, vividly illustrated in the American experience. In slighting this dynamic she reveals more about the academic culture in which she did her work than about the nature of work in general. Thus she also missed the wellspring of American democratic energy and possibility: the tie between everyday labor and a public world.

Jürgen Habermas and the Public Sphere

In the last twenty years discussions of the public sphere have been shaped strongly by Jürgen Habermas, the German social theorist. Habermas is perhaps the leading theorist of a public world aimed at mutual communication. Communicative theory for Habermas holds potential to "locate a gentle, but obstinate, a never silent although seldom redeemed claim to reason, a claim that must be recognized de facto whenever and wherever there is to be consensual action."[8]

In the 1990s, Jürgen Habermas has many offspring. Calls for "deliberation" have proliferated. Deliberation appeared as a central theme at the 1994 convention of the American Political Science Association. Sheldon Hackney, Chair of the National Endowment for the Humanities, has undertaken a "National Conversation" aimed at recreating a public realm for public discussion to improve common understanding across the sharp and bitter divides that separate Americans.

Deliberative citizenship challenges the instrumental politics of conventional liberal theory and the practices of interest groups in the welfare state. In John Dewey's terms, a deliberative vision rests on a notion of democracy as a "shared way of life." Here, such theorizing draws heavily from the work of Habermas.[9]

A number of elements formed the background for the emergence of what Jürgen Habermas calls "the bourgeois public sphere." Long-term trends toward long-distance trade and commercialization undermined the household economy and created pressures toward a commodity market that reworked political relations and also created new "public knowledge" across communal and even national boundaries. A politicized and self-conscious language of public opinion was closely connected, moreover, to the development of a vibrant urban culture. Urban sites of many kinds formed a spatial environment for the public sphere: lecture halls, museums, public parks, theaters, meeting houses, opera houses, coffee shops, and the like. Associated with such changes was an emergent infrastructure of new social information created through institutions like the press, publishing houses, lending libraries and literary societies.

Finally, the explosion of voluntary associations in the eighteenth and nineteenth century created a social setting in which a sense of far-ranging and self-conscious "public" could take shape. Habermas drew particular attention to associations of debate and discussion occurring in these public settings. These formed a context in which older hierarchical principles of deference and ascribed social status gave way to public principles of rational discourse. New professional and business groups nourished and asserted their claims to a more general social and political leadership.

By the late eighteenth or the beginning of the nineteenth century, depending on the nation, the public sphere "was casting itself loose as a forum in which the private people, come together to form a public, readied themselves to compel public authority to legitimate itself before public opinion. The *publicum* developed into the public, the *subjectum* into the reasoning subject, the receiver of regulations from above into the ruling authorities' adversary."[10]

Habermas's focus on public opinion drew on the history of word usage in the eighteenth century. In 1765, the article on "Opinion" in the French *Encyclopedie* defined the word in terms of the classically rationalist distinction between *knowledge,* which was based on science ("a full and entire light which reveals things clearly, shedding demonstrable certainty upon them") and *opinion,* which was seen as shifting and unreliable ("but a feeble and imperfect light which only reveals things by conjecture and leaves them always in uncertainty and doubt.")

By 1789, the "Opinion" entree had disappeared from the *Enclyclopedie Methodique*. Instead, under politics, "opinion" had become "public opinion." Moreover, its resonances had been radically transformed. "Public opinion," said Jacques Necker, former minister to Louis XVI, was "an invisible power that, without treasury, guard or army, gives its laws to the city, the court, and even the palaces of kings." Or as editor Jacques Peuchet elaborated in the same work, public opinion was the highest form of political knowledge, designating "the sum of all social knowledge . . . [the] judgments made by a nation on the matters submitted to its tribunal. Its influence is today the most powerful motive for praiseworthy actions."[11]

Opinion in this sense was an integrative process. One's views were understood to become more multi-dimensional and fuller by engagement with perspectives of others and with insights and knowledge with which one had not previously been acquainted. The eighteenth-century philosopher, Immanuel Kant captured this distinction in his contrast between the *sensus privatus*—views that are only formed through private experience—and the *sensus communis,* common or public sense. The former he also called "cyclopean thinking," based on the character from Greek mythology who had only one eye.

In terms that have relevance for expert training today, Kant argued it was entirely possible to be a learned cyclops: "A cyclops of mathematics, history, natural history, philology and languages." But without the "enlarged thought," or public judgment, that comes from engagement with a diversity of other viewpoints and perspectives, the learned person fails to think "philosophically": in Kant's terms, as a member of a living human community. Kant argued that the most severe insanity was that defined by *sensus privatus,* those cut off from *sensus communis,* who had radically lost touch with public conversation.[12]

By the last decades of the nineteenth century, Habermas argues, the public sphere decayed. The replacement of a competitive economy with a monopolized economy dominated by large industrial and financial interests undermined the power and authority of the commercial and professional middle classes. The state itself increasingly took on the role of social regulator of conflicts. The public began to break apart into a myriad of special interests. Most importantly, a technical rationality focused on means replaced more interactive public dialogue. Technical rationality depends on a prior assumption of what the "ends" entail—how problems are defined and what solutions are desirable—and concerns itself with the most efficient means to accomplish the task.

Habermas has focused on the process of communication in an effort to sustain the democratic ideal in the modern world. After his first book, *Transformation of the Public Sphere,* he has had the goal of understanding conditions for public deliberation in a world which undermines it. He has sought to describe the public spaces for "uncoercive interaction on the basis of communication free from domination."[13]

His primary strategy has been to distinguish between types of reason. For Habermas practical reason—thinking directed to solving problems—should be seen as different than communicative reason directed to common understanding. Practical, "purposive-rational actions" are the province of the larger "system world" of big, impersonal institutions and bureaucracies.

"Communicative actions" survive—though endangered by the colonizing of large institutions—in everyday experience, the "life worlds" of ordinary people and communities.[14] The patterns of each are qualitatively different, he suggests:

> *Purposive-rational actions* can be regarded under two different aspects—the empirical efficiency of technical means and the consistency of choice between suitable means. Actions and action systems can be rationalized in both respects. The rationality of means requires technically utilizable, empirical knowledge. The rationality of decisions requires the explication and inner consistency of value systems and decision maxims, as well as the correct derivation of acts of choice.[15]

In contrast, the "rationalization of communicative action" for Habermas involves the end of hierarchies of power:

> Rationalization here means extirpating those relations of force that are inconspicuously set in the very structure of communication and that prevent conscious settlement of conflicts, and consensual regulation of conflicts by means of . . . interpersonal communication. Rationalization means overcoming such systematically distorted communication.[16]

Habermas distills from examinations of these processes an account of what he sees as the preconditions for "ideal speech situations," free of domination.

Habermas's approach has generated many creative insights. His interests are echoed, in different accents, in the concerns and practices of those promoting deliberative democracy in many settings.

Yet there are also major limits in his version of the public sphere. The very specialized language that Habermas uses is full of irony: He describes public spaces "free of domination" in a specialized and arcane vocabulary that shows how far contemporary academic discussion is removed from democratic talk and the real world in which most people live.

Some of the limits of this idealized treatment of the public world are named by critics of Habermas writing from a left-wing perspective. Critics like Nancy Fraser, Mary Ryan, and Geoff Eley focus on problems of power and interest. They do not generally observe the exclusivity built into an academic language like Habermas's, but they do argue that Habermas's theory embodies a notably middle-class bias. They describe the ways in which the nineteenth-century public sphere took shape partly through excluding groups. Women were consigned to the household; lower-class groups were viewed as unruly.

In the critics' view a more dynamic historical understanding of public life comes from looking at it as a series of diverse publics rather than a singular "public sphere." Democratic publics were created through a turbulent, provisional, and open-ended process of struggle, change, and challenge. Mary Ryan artfully depicts the diverse worlds of street corner and outdoor society, far removed from the reading rooms and clubs of polite society. Similarly, she describes political judgment and citizenship as always infused with interests, power relationships, and divergent points of view that could rarely reach "consensus." Public conversations were not shaped by abstract universal categories like "deliberation" or "search for the common good." Public judgment was not a search for truth or consensus in the ways Habermas suggests should be the aim of public discussion. In real life, judgments are always dependent on *context* and perspective. They are suffused with power dynamics and conflicts that may well never be resolved.[17]

Like Ryan, most of the academic left today—theorists like Cornel West, Roberto Unger, Stanley Fish, and Iris Young—argue that the public world needs to be seen as open, diverse, full of conflict and change. Interestingly, for all the disagreements, Habermas and his left-wing critics share a fundamentally similar position on citizens and power in the modern world. All see citizens as excluded from governance, public policy, and in the broadest sense, public creation. This assumption of the separation of citizens from actual public work is widespread today. Thus, the language of citizen participation focuses on process, not on decisions about what is produced or the accountable work of production itself.

Separating decision making from everyday work settings corresponds to the formal structures of modern governments. Political authority is delegated through elections to representatives. It is not exercised by the citizenry as a whole. The problem is that Habermas and left-wing theorists take formal structures too literally. Habermas and deliberative theorists put citizens in the role of judicious audience. Left-wing theorists put citizens in the role of outsiders and victims.

Such theorists advance a moralized, heavily ideological politics, where the forces of righteousness are arrayed against the forces of oppression. Public encounters are organized around the struggle for justice. Power largely is zero-sum and one-directional in which the people are acted upon. "The wretched of the earth," in West's phrase, are innocent victims. The role of progressive intellectuals is to champion their cause.[18]

Yet the very division between everyday work of ordinary people and formal structures of government and other big institutions obscures the multiple ways in which people act along the borders. Power never operates simply in a monochromatic, uni-directional fashion but always is an ensemble of relationships.[19]

In fact, as we have seen throughout the whole book, ordinary people have regularly created public spaces through which they exercised power in the central corridors of policy and decision making. In public spaces people draw on local and communal identities, but they also create larger publics with power and purpose that cross lines of division.[20]

Separating public life from everyday work results in an abstract "public sphere" of action and deed, or communicative consensus. Public life in the real world, by way of contrast, includes negotiation, bargaining, messy compromise, and also creative work in building the commonwealth. To bring back a fuller account of public life, it is useful to advance a third version of citizenship, aimed at developing the capacities of citizens for public work.

Work and Politics

Despite the technocratic, therapeutic, and moralized temper of our age, a sense of citizenship that combines practical work with a larger civic vision, an understanding of the citizen as producer of our commonwealth, has renewed relevance.

Today the inability of a specialized expert approach to solve virtually any serious public problem is increasingly apparent. Moreover, the richest accounts of professional practice in Habermas's "system world," suggest a much more complex reality than simply means-focused technical rationality. For example, Donald Schön's studies of creative professional craft indicate that professionals who do their work well learn an attentiveness to context, learn to interact with others, and learn an open-ended fluidity about how to define what problems are and how to address them. As Schön puts it, technical rationality leaves out "problem setting;" it mistakenly "leads us to think of intelligent practice as an application of knowledge to instrumental decisions." Creative practice is in most instances a highly contextual art: "The know-how is *in* the action." The practitioner "does not keep means and ends separate, but defines them interactively as he frames a problematic situation."[21]

A vocabulary of technical rationality not only constricts creativity of work, it also neglects its broader purposes, meaning, and value, through which we collectively determine the shape of our world.

Neither a language of deliberation and community, nor a language of justice is sufficient to move beyond fragmented purposes and rights-based political activism. Citizenship understood as public work among groups with widely differing interests and values offers different resources for democratizing power and for integrating public relations.

Simone Weil is one of the few in modern political theory to take work seriously. In *Oppression and Liberty,* Weil drew on her actual experiences among working people. The richness of Weil's analysis of the cooperative, democratic aspects of work contrasts sharply with the limitations of Arendt's. "A . . . free life would be one wherein all real difficulties presented themselves as kinds of problems, wherein all successes were as solutions carried into action," wrote Weil. She argued that work and problem solving, involving both reflective thought and action, entailed practical relationships that could disrupt hierarchies of power and status which otherwise operate unquestioned:

> [In a 'free' society] social relations would be directly modeled upon the organization of labour; men would group themselves in small working collectivities . . . it is a fine sight to see a handful of workmen in the building trade, checked by some difficulty, [who] ponder the problem each for himself, make various suggestions for dealing with it, and then apply unanimously the method conceived by one, who may or may not have any official authority . . . at such moments, the image of a free community appears.[22]

Serious citizenship requires public action as the everyday, demanding craft of addressing the challenges and problems of our common existence and creating larger spaces that have diversity of interest and viewpoint. This means acknowledging differences in interest and power (at the same time not accepting them as static or absolute). It also means working alongside people with whom we may disagree about moral issues or with whom we may not wish to "live in community," for the sake of broader objectives.

What gets lost when public life is separated from everyday work is the moral ambiguity, the open-ended, provisional quality, and sense of productiveness involved in the pragmatic tasks of the public world. In public settings the search is not for "truth" or final vindication; rather, there are many truths, reflecting the multiplicity of experiences and stories that bring diverse groups into politics. The challenge is finding appropriateness, fit, agreement, adjudication, and provisional resolution of pressing concerns. In a problem-solving and work-centered public, there are few saints or sinners but rather an interplay among a variety of interests, values, and ways of looking at experience.

Principles of action are different in public. The aim of politics is action on significant problems—not bonding, or intimacy, or communal consensus. In public, principles such as recognition, respect, and accountability are appropriate bases for action.

Public work which develops people's sense of themselves as contributors on a larger stage can generate new confidence and strategic capacity. Most important, it also renews hope that the world is ours to create over again.

NOTES

INTRODUCTION

1. Joseph Wood, *Commonwealth*, vol. 1, no. 1 (1893), p. 1. Work in America once had a far more public resonance and larger significance than it commonly does today. Commonwealth meanings of work have disappeared. Joseph Wood's comment above would have had a wide audience who understood exactly what he meant. People saw themselves as "producers," and America developed a producer culture. Thus, ordinary people understood the meaning of democracy and their role in it far differently than we do in our time.
2. John Hannah, quoted from speech, "The Place of the Land-Grant College in Public Educational System of the Future," to annual Land Grant-College meeting, 1944; Boyte possession.
3. Simone Weil, "On the Portrait of a Free Society", in *Oppression and Liberty* (Amherst: University of Massachusetts, 1973), pp. 83, 106, 101. For a fine treatment of Weil's thought, see Mary Dietz, *Between the Human and the Divine: The Political Thought of Simone Weil* (Totowa, N.J.: Rowman and Littlefield, 1988).

4. Joe Klein, "How to Capture the Radical Middle," *Newsweek*, September 27, 1995.

5. Figures from *Business Week*, March 13, 1995; *New York Times*/CBS News poll, August 12, 1995. Fifty-nine percent of the *Times*/CBS poll said there was not a single elected official they admired.

6. Robert Putnam et al., *Making Democracy Work* (Princeton: Princeton University Press, 1993); Robert Putnam, "Bowling Alone," *Journal of Democracy*, vol 9, January, 1995, pp. 65–78.

7. Current works on politics, citizenship, and democracy of importance include Benjamin Barber, *Jihad Versus McWorld*, Robert Bellah et al., *Habits of the Heart*, E. J. Dionne, *Why Americans Hate Politics*, Alan Ehrenhalt, *The United States of Ambition*, Jean Bethke Elshtain, *Democracy on Trial*, Amitai Etzioni, *The Spirit of Community*, William Galston, *Liberal Virtues*, William Grieder, *Who Will Tell the People?*, Michael Kazin, *The Populist Persuasion*, Frances Moore Lappé and Paul Dubois, *Quickening of America*, Michael Lind, *The Next American Nation*, David Mathews, *Politics for People*, David Osborn and Ted Gaebler, *Reinventing Government*, and Robert Wiebe, *Self-Rule: A Cultural History of Democracy*. For treatments on work and the "obstacles" it presents to civic involvement, see Robert Putnam's forthcoming, *Bowling Alone*, Jeremy Rifkin, *The End of Work*, and Juliet Schor, *The Overworked American*. The late Christopher Lasch, especially in *Revolt of the Elites*, is a rare voice in contemporary discussions, tying the crisis in democracy to loss of people's identities as "producers."

8. These patterns have not remained unnoticed by political theorists. Thus, for instance, a common complaint among theorists in our time is the separation of most theorizing from actual public practice. On the specific topic here, John Dunn, the distinguished British political theorist, made the argument that conventional political theorizing has almost nothing of use to say about effective democratic action, in "Why Democracies Succeed," a presentation to the Department of Political Science at the University of Minnesota, April 6, 1994.

In intellectual discussion today, social movement theorists are those who most directly address questions of "capacities for action," but their treatment has generally slighted questions of what makes for specifically *democratic* (as opposed to authoritarian) action. Indeed, for all the sophistication of contemporary social movement theory on some questions, it lags behind social theory of the 1950s on this critical axis. For a summary of some of the literature and a critique, see Sara M. Evans and Harry C. Boyte, *Free Spaces: The Sources of Democratic Change in America* (Chicago: Chicago University Press, 1992).

9. This was pointed out by the historian Cliff Kuhn, one of the first researchers with the Textile Oral History Project at the University of North Carolina, Chapel Hill, who said the Project's interviews with blue-collar workers in the South found "public work" a very common term. Discussion with Harry Boyte, September 29, 1995, Atlanta, Ga.

10. This explicit naming corresponds well to what James Farr has called conceptual innovation. See James Farr, "Understanding Conceptual Change Politically," in Terrence Ball, James Farr, and Russell Hanson, eds., *Political Innovation and Conceptual Change* (Cambridge: Cambridge University Press, 1989), Chapter 2.

11. Interview with Deborah Meier (phone), August 14, 1995, interviewer, Harry Boyte. See also, Deborah Meier, *The Power of Their Ideas* (Boston: Beacon Press, 1995).

12. Walzer's views are described in Peter Steinfels, "Beliefs: Battling for the Backing of Judaism in the Country's Cultural Wars," *The New York Times,* November 4, 1995.

13. Adam Smith, *An Inquiry into the Nature and Causes of the Wealth of Nations.* (Chicago: University of Chicago Press, 1975), p. 244.

14. These themes of freedom in civil rights are well described in Richard H. King, "Citizenship and Self-Respect: The Experiences of Politics in the Civil Rights Movement," *Journal of American Studies,* vol. 22 (1988), pp. 7–24.

CHAPTER 1

1. Program Notes, in Boyte possession, written by Martin Luther King, John Lewis, James Farmer, and other civil rights leaders to describe the purpose of the March on Washington for Jobs and Freedom, August 28, 1963.

2. Paul Leichester Ford, ed., Thomas Jefferson, *The Works of Thomas Jefferson* (New York: Knickerbocker Press, 1903), p. 278.

3. For discussion of Lincoln's views on freedom and self-governance see, Garry Wills, *Lincoln at Gettysburg.* (New York: Simon and Schuster, 1992).

4. Interviews with Mike Gecan, Brooklyn, N.Y., November 14, 1984, Harry Boyte; Interview with Ed Chambers, New York, February 22, 1983, Harry Boyte; Youngblood and Jamieson quoted from Jim Sleeper, "East Brooklyn's Second Rising," *City Limits,* December, 1982, p. 13.

5. "What Works," *Newsweek,* May 29, 1995.

6. "Who Built the Pyramids?" Studs Terkel, *Working* (New York: Avon, 1972), p. 2.

7. Leonard W. Levy, *The Law of the Commonwealth and Chief Justice Shaw* (New York: Oxford University Press, 1957), pp. 120–21.

8. For a discussion of the ways these versions of citizenship are discussed in contemporary political and social theory—what is called the "liberal-communitarian" debate—and the way in which public work offers an alternative, see Harry Boyte, "Beyond Deliberation: Citizenship as Public Work," *The Good Society,* vol. 5, no. 2 (1995), pp. 15–19.

9. Robert Bellah et al., *Habits of the Heart: Individual and Commitment in American Life* (Berkeley: University of California Press, 1986), p. 121.

10. Kevin Sack, "Volunteering Made Easier for Busy Young Workers," *The New York Times,* November 25, 1995, p. 1.

11. Interview with Al Hammer, Minneapolis, May 27, 1995, Nancy Kari.

12. Interview with David Cohen (phone), November 15, 1994, Harry Boyte.

13. Interviews with Jean Carls, March 14, 1995, Minneapolis, Harry Boyte; Dave Berner, April 21, 1995, Tomah, Wis., Nancy Kari and Harry Boyte.

14. Interview with Gerald Taylor (phone), January 18, 1995, Nancy Kari and Harry Boyte.

15. The trends of bureaucracy and expert-dominated decision making have reflected not only the rise of large economic enterprise, the modern state, and communications systems, but also the practical dilemmas of political decision making in technological,

large-scale, and complex societies. Scientific language gains its power through the fact that a marked process of abstraction is inevitable, given such complexity. See Kenneth Boulding, *Economics as a Science* (New York: McGraw–Hill, 1970), p. 2.

The possibility of significant democratization of such systems comes from the fact that public judgment or wisdom generated through citizen deliberation and action is necessary, when "knowledge" is not sufficient to solve the most pressing social problems of our time. This argument is developed in Harry Boyte, *CommonWealth: A Return to Citizen Politics* (New York: Free Press, 1990); see also Alain Touraine, *Post-Industrial Society* (New York: Random House, 1971).

CHAPTER 2

1. Quoted in Michael Kazin, *The Populist Persuasion: An American History* (New York: Basic Books, 1995), p. 9.
2. Jane Addams, *Twenty Years at Hull-House* (New York: Macmillan, 1938), p. 179.
3. Robert Wiebe, *Self-Rule: A Cultural History of American Democracy* (Chicago: The University of Chicago Press, 1995), pp. 45–46.
4. For an illustration of feminist arguments about the Greeks, see for instance, Jean Bethke Elshtain, *Public Man, Private Woman: Women in Social and Political Thought* (Princeton: Princeton University Press, 1981); and Helen P. Foley, ed., *Reflections on Women in Antiquity* (New York: Cordon and Breach Science, 1981).
5. Christian Meier, *The Greek Discovery of Politics* (Cambridge: Harvard University Press, 1990), p. 145.
6. *Ibid.*, p. 141.
7. Wiebe, *Self-Rule*, p. 281.
8. Quoted from Gordon Wood, *Creation of the American Republic: 1776–1787* (Chapel Hill: University of North Carolina, 1969), p. 32.
9. John Adams, quoted in Wood, *Creation*, p. 574; Hamilton, quoted in Vernon Louis Parrington, *Main Currents in American Thought: An Interpretation of American Literature From the Beginnings to 1920*, vol. 1, 1620–1800 (New York: Harcourt, Brace and Co., 1927), p. 298.

10. Gordon S. Wood, *The Radicalism of the American Revolution* (New York: Vintage, 1991), p. ix.
11. *Ibid.*, pp. 277–278.
12. *Ibid.*, pp. 278–279.
13. Wiebe, *Self-Rule*, p. 43.
14. Bruce Laurie, *Artisans into Workers: Labor in 19th-century America* (New York: Farrar, Straus, and Giroux, 1989), p. 15.
15. *Ibid.*, p. 280.
16. Grund, Chevalier, Tocqueville, quoted in Wood, *Radicalism*, p. 285.
17. John Michael Vlach, *By the Work of Their Hands: Studies in Afro-American Folklife* (Charlottesville: University of Virginia, 1991), p. 222. For a description of the "free spaces" in which black slaves created their own religious traditions, see for instance Sara M. Evans and Harry C. Boyte, *Free Spaces: The Roots of Democratic Change in America* (Chicago: University of Chicago Press, 1992), Chapter 2.
18. Wiebe, *Self-Rule*, pp. 104–111, summarized the literature on women's roles and their relation to democracy. See also Nancy Cott, *The Bonds of Womanhood* (New Haven: Yale University Press, 1977); Mary Ryan, *Women in Public* (Baltimore: Johns Hopkins, 1990); Sara M. Evans, *Born for Liberty: A History of Women in America* (New York: Free Press, 1989), especially Chapters 3 and 4; Evans and Boyte, *Free Spaces*, Chapter 3.
19. Historians Oscar and Mary Handlin have described the association of the word in Massachusetts with the founding of towns, churches, schools, and a variety of other institutions: "For the farmers and seamen, for the fishermen, artisans and new merchants, commonwealth . . . embodied . . . the value of common action." Oscar and Mary Handlin, *Commonwealth: A Study of the Role of Government in the American Economy, Massachusetts, 1774–1861* (Cambridge: Harvard University Press, 1969), p. 30.
20. Edward Miller and John Hatcher, *Medieval England: Rural Society and Economic Change, 1086–1348* (London: Longman, 1978), pp. 105, 106, 108–109. On traditions of open-field agriculture in England, see Tremor Rowley, ed., *The Origins of Open-Field Agriculture* (London: Croom Helm, 1981).
21. Richard Lingeman, *Small-Town America: A Narrative History, 1620 to the Present* (Boston: Houghton Mifflin, 1980), p. 29.

Commons, as Ivan Illich has described, bears close resemblance to German terms *Almende* and *Gemeinschaft* and the Italian *gli usi civici.* Illich defines the commons as "that part of the environment which lay beyond the person's own threshold and outside his own possession, but to which, however, that person had a recognized claim of usage—not to produce commodities but to provide for the subsistence of kin. Neither wilderness nor home is commons, but that part of the environment for which customary law exacts specific forms of community respect." Illich conveys the nonprivate nature of the commons, and concepts of stake-holding and responsibility—but he neglects the public and power dimensions. See Chapters 6 and 7 and Appendix 2. Ivan Illich, *Gender* (New York: Pantheon, 1982), pp. 17–18.

22. Ruth Bordin, *Woman and Temperance: The Quest for Power and Liberty, 1873–1900* (Philadelphia: Temple University Press, 1980), p. 98.

23. Quoted from Barbara Epstein, *The Politics of Domesticity: Women, Evangelism and Temperance in Nineteenth Century America* (Middletown: Wesleyan University Press, 1981), p. 100.

24. John Adams, quoted in David Mathews, *The Promise of Democracy* (Dayton: Kettering Foundation, 1988), p. 5.

25. Paul Starr, *The Social Transformation of American Medicine* (New York: Basic Books, 1982), pp. 32–34.

26. Sean Wilentz, *Chants Democratic: New York City and the Rise of the American Working Class, 1788–1850* (New York: Oxford University Press, 1984), p. 156.

27. Gary B. Nash, *Race, Class and Politics: Essays on American Colonial and Revolutionary Society* (Urbana: University of Illinois Press, 1986), p. 249.

28. Gary Kulik, "Dams, Fish and Farmers: The Defense of Public Rights in Eighteenth-Century Rhode Island," in Steven Hahn and Jonathan Prude, *The Countryside in the Age of Capitalist Transformation* (Chapel Hill: University of North Carolina, 1985). As Gary Kulik puts it: "Farmers saw their rights to fish threatened by powerful ironmasters closely tied to the colony's political leadership. They drew upon a common sensibility— distrust of corrupt and arbitrary power." Kulik, "Dams," pp. 36–41.

29. Leonard W. Levy, *The Law of the Commonwealth and Chief Justice Shaw* (New York: Oxford University Press, 1957), pp. 306, 309; Shaw quoted from p. 306.

30. For background see Eric Foner, *Nothing but Freedom: Emancipation and Its Legacy* (Baton Rouge: Louisiana State University Press, 1983).

31. On early nineteenth-century popular republicanism based among artisans, see Sean Wilenz, *Chants Democratic: New York City and the Rise of the American Working Class, 1788–1859* (New York: Oxford University Press, 1984). Harper quoted in Eric Foner, *The Voice of Black America* (New York: Simon & Schuster, 1972), p. 431. On the maternal commonwealth, see Sara M. Evans, *Born for Liberty: A History of Women in America* (New York: Free Press, 1989); on labor organizations—especially the Knights of Labor, the largest nineteenth-century workers' organization—see Leon Fink, *Workingmen's Democracy: The Knights of Labor and American Politics* (Urbana: University of Illinois, 1983). Also, Eric Foner, *Reconstruction* (New York: Harper & Row, 1988).

32. See Lawrence Goodwyn, *Populist Moment* (New York: Oxford, 1978); and also Steven Hahn, *The Roots of Southern Populism* (New Haven: Yale University Press, 1982); on a rich and fascinating view of the Knights of Labor's republican themes in this vein, see Leon Fink, *Workingmen's Democracy: The Knights of Labor and American Politics* (Urbana: University of Illinois Press, 1983); for a detailed discussion of the Populist Party platform, see Bruce Palmer, *Man Over Money;* for a discussion of Populism's relative democracy, see Walter K. Nugent, *The Tolerant Populists: Kansas Populism and Nativism* (Chicago: University of Chicago Press, 1963). See also John Bodnar's extensive studies of immigrants which largely reinforce this portrait in *The Transplanted: A History of Immigrants in Urban America* (Bloomington: Indiana University Press, 1985).

33. The quotes from Pettus are taken from interviews on March 14, 17, and 18, 1983, Seattle. Other accounts of the Seattle houseboat story are found in "Subversive?" a special documentary by John de Graaf for KCTS, aired in Seattle, September 5, 1983; and Howard Droker, *Seattle's Unsinkable Houseboats* (Seattle: Watermark Press, 1977). For a detailed description of the Lake Union

effort and other "commonwealth" stories of the seventies and eighties, see Harry C. Boyte, *Community Is Possible: Repairing America's Roots* (New York: Harper & Row, 1984).

34. Howard Drucker, *Seattle's Unsinkable Houseboats* (Seattle: Watermark Press, 1977), p. 75.

35. Steinbrueck's battle is described in detail in Alice Shorett and Murray Morgan, *The Pike Place Market: People, Politics and Produce* (Seattle: Pacific Search Press, 1982); Ellis quoted from Leonard Silk, "Seattle Looks for its Future," *New York Times*, April 22, 1983.

CHAPTER 3

1. Liberty Hyde Bailey, *The Holy Earth* (New York: Charles Scribner & Sons, 1915), p. 41.

2. For a depiction of the late-nineteenth-century attack on farms and rural life, see Clayton S. Ellsworth, "Theodore Roosevelt's Country Life Commission," *Agricultural History* 34 (October, 1960), p. 155. This chapter benefits greatly from the pioneering work of Scott J. Peters, a graduate assistant of Harry Boyte's at the Humphrey Institute. See Peters's publication, *Cooperative Extension and the Democratic Promise of the Land-Grant Idea* (Minneapolis: Minnesota Extension Service, 1995).

3. Daniel Kemmis, "Barn Building: Cooperation and the Economy of the West," *Kettering Review,* Summer, 1988, pp. 6–14; quotes from pp. 6, 7, 8.

4. Bruce Laurie, *Artisans into Workers: Labor in 19th-century America* (New York: Farrar, Straus, and Giroux, 1989), p. 15.

5. The history of the agricultural basis of democracy in America has an interesting parallel to the way that Greeks created the actual substance, if not the formal language and categories, of democracy more than 2,000 years ago. Recent scholarship on Greece has cast doubt on the conventional interpretations that focus on the urban Greek experience and its intellectual interpreters, who held that democracy was a qualitatively different arena sharply removed from the world of work.

Thus, for instance, Victor Hanson argues that democracy is best understood as the outgrowth not of exceptional circumstances, but rather of everyday agricultural work among the

Greeks. The emergence of a new practice of family farming—individual, small farms, worked by fiercely independent, ingenious farmers—generated the ethos and practice of democracy. Victor Davis Hanson, *The Other Greeks: The Family Farm and the Agrarian Roots of Western Civilization* (New York: Free Press, 1995), pp. 27, 82, 93, 98–99.

6. William Leach, *Land of Promise: Merchants, Power, and the Rise of a New American Culture* (New York: Vintage, 1993), pp. 248–49.

7. Merchant and *Emerald City* quoted from Leach, *Land*, pp. 3, 259.

8. Marx is here quoted from Lucio Colletti, *From Rousseau to Lenin: Studies in Ideology and Society* (New York: Monthly Review, 1972), pp. 86–88.

9. *Culture and Society in Industrializing America* (New York: Vintage, 1977); Everett quoted in John Kasson, *Civilizing the Machine: Technology and Republican Values in America, 1776–1900* (New York: Penguin, 1976), p. 45.

10. These descriptions of America's transformation are taken from Robert Reich, *The Next American Frontier* (New York: Times Books, 1983), pp. 30–32.

11. Quoted from Jeremy Rifkin, *The End of Work* (New York: Tarcher/Putnam, 1995), pp. 47–48.

12. Walter Lippmann, *A Preface to Morals* (New York: Macmillan, 1929), p. 120.

13. Robert Wiebe, *Self-Rule: A Cultural History of American Democracy* (Chicago: The University of Chicago Press, 1995), pp. 139, 136.

14. Quoted from Jeremy Rifkin, *The End of Work* (New York: Putnam, 1995), p. 51.

15. Wiebe, *Self-Rule*, p. 122.

16. *Ibid.*, p. 134.

17. On vagrancy; socialism, *ibid.*, p. 133. On ethnic stereotypes, see Colin Greer, *The Great School Legend* (New York: Penguin, 1972).

18. Ellsworth, "Country Life Commission," p. 155.

19. Jefferson quoted from Suzanne Morse, *Renewing Civic Capacity: Preparing College Students for Service and Citizenship* (Washington: Association for the Study of Higher Education, 1989), p. 27. Morse points out that early colleges and universities had three aims: the promotion of common culture; the teaching of moral

philosophy which was to guide students; and the production of civic leadership. On the early years of land-grant education, see Earle D. Ross, *Democracy's College: The Land-Grant Movement in the Formative Stage* (Ames, Iowa: Iowa State College, 1942); on the Association, p. 22.

20. History from Clarence Beaman Smith and Meredith Chester Wilson, *The Agricultural Extension System of the United States* (New York: John Wiley & Sons, 1930).

21. For a discussion of these contending currents and the "craft based" approach favored by farmers, see G. W. Stevenson and Richard M. Klemme, "Advisory/Oversight Councils: An Alternative Approach to Farmer/Citizen Participation in Agenda Setting at Land-Grant Universities," *American Journal of Alternative Agriculture*, vol. 7 (1992), pp. 111–17.

22. This line of argument follows closely Scott Peters, "The Civic Nature of the Land-Grant Idea," unpublished paper for Independent Study, Humphrey Institute, 1994. Ohio Trustees quoted in Edward Danforth Eddy, *Colleges for Our Land and Time: The Land-Grant Idea in American Education* (New York: Harper & Brothers, 1956), p. 55. See also Ross, *Democracy's College*.

23. The widespread use of these phrases was pointed out by Gerald Campbell, Vice Chancellor of the University of Wisconsin, in private correspondence with Boyte, December 22, 1993; see also Robert C. Nesbitt, *Wisconsin: A History* (Madison: University of Wisconsin Press, 1973), p. 426.

24. Russell Lord, *The Agrarian Revival* (New York: George Grady Press, 1939), pp. 42, 43.

25. L. H. Bailey, *York State Rural Problems* (Albany: J. B. Lyon Co., 1913), pp. 11–12.

26. *Ibid.*, 133, 29–30.

27. L. H. Bailey, *The State and the Farmer* (New York: Macmillan, 1908), pp. 1, 120.

28. *Ibid.*, pp. 173–74, 120, 123, 139.

29. Survey rationale from Ellsworth, "Commission," p. 158.

30. Quote on truth and dogma, from L. H. Bailey, *Ground-Levels in Democracy* (Ithaca: Cornell, 1916, p. 12); on his view of spirituality and the new age, *Outlook to Nature* (Ithaca: Cornell, 1905), pp. 4, 9–10, 91, 106–7.

31. Lord, *Revival* (New York: George Grady Press, 1939), pp. 42, 43; on political successes, see Ellsworth, "Commission," p. 157; Bailey on relevance to higher education, *Rural Problems*, p. 113.

32. Roosevelt, quoted from Peters, *Cooperative Extension*, p. 32.

33. For a description of the politics of the Commission—especially the opposition it provoked—see Clayton S. Ellsworth, "Theodore Roosevelt's Country Life Commission," *Agricultural History*, 34 (October, 1960), pp. 155–172.

34. *Ibid.*, p. 33. In a series of popularly written subsequent books Bailey further elaborated the democratic philosophy of extension based on what he called "democratic public work." In terms that bore striking resemblance to contemporary environmentalists' stress on an ethos of stewardship, Bailey argued in his 1915 book, *The Holy Earth*, that farmers needed not mainly regulation but rather education. The farmer was a "guardian" over land that "he really does not even own." More generally, Bailey stressed education for cooperative work by rural communities to solve their own problems. This required the democratic "training of a people," in ways much more expansive than narrowly professionalized or technical training. "We are to avoid the mechanistic standardization of society," wrote Bailey. "Democracy cannot be maintained on the mental habits of quantity-production." Bailey contrasted democratic public work with the technical approach and focus on "vast quantity production" that characterized most business. Democracy necessarily was messy, open ended and unpredictable, in his view. It could not be captured or even be well promoted by "programs" or bureaucracies: The most effective "program" for Bailey was always men and women working together cooperatively, with a sense of craft, spirit, and larger purpose. Bailey warned prophetically of "the tendency of all government to formality and to crystallization to machine work and to armchair regulations." *Holy Earth*, pp. 142–43.

In his 1918 book, *What Is Democracy*, Bailey defined public work further as he sought to distinguish democratic agriculture from the growing emphasis on farming as a commerical business aimed at maximizing production: "For public work we need much more than so-called business ability. We need broad views on public questions, outlook into future results, passion for public service." L. H. Bailey, *What Is Democracy?* (Ithaca: Comstock Publishing, 1918), pp. 87–88.

35. Smith and Wilson, *Extension System,* pp. 25–44; Smith Lever, quoted p. 4.

36. Quoted from *ibid.,* frontispage.

37. Knapp quoted from O. B. Martin, *The Demonstration Work: Dr. Seaman A. Knapp's Contribution to Civilization* (San Antonio: Naylor Co., 1941), pp. 179, 188, 170, 2, 22.

38. Herbert Croly, *The Promise of American Life* (New York: Macmillan, 1909, pp. 139, 453; see also William A. Schambra, *The Quest for Community and the Quest for a New Public Philosophy* (Washington: American Enterprise Institute, 1983).

39. Lippmann quoted from Robert H. Wiebe, *Self-Rule: A Cultural History of American Democracy* (Chicago: University of Chicago Press, 1995), pp. 174–75.

40. These developments are summarized in Stevenson and Klemme, "Oversight Councils," pp. 112–13; tendencies toward work with more affluent farmers especially in the 1920s are widely noted in descriptions of twenties extension work. See for instance Gladys Baker, *The County Agent* (Chicago: University of Chicago Press, 1939); and Lord, *The Agrarian Revival.*

41. Lord, *Agrarian Revival,* p. 49; Eddy, *The Land-Grant Idea,* p. 175.

42. Smith and Wilson, *System,* p. 2.

43. Baker, *Agent,* descriptions of involvement in programs 1969–1992; quote, p. 69.

CHAPTER 4

1. Jane Addams, *Twenty Years at Hull-House* (New York: Macmillan, 1938), pp. 235–37.

2. Robert Slayton, *Back of the Yards: The Making of a Local Democracy* (Chicago: University of Chicago, 1986), pp. 15, 20.

3. *Ibid.,* p. 38.

4. Quoted from Harry C. Boyte, "Reinventing Citizenship," *Kettering Review,* Winter, 1994, pp. 80–81.

5. Y public affairs principles quoted from Paul M. Limbert, *Educating for Civic Responsibility: A Guide Policy and Practice in Public Affairs Education* (New York: Association Press, 1941), p. 10; H. A. Overstreet, quoted from Scott J. Peters, "Agency or Association?"

unpublished paper for Public Affairs 5193 (Independent Studies), frontispiece, in Boyte collection.

6. See Lizbeth Cohen, *Making a New Deal: Industrial Workers in Chicago, 1919–1939* (New York: Cambridge Press, 1990).

7. Cohen, *Making a New Deal*, p. 65.

8. Mike Royko, *Boss* (New York: Penguin, 1971), p. 68.

9. Cohen, *Making a New Deal*, p. 77.

10. *Ibid.*, p. 78.

11. Addams, *Twenty Years*, p. 116.

12. Addams, quoted in William Sullivan, *Work and Integrity* (New York: HarperCollins, 1995), p. 77.

13. Addams, *Twenty Years*, pp. 121–122.

14. *Ibid.*, p. 236.

15. Interview with Helen Gransberg Turner, March 23, 1983, St. Paul, Harry Boyte; descriptions of the West Side are also taken from Edward D. Neill, *History of Ramsey County and the City of St. Paul* (Minneapolis: North Star Publishing, 1881), pp. 330–34.

16. Figures from School Ledgers, in possession of Helen Turner.

17. Interview with Mat Moreno, April 27, 1983, St. Paul, Harry Boyte.

18. Interview with Bill Kuehn, February 7, April 12, April 20, 1983, St. Paul, Harry Boyte.

19. Interview with Nellie Stone Johnson, November 10, 1994, Minneapolis, Nancy Kari and Harry Boyte.

20. Ellen Condliffe Lagemann, *The Politics of Knowledge: The Carnegie Corporation, Philanthropy, and Public Policy* (Chicago: University of Chicago Press, 1989), pp. 67–68.

CHAPTER 5

1. Interview with James Ronning, June 15, 1995, Rochester, Minnesota, Nancy Kari and Harry Boyte.

2. Writers and Tugwell, quoted in William E. Leuchtenburg, *Franklin D. Roosevelt and the New Deal* (New York: Harper & Row, 1963), pp. 18–19.

3. Leuchtenburg, *New Deal*, p. 231.

4. The political connections between Roosevelt and the CIO are described in Steve Fraser, "The 'Labor Question,' " in Steve Fraser and Gary Gerstle, eds., *The Rise and Fall of the New Deal Order:*

1930–1980 (Princeton: Princeton University Press, 1989), especially pp. 70–71, from which the Non-Partisan League quotes are taken.

5. Wilson, quoted from *ibid.,* p. 55.

6. Cooke, quoted in *ibid.,* p. 61.

7. See David Brody, "The Emergence of Mass Production Unionism," in John Braeman, Robert H. Bremner and Everett Walters, eds., *Change and Continuity in Twentieth-Century America* (Columbus: Ohio State University Press, 1964), pp. 221–264; on communist neighborhood approaches, Fisher, *Neighborhood,* pp. 34–46 (Nelson quoted p. 38); on communist use of democratic themes, Irving Howe and Lewis Coser, *The American Communist Party: A Critical History* (New York: Praeger, 1962); interview with Terry Pettus, March 14, 1983, Harry Boyte.

8. Louis Adamic, quoted from Jeremy Brecher, *Strike!* (San Francisco: Straight Arrow Press, 1972), pp. 182–83; worker in Studs Terkel, *Hard Times: An Oral History of the Depression* (New York: Pantheon, 1970), p. 158.

9. Quote from John Bodnar, *Immigration and Industrialization: Ethnicity in an American Mill Town, 1870–1940* (Pittsburgh: University of Pittsburgh Press), pp. 112; Bodnar, *Immigration,* pp. 150–51.

10. *Ibid.,* pp. 92–99, for an account of earlier organizing campaigns.

11. Statement quoted in Slayton, *Back,* p. 203 (cited in Chapter 4); see also Fisher, *People Decide,* pp. 54–56.

12. Marlene Park and Gerald E. Markowitz, *Democratic Vistas: Post Offices and Public Art in the New Deal* (Philadelphia: Temple University Press, 1984), p. 5.

13. Stan Cohen, *The Tree Army* (Missoula: Pictorial Histories Publishing Company, 1980), p. 6.

14. E. Leake and Ray S. Carter, "Roosevelt's Tree Army: A Brief History of the Civilian Conservation Corps," distributed by the National Association of Civilian Conservation Corps Alumni, January 1987, edited by Richard A. Long and John C. Bighee.

15. Leake and Carter, "Roosevelt's Tree Army," p. 6.

16. Interview with James Ronning, June 15, 1995, Rochester, Nancy Kari and Harry Boyte.

17. Interview with William Cleveland, May 27, 1995, Askow, Minn., Nancy Kari and Jonathan Kari.
18. Ronning interview.
19. Interview with Francis Crowdus, July 29, 1995 (phone), Nancy Kari and Harry Boyte.
20. Donald Dale Jackson, *Smithsonian*, December 1994, p. 66–78.

CHAPTER 6

1. Editors of *Daedalus* magazine, quoted from Donald Schön, *The Reflective Practitioner* (New York: Basic Books, 1983), pp. 5–6.
2. Alan Brinkley, "For America, It Truly Was a Great War," *The New York Times Magazine*, May 7, 1995, pp. 54–57.
3. Lewis Mumford, *The Conduct of Life* (New York: Harcourt, Brace and Co., 1951), pp. 276, 278.
4. Steven Mintz and Susan Kellogg, *Domestic Revolutions: A Social History of American Family Life* (New York: The Free Press, 1989), p. 182.
5. Dolores Hayden, *Redesigning the American Dream: The Future of Housing, Work, and Family Life* (New York: W. W. Norton & Company, 1984), p. 19.
6. *Ibid.*, p. 33.
7. Alan Brinkley, "The New Deal and the Idea of the State" in Steve Fraser and Gary Gerstle, eds., *The Rise and Fall of the New Deal Order 1930–1980* (Princeton: Princeton University Press, 1989), pp. 85–121.
8. Interview with Janet Ferguson, August 17, 1995, Clayton, Georgia, Harry Boyte.
9. David Halberstam, *The Fifties* (New York: Ballantine Books, 1993), pp. 142–143.
10. For a discussion of these criticisms see Dolores Hayden, *Redesigning the American Dream*, and David Halberstam, *The Fifties*.
11. Mintz and Kellogg, *Domestic Revolutions*, p. 181.
12. *Ibid.*, p. 181.
13. *Ibid.*, pp. 178–179.
14. For a vivid analysis of television sitcoms in the 1950s and their shaping of the American ideal see, Halberstam's *The Fifties*, Chapter 34.

15. Mintz and Kellogg, *Domestic Revolutions,* p. 185.
16. See Sara M. Evans, *Born for Liberty* (New York: The Free Press, 1989) for comprehensive discussion of women's roles and the broader political culture.
17. Interview with Betty A. Newland, August 10, 1995, LaCrosse, Wis., Nancy Kari.
18. *Ibid.*
19. Halberstam, *The Fifties,* p. 510.
20. Ferguson interview, August 17, 1995.
21. *Ibid.,* p. 52.
22. Elaine Tyler May, "Cold War—Warm Hearth: Politics and the Family in Postwar America," in Steve Fraser and Gary Gerstle, eds., *The Rise and Fall of the New Deal Order 1930–1980* (Princeton: Princeton University Press, 1989), p. 156.
23. Philip Cushman, *Constructing the Self, Constructing America: A Cultural History of Psychotherapy* (New York: Addison-Wesley Publishing Company, 1995), pp. 222–223.
24. May, "Cold War—Warm Hearth," p. 158.
25. *Ibid.* p. 158.
26. Christopher Lasch, *The True and Only Heaven* (New York: W. W. Norton, 1991), pp. 518–522.
27. Quoted from Donald Schön, *The Reflective Practitioner* (New York: Basic Books, 1983), p. 6.
28. See for instance Burton Bledstein, *The Culture of Professionalism: The Middle Class and the Development of Higher Education in America* (New York: W. W. Norton, 1976); Thorstein Veblen, *The Engineers and the Price System* (New York: Viking, 1932); Robert Wiebe, *The Search for Order, 1877–1920* (New York: Hill and Wang, 1967); James Weinstein, *The Corporate Ideal in the Liberal State, 1900–1918* (Boston: Beacon Press, 1968); Raymond E. Callahan, *Education and the Cult of Efficiency* (Chicago: University of Chicago Press, 1962); Michael B. Katz, *In the Shadow of the Poorhouse: A Social History of Welfare in America* (New York: Basic Books, 1985); and John Kenneth Galbraith, *The New Industrial State* (New York: Signet, 1967), p. 326.
29. Guidance counselors quoted from Christopher Lasch, *Haven in a Heartless World: The Family Besieged* (New York: Basic Books, 1977), p. 18; on domestic science, see Laura Shapiro, *Perfection*

Salad: Women and Cooking at the Turn of the Century (New York: Farrar, Straus and Giroux, 1987), pp. 91–95.

30. Spock quoted in Mintz and Kellogg, *Domestic Revolutions: A Social History of American Family Life*, p. 188.
31. *Ibid.*, p. 189.
32. May, "Cold War—Warm Hearth," p. 164–165.
33. Myrdal quoted in Jeffrey Galper, *The Politics of Social Services* (Englewood Cliffs: Prentice Hall, 1975), p. 113. Note literature on professional-managerial class as the most promising exploration of these issues, but weakened by lack of attention to the specific power dynamics characteristic of information-based environments.
34. Toynbee quoted in John Kenneth Galbraith, *New Industrial State* (New York: Signet, 1967), p. 109.
35. Interview with William Myers, St. Paul, March 12, 1995, Nancy Kari.
36. Interview with Pat Borich, Minneapolis, May 1, 1995, Harry Boyte.
37. Interview with Paul Light, Minneapolis, May 1, 1995, Harry Boyte.
38. Gill quoted from Sylvia Shaw Judson, *The Quiet Eye* (Washington: Regency Gateway, 1982), p. 27.
39. Interview with Elizabeth McPike, South Bend, August 20, 1977; interview with Darlene Stille, Chicago, Ill., April 28, 1977, interviewer, Harry Boyte.
40. Studs Terkel, *Working* (New York: Avon, 1972) p. xxix.

CHAPTER 7

1. Saul Alinsky, *Reveille For Radicals* (New York: Vintage, 1946), p. 40.
2. Ginsberg and Kerouac quoted from Todd Gitlin, *The Sixties: Years of Hope, Days of Rage* (New York: Bantam, 1988), pp. 44, 47; Gitlin has a marvelous depiction of these dissenting cultural strands of the fifties in Chapters 2 and 3 of his book.
3. Quotes from Appendix, James Miller, *"Democracy Is in the Streets: From Port Huron to the Siege of Chicago"* (New York: Simon & Schuster, 1987), pp. 330, 333, 336.
4. Miller, *Democracy*, pp. 329, 360, 354, 330.

5. Interview with Bertha Gilkey, St. Louis, August 20, 1983.

6. *Christian Science Monitor* poll, December 23, 1977; see also Renee Berger, *Against All Odds: The Achievements of Community-Based Development Organizations* (Washington: NCCED, 1989).

7. Ralph Ellison, *Invisible Man* (New York: Vintage, 1989), p. 11.

8. Richard H. King, "Citizenship and Self-Respect: The Experience of Politics in the Civil Rights Movement," *Journal of American Studies,* 22 (1988), pp. 7–24.

9. Devine and Hulett, quoted from King, "Citizenship," pp. 18–19.

10. See Sara M. Evans and Harry C. Boyte, *Free Spaces: The Sources of Democratic Change in America* (Chicago: University of Chicago Press, 1992).

11. Interview with Myles Horton, Highlander, July 4, 1977, see Evans and Boyte, *Free Spaces,* p. 64.

12. On the background and dynamics of the boycott, see Stephen B. Oates, *Let the Trumpet Sound: The Life of Martin Luther King, Jr.* (New York: Harper & Row, 1982), pp. 63–69; also Morris, *Origins,* pp. 43–44.

13. King's social and political thought is discussed in Oates, *Trumpet,* pp. 25–41; one evening in St. Augustine, Florida, in August, 1964, King discussed at some length his identification with the southern Populist tradition, which conveyed these themes with Harry Boyte.

14. King's speech quoted from Oates, *Trumpet,* p. 71; "Letter from a Birmingham Jail," from Martin Luther King, Jr., *Why We Can't Wait* (New York: Harper & Row, 1963), p. 99.

15. Interview with Dorothy Cotton, Minneapolis, May 10 and September 17, 1991, Harry Boyte and Kate Stoff Hogg.

16. Cotton interview, September 17, 1991.

17. Heather Booth, speech to Democratic Agenda conference, Washington, D.C., November 13, 1977; Boyte interview with Bill Thompson, Boston, April 18, 1977; Boyte interview with Waymer Thomas, Oakland, May 12, 1977.

18. Interview with Wade Goodwyn on Chambers' "relational" quality, November 8, 1987, Baltimore; on COPS depictions, interviews with Beatrice Cortes, July 8, San Antonio; Christine Stephens, Ernie Cortes, San Antonio, July 4, 1983. Cortes was the first to begin describing COPS as like a "university of public life." See also Peter Skerry, "Neighborhood COPS," *New Republic,* February 6, 1984, p. 23.

19. An exchange between Boyte and Ed Chambers, the successor of Alinsky as head of the IAF training institute, illustrated their epistemology. Chambers, describing the importance that IAF organizing has come to place on people's disentangling of "public" and "private" realms, said that people lose the "public" side of "mediating institutions," associations between the individual and the state or large-scale systems. "They think of things like churches simply as private, so they make all sorts of inappropriate demands," he argued. Boyte replied that the very concept of mediating institutions (seeing them as private) maintains a narrow view of public life.

Chambers went off on another track: "I haven't read Berger in years. The only thing I know is that this thing is very close to the truth." He continued, "I've seen the response to this now in hundreds of meetings across the country over ten years now. It strikes home. People come up, sometimes with tears in their eyes, priests, women religious, lay leaders, saying 'I wish I'd known this years ago.'" Interview in Baltimore, November 6, 1987.

The exchange illustrated IAF's feedback process. What it calls "universals" of organizing are always contextualized, provisional, and aimed at the particular *problems* they encounter in their work. As Ernie Cortes, a key figure in their network, pointed out, the IAF methodology bears resemblance to the "critical method" of Karl Popper, philosopher of science, who argued for a view of "truth" not as positive assertion, but as theories formulated out of practice and aimed at problem solving.

IAF's epistemology combines "qualitative" and "quantative" methods—a vast process of detailed information gathering about particular individuals, cultures and settings with a rigorous analysis of the economic dimensions of issues and the like—which is rarely practiced today. But it is in keeping with what Michael Patton, a leading theorist in the field of evaluation, has called the growing consensus about what *should* be done: "pragmatism, methodological tolerance, flexibility and concern for appropriateness rather than orthodoxy now characterize the practice, literature and discussions of evalution." Michael Quinn Patton, *Utilization-Focused Evaluation* (London: Sage, 1986), p. 210.

20. Interview with Douglas I. Miles, Baltimore, November 14, 1987, Harry Boyte.

CHAPTER 8

1. W. E. B. Du Bois, *The Souls of Black Folks* (New York: Vintage Edition, 1990), p. 69.
2. Interview with Ed Chambers, New York, June 1, 1988, Harry Boyte.
3. Ira De Reid, *The Negro Community of Baltimore: A Social Survey* (Baltimore: Urban League, 1934), pp. 207–08; interview with Gerald Taylor, Baltimore, November 11, 1987.
4. Reid, *Negro Community;* Suzanne E. Greene, *Baltimore: An Illustrated History* (Woodland Heights, Cal.: Windsor Publications, 1980); interview with Vernon Dobson, Baltimore, November 13, 1987.
5. Reid, *Negro Community,* see especially pp. 191–205; Leroy Graham, *Elisha Tyson, Baltimore and the Negro* (Baltimore: Morgan State, 1975).
6. Interview with Dobson, Baltimore, November 13, 1987; Miles, Baltimore, November 14, 1987, Harry Boyte.
7. Miles interview.
8. The story of the Inner Harbor and Center City is detailed in Greene, *Baltimore;* interview with Michael Fletcher, Baltimore, November 13, 1987; interview with Michael Ollove, Baltimore, November 13, 1987; Miles interview.
9. Figures on schools and unemployment from DeWayne Wickham, *Destiny 2000: The State of Black Baltimore* (Baltimore: Baltimore Urban League, 1987); and also Frank Defilippo, "'Baltimore 2000' Revives the Notion of Two Baltimores," *City Paper,* February 13, 1987; interview with Irene Dandridge, Baltimore, November 16, 1987; interview with Alice Pinderhughes, Baltimore, November 16, 1987.
10. Interview with Carl Stokes, Baltimore, November 5, 1987; interview with Robert Keller, Baltimore, November 16, 1987, Harry Boyte.
11. Interview with Father Joe Muth, November 13, 1987, Baltimore, Harry Boyte; Graf acknowledged that when he arrived, the organization was deeply in debt and had a core of only six or eight leaders.
12. Interview with Arnie Graf, Baltimore, November 6, November 16, 1987, Harry Boyte.
13. *The Baltimore Morning Sun,* July 10, 1981, front page.

14. Interview with Gary Rodwell, Baltimore, November 13, 1987, Harry Boyte; the campaign was also described in the *Afro American;* see especially "BUILD Reaches Agreement with Baltimore Federal," Tuesday, June 30, 1981.

15. *The Baltimore Sun,* July 10, 1981, front page.

16. Rodwell interview; Miles interview.

17. Miles interview.

18. Interview with Marian Dixon, Baltimore, March 31, 1988, Harry Boyte.

19. John Langston Gwaltney, *Drylongso* (New York: Vintage, 1981), p. 6; Dixon interview.

20. Interview with Mike Gecan, Baltimore, November 11, 1987, Harry Boyte.

21. Gecan interview.

22. "BUILD convention attracts politicians, gains credibility," *The Baltimore Sun,* Oct. 22, 1984.

23. Graf interview, Baltimore, November 16, 1987, Harry Boyte.

24. Graf interview, November 16; also Pinderhughes interview, November 16; information on school supplies from "Schools Need Paper," *The Baltimore Sun,* March 7, 1984.

25. Interview with Alan Hoblitzel, Baltimore, April 18, 1988.

26. Miles interview; Hoblitzel interview; also interviews with Graf, November 16, Keller.

27. Interviews with Gerald Taylor, Baltimore, November 11, November 12, 1987, Harry Boyte; Keller interview.

The initial *Commonwealth Agreement* was signed April 24, 1985. Its preamble read:

> The Commonwealth Agreement evolved out of a series of meetings held between leaders of the Baltimore City Public Schools, the Greater Baltimore Committee and BUILD over the course of the past six months. It represents a partnership between these parties to take dramatic steps to improve public educational opportunities.
>
> The largest segment of today's workforce is composed of high school graduates who will not attend college. Numerous national studies indicate that many of these graduates lack the basic skills necessary for the employment opportunities open to them. Other students do not graduate from high school, further restricting their opportunities for the future. Well-educated citizens are essential to the economic well-being of our metropolitan area; our vitality is linked to our youth gaining appropriate job skills.

> The Commonwealth Agreement commits the Baltimore City Public Schools, the Greater Baltimore Committee (GBC) and BUILD (Baltimoreans United in Leadership Development) to improve educational opportunities, to prepare students for careers, post secondary education and to improve access for jobs. The Commonwealth Agreement is about a common vision, a common focus, a common wealth—One Greater Baltimore.

Document in Boyte's possession.

28. Interview with Gerald Taylor, September 6, 1995 (phone), Harry Boyte.
29. On the Baltimore Commonwealth, see Carol Steinback, "Investing Early: Education Report on Baltimore," *National Journal,* September 3, 1988, pp. 2192–2195; interview with Charlotte Brown, Baltimore, November 16, 1987.
30. Interview with Taylor, Baltimore, November 12, 1987, Harry Boyte.
31. Interview with Hoblitzel, Minneapolis-Baltimore, April 18, 1988; interview with Kurt Schmoke, Minneapolis-Baltimore, May 5, 1988, Harry Boyte.

CHAPTER 9

1. David Broder, and "Democracy and the Press," *Washington Post,* January 3, 1990.
2. David Broder, *A New Assigment for the Press,* Press Enterprise Lecture no. 26 (Riverside, Cal.: The Press Enterprise, 1991); and "Democracy and the Press," *Washington Post,* January 3, 1990.
3. Philip Meyer, "An Ethic for the Information Age," in L. Hodges, ed., *Social Responsibility: Business, Journalism, Law, Medicine* (Lexington, Va.: Washington and Lee University, 1990), p. 15.
4. Meyer details the economic ground for journalistic independence historically in "An Ethic for the Information Age," pp. 14–21.
5. Interview with Jay Rosen, August 24, 1995 (phone), Harry Boyte.
6. On views of the press, *The New Political Landscape* (Washington: Times Mirror Center, 1994), p. 160; on readership, *Report on the Press* (Washington: Times Mirror Center, April 6, 1995), pp. 9, 29. On dissatisfaction with the profession, G. Cleveland Wilhoit and David Weaver, "U.S. Journalists at Work, 1971–1992," paper at the

Association for Education in Journalism and Mass Communications, Atlanta, Ga., August 10–13, 1994, p. 41; on plans to leave the profession, David Weaver and G. Cleveland Wilhoit, "The American Journalist in the 1990s" (Arlington, Va.: The Freedom Forum, 1992).

7. Leslie Stahl quoted from "Talking about the Media Circus," *The New York Times Magazine,* June 28, 1994, p. 53; Cokie Roberts, quoted in Thomas E. Patterson, *Out of Order* (New York: Knopf, 1993), p. 115; *Washington Post* critic is Howard Kurtz, from his book, *Media Circus: The Trouble with America's Newspapers* (New York: Times Books, 1993), pp. 6–7.

8. This project was incubated at the Kettering Foundation and is sponsored by New York University, the American Press Institute, and the Knight Foundation.

9. Interview with Cole Campbell, September 5, 1995 (phone), Harry Boyte.

10. Campbell quoted from Jay Rosen, "Getting the Connections Right: Public Journalism and its Message to the Press," unpublished paper in Boyte possession, p. 55; Warhover interview, Reston, Virginia, August 13, 1995, Harry Boyte.

11. Rosen interview.

12. See James C. Collins and Jerry I. Porras, *Built to Last: Successful Habits of Visionary Companies* (New York: Harper/Business, 1994).

13. The Center is codirected by Harry Boyte and Edwin Fogelman. Project Public Life, the Center's fieldwork effort from 1989 to 1994, was founded by Harry C. Boyte and Frances Moore Lappé, with Peg Michels serving as associate director and later codirector; Carol Johnson was Training Director of Project Public Life; Nan Skelton now serves as Director of Training and Youth Development for the Center. Carmen Sirianni, Professor of Sociology at Brandeis, was the Research Director of the New Citizenship effort.

The framework has been developed by partners including Rebecca Breuer, David Cohen, Dorothy Cotton, Dennis Donovan, Walter Endloe, Sara M. Evans, James Farr, Pamela Hayle, Kathryn Hogg, Juan Jackson, Rick Jackson, Carol Johnson, John Kari, Nancy Kari, Anthony Massengale, Judy Meath, Miaisha Mitchell, Nan Skelton, and Carol Shields. It was enriched by commentary and contributions from many colleagues, including especially Benjamin Barber, Gil Clary, Steve Clift, Ernesto Cortes, Mary

Dietz, E. J. Dionne, Edwin Fogelman, Alan Isaacman, Lew Fried-land, Bruce Jennings, Paul Light, David Lisman, Gregory Markus, Paul Martinez, Lary May, David Mathews, Deborah Meier, Suzanne Morse, Fraser Nelson, Scott Peters, Jay Rosen, Harold Saunders, William Schambra, Jim Scheibel, Carmen Sirianni, Gerald Taylor, Alex Waegenaar, Robert Woodson, and Kathryn Zurcher. The seminar on the meaning of populism in the 1990s organized by the Center and the Bradley Foundation was especially helpful in illustrating common themes of civic work across wide ideological differences.

Institutions and groups of associates with which the Center has collaborated and from which it has learned have included the Minnesota Extension Services, the Asili Institute for Women of African Descent, the Association of Retarded Citizens, schools like St. Bernards, Breck Academy, and J. J. Hill; faculty at the College of St. Catherine, a Catholic women's college; Augustana Home, a nursing home in Minneapolis; the Metropolitan Council, a regional governing and planning body in the Twin Cities area; Central Medical Center, an historically black hospital in St. Louis; the Korean Youth Cultural Center, a major youth services group in Koreatown, Los Angeles; and a joint project with the Department of Epidemiology at the University of Minnesota, exploring community-based approaches to underage drinking in seven Wisconsin and Minnesota communities. Working partnerships nationally on the New Citizenship included the Kettering Foundation, the Whitman Center at Rutgers, the Corporation for National Service, Alabama Cooperative Extension, the National Easter Seal, the Indiana Youth Institute, the Council for the Advancement of Citizenship, and Eisenberg Associates.

Major funding partners have included the W. K. Kellogg Foundation, which provided an initial three-year core support grant; the Lilly Endowment; the Ford Foundation; the Haas Fund; the Surdna Foundation; the City of St. Paul; and the General Mills Foundation, among others.

14. Jane Addams, *Twenty Years at Hull-House* (New York: Basic Books, 1995), p. 120.

15. For figures on youth disenchantment from politics, see for instance, Michael Oreskes, "Profiles of Today's Youths: Many Just Don't Seem to Care," *New York Times,* June 28, 1990; "An Indiffer-

ent Age?" *Christian Science Monitor,* July 9, 1990; and "Children's Moral Compass Wavers," *Christian Science Monitor,* May 16, 1990.

16. These are conclusions that emerge from work with several thousand youth and young adults in the last seven years, at the Center for Democracy and Citizenship.

17. Grant Commission, "Pathways to Success: Citizenship Through Service," in Jane Kendall, ed., *Combining Service and Learning* (Raleigh: NSIEE, 1990), p. 441.

18. Figures on service from Alonzo Crim, "The Obligation of Citizenship," *ibid.,* pp. 240–41.

19. For a representative listing of learner outcomes, *ibid.;* also Sandra LaFave, "Letter to the Editor," *Harper's,* February, 1991.

20. This discussion draws heavily from the splendid master's thesis by Melissa Bass, "Toward a New Theory and Practice of Civic Education: An Evaluation of Public Achievement," Minneapolis, Humphrey Institute, 1995.

21. Interview with Juan Jackson, September 7, 1995, Minneapolis, Harry Boyte.

22. Interview with Dennis Donovan, August 30, 1995, St. Paul, Harry Boyte.

23. Interview with Dennis Donovan, September 4, 1995, Minneapolis, Harry Boyte.

24. Interview with Matt Musl, August 19, 1995, Minneapolis, Harry Boyte.

25. Interview with James Farr, August 30, 1995, Minneapolis, Harry Boyte.

26. Jay Rosen, phone interview, August 24, 1995; quotes from Children's Express staff from *REPORT to Lilly Endowment* (Indianapolis: Children's Express Indianapolis News Bureau, 1995), pp. 10, 13.

27. Interview with Nan Skelton, Minneapolis, September 6, 1995, Harry Boyte and Nancy Kari.

28. Mary Reilly, "Occupational Therapy Can Be One of the Great Ideas of Twentieth Century Medicine," in *A Professional Legacy: The Eleanor Clark Slagle Lectures in Occupational Therapy, 1955–1984* (Rockville: The American Occupational Therapy Association, Inc., 1985), pp. 92, 101.

29. *Ibid.,* p. 89.

30. The Lazarus Project, under the auspices of Project Public Life, the Center's field-testing effort for several years, was codirected by Pam Hayle, Nancy Kari, and Peg Michels.
31. Interview with Pamela Hayle, September 1, 1995, Minneapolis, Harry Boyte and Nancy Kari.
32. Interview with Judy Meath, September 13, 1995, Minneapolis, Harry Boyte.
33. Adapted from N. Kari, H. Boyte, B. Jennings, et al., "Health as a Civic Question," prepared for and published by The American Civic Forum, Minneapolis, 1994.
34. Joanne Cavallaro describes these dynamics well in "The Renewal of Civic Life: One College's Journey," *Higher Education Exchange,* 1995, pp. 56–65.
35. Interview with Gil Clary, September 7, 1995, Minneapolis, interviewer, Nancy Kari.
36. Interview with Anita Pampusch, December 11, 1995, St. Paul, interviewers, Nancy Kari and Harry Boyte.
37. Interview with Gloria Scott, November 21, 1995, Greensboro, (phone) Nancy Kari.

CHAPTER 10

1. "Theodore Roosevelt's New Nationalism," Sidney Hyman, ed., *Law, Justice and the Common Good: Reading for Leadership Program* (Minneapolis: Humphrey Institute, 1981), pp. 334–335.
2. Tony Horwitz, "These Six Growth Jobs Are Dull, Dead-End, Sometimes Dangerous," *Wall Street Journal,* December 1, 1994.
3. Adams from Oscar and Mary Flug Handlin, *Commonwealth: A Study of the Role of Government in the American Economy: Massachusetts, 1774–1861* (Cambridge: Harvard University Press, 1969), pp. 29–30. Adams drew very directly on the writings of Harrington, especially for his theories of property and of balanced government; for the most elaborate treatment of Harrington's thought and its influence in the "Country" tradition of opposition to the Crown, see J.G.A. Pocock, *The Machiavellian Moment: Florentine Political Thought and the Atlantic Republic Tradition* (Princeton: Princeton University Press, 1975).
4. Lester C. Thurow, "Companies Merge; Families Break Up," *New York Times,* September 3, 1995.

5. Timothy Egan, "Many Seek Security in Private Communities," *New York Times,* September 3, 1995.
6. Interview with Elizabeth Kautz, August 10, 1995, Burnsville, Nancy Kari and Harry Boyte.
7. Greenberg asked people their opinions on what he called the "view of traditional Democrats who believe government's role is to solve problems and protect people from adversity." He also asked for opinions on what he termed the "traditional Republican position that government should leave people alone to solve their own problems." Though the traditional Republicans received more support than the traditional Democrats, neither were popular at all—both had less than 30 percent approval.

   When Greenberg proposed an alternative that government's role should be to "equip people to solve their own problems," it re-cast responses entirely. Posed in contrast with "traditional Republicans," this third approach, which he labeled "New Democrats," won 52 to 38 percent among the general public. These figures were presented by Al From, President of the DLC, to President Clinton and other members of his administration at a Camp David Roundtable on Democracy, Citizenship, and Civil Society, January 14, 1995; Boyte participated in the roundtable.
8. Interview with Tony Massengale, September 12, 1995 (phone interview), Harry Boyte.
9. Interview with Paul Light, Minneapolis, May 1, 1995, Harry Boyte.
10. Interview with John Kari, September 13, 1995, Minneapolis, Nancy Kari.
11. Interview with Carol Shields, June 15, 1995, St. Paul, Harry Boyte.

APPENDIX

1. We are indebted for this distinction between "making history" and "making life" to the sociologist Richard Flacks, who used it to describe the exhiliration of new left and student activists involved in the 1960s social movement, in contrast to the resignation and diminished expectations they experienced in their later years.

2. Christian Meier, *The Greek Discovery of Politics* (Cambridge: Harvard University Press, 1990). For an illustration of feminist arguments about the Greeks, see for instance, Jean Bethke Elshtain, *Public Man, Private Woman: Women in Social and Political Thought* (Princeton: Princeton University Press, 1981); and Helen P. Foley, ed., *Reflections on Women in Antiquity* (New York: Cordon and Breach Science, 1981).

3. Meier, *The Greek Discovery of Politics* p. 146.

4. For a dissenting view that challenges the way scholars have separated work from democracy in Greek experience, see Victor Hansen, *The Other Greeks* (Berkeley: University of California Press, 1994).

5. *Ibid.,* p. 161.

6. Hannah Arendt, *The Human Condition* (Chicago: University of Chicago Press, 1958), pp. 57, 19.

7. *Ibid.,* 57.

8. Jürgen Habermas, "Historical Materialism and the Development of Normative Structures," in *Communication and the Evolution of Society* (Boston: Beacon, 1979), p. 97.

9. Benjamin Barber, whose criticism of liberal or "thin" democracy has helped to shape much of the deliberative position in America, lists these characteristics of deliberation: commonality; deliberateness; inclusiveness; provisionality; listening; learning; lateral communicatoin; imagination; and empowerment. See Benjamin R. Barber, "An American Civic Forum," *The Good Society: A PEGS Journal,* vol. 5, no. 2 (1995), pp. 10–14.

10. Jürgen Habermas, *The Transformation of the Public Sphere* (Cambridge: MIT Press, 1989), pp. 25–26.

11. Quoted from Keith Baker, "Politics and Public Opinion under the Old Regime," in J. Censer and J. Popkin, eds., *Press and Politics under the Old Regime* (Berkeley: University of California, 1987), pp. 238, 240.

12. Kant quoted from Raul Tyson, *Odysseus and the Cyclops* (Dayton: Kettering Foundation, 1988), p. 1.

13. Habermas, *Knowledge and Human Interests* (Boston: Beacon, 1971).

14. *Ibid.,* p. 58.

15. Habermas, "Historical Materialism," p. 117.

16. *Ibid.,* pp. 119–20.

17. See for instance Nancy Fraser, "Rethinking the Public Sphere," Mary P. Ryan, "Gender and Public Access," and Geoff Eley, "Nations, Publics, and Political Cultures," in Craig Calhoun, ed., *Habermas and the Public Sphere* (Cambridge: MIT Press, 1992), pp. 99–108, 259–288, 289–339.

18. For examples, see Ernesto Laclau and Chantel Mouffe, *Socialism and the Struggle for Hegemony: Towards a Radical Democratic Politics* (London: Verso, 1985); Cornel West, *American Evasion of Philosophy* (Madison, Wis.: University of Wisconsin, 1987) Nancy Fraser, "Rethinking the Public Sphere," in Calhoun, *Public Sphere;* Roberto Unger, *Social Theory, Its Situation and Its Task: A Critical Introduction to Politics—A Work in Constructive Social Theory* (Cambridge: Cambridge University Press, 1987); Iris Young, "Impartiality and the Civic Public: Some Implications of Feminist Critiques of Moral and Political Theory," *Praxis International,* vol. 5, no. 4 (January, 1986), pp. 381–401. The characteristic feature of all such argument is the fashion in which political life is seen to revolve singularly around the struggle for justice and equality, creating a stark division of the world between the powerless, oppressed, who are change-oriented, radical or proto-radical, and innocent victims of injustice, and the oppressors, who are seen as degraded, all-powerful, and above all wedded to the unjust status quo. Frank Lentricchia is emblematic here. In *Criticism and Social Change,* he begins by "dividing the world between those who like it and those who do not." *Criticism and Social Change* (Chicago: University of Chicago Press, 1984), p. 1.

19. This sort of division is in fact reproduced widely, across many academic disciplines. There is a "return of the agent" in a variety of recent academic work on political and social theory, history, linguistic analysis, and other fields—awareness that people are never simply victims or objects of impersonal forces. Rather, people constantly help to create and shape their environments.

    In history, this theme has been expressed in the renewed attention to narrative. In sociology, Alain Touraine observes the "return of the actor." This is visible in the focus on social movements, prompted by a variety of real-world actors—"dominated classes, colonized nations, censored creators, actors stigmatized as deviants or marginals"—who refuse prescribed roles or a status as simply statistical ensembles. See, for instance, Hayden

White, *The Content of the Form: Narrative Discourse and Historical Representation* (Baltimore: University of Maryland, 1987). Alain Touraine, *Return of the Actor: Social Theory in Postindustrial Society* (Minneapolis: University of Minnesota, 1988), p. 5.

Political theory and moral philosophy have recently addressed questions of citizenship, the public sphere and an anti-foundationalist theory of knowledge and action. Cornel West captures well the democratic implications of neo-pragmatism: "What was the prerogative of philosophers, i.e., rational deliberation, is now that of the . . . citizenry in action." Cornel West, *The American Evasion of Philosophy: A Genealogy of Pragmatism* (Madison: University of Wisconsin, 1989), p. 213.

Yet this democratic impulse is also undercut by the failure of academics of various persuasions to complete their escape from a self-referential, enclosed, and idealized set of categories. For example, advocates of neo-pragmatism such as Richard Rorty reimagine democratic politics as the playfulness of talk, generating language games and discursive communities. This politics of deliberation has counterparts today in those strands of liberalism which, while declaring the triumph of "democratic capitalism" or even "the end of history," also propose a role for the citizen as judicious critic adjunct to representative government. But such a politics is far removed from the conflicts, differences, and power-laden encounters of the actual public world, in which a search for common understanding—or talking itself—is, at most, one objective among many. Richard Rorty, *Contingency, Irony, and Solidarity* (Cambridge: Cambridge University Press, 1989); and also James S. Fishkin, *Democracy and Deliberation* (New Haven: Yale University Press, 1991). Though far less ironic than Rorty, critical of pragmatism, and not nearly as fatalistic about liberal capitalism, Jürgen Habermas's consignment of modern publics to an entirely deliberative function (built on his assumption that what he calls "instrumental rationality" is ineluctably constituted in a technocratic, anti-democratic fashion in the modern world) leads to similar political conclusions, as Rorty points out. See, for instance Jürgen Habermas, *The Transformation of the Public Sphere* (Cambridge: MIT, 1989); and the collection edited by Craig Calhoun, *Habermas and the Public Sphere* (Cambridge: MIT, 1992).

Both liberals and critical intellectuals ironically reproduce the spectator role for citizens that they excoriate in epistemology. Citizens lose the middle ground of public action, where the point is neither vindication nor talk but rather practical engagement in the complex, messy process of creating the world. Yet without a framework for politics that puts citizens into the equation as central agents, ordinary people remain childlike, unaccountable outsiders. The resonances of citizens are narrowed to roles such as voter, volunteer, ideological partisan, client, expert, and community member.

20. For a discussion of contemporary social history, in which this Habermasian distinction between "life worlds" and "system worlds" is embodied in the distinction between "micro" and "macro" social processes, see Steve Fraser and Gary Gerstle, eds., *The Rise and Fall of the New Deal Order: 1930–1980* (Princeton: Princeton University Press, 1989). Like many other works in this vein, their book is a splendid treatment, shedding light on otherwise unexplored topics and questions. But because it lacks any substantial category and treatment of public spaces, it also ultimately has the tone of despair and hopelessness about the prospects for democracy that is now nearly universal among intellectuals.

21. Donald Schön, *The Reflective Practitioner: How Professionals Think in Action* (New York: Basic Books, 1983), pp. 40, 68. For an important new statement of civic possibilities for professional action, combining practical intelligence with attention to values of integrity, autonomy, responsibility, and craft, which represent the best of the professional tradition, see William Sullivan, *Work and Integrity: The Crisis and Promise of Professionalism in America* (New York: HarperCollins, 1995).

22. Simone Weil, *Oppression and Liberty* (Amherst: University of Massachusetts, 1973), pp. 83, 106, 101. For a fine treatment of Weil's thought, see Mary Dietz, *Between the Human and the Divine: The Political Thought of Simone Weil* (Totowa, N.J.: Rowman and Littlefield, 1988). See also Mary G. Dietz, " 'The Slow Boring of Hard Boards': Methodical Thinking and the Work of Politics," *The American Political* Science Review, vol. 5, no. 4 (December, 1994) pp. 873–886.

INDEX

ABC News, 167
Abernathy, Ralph, 140
Abramovitz, Gershon, 89-90
Adamic, Louis, 101
Adams, Abigail, 45
Adams, John, 37-38, 43, 45, 191
Addams, Jane, 8, 34, 78, 82, 86-88, 102,
   142, 173, 178, 186
   democratic philosophy of, 86
   education of young people, 86-88
Advocacy Institute, 30
Aeschylus, 203
African Methodist Episcopals, 151
African School, 151
Agranoff, Betty, 89
Alinsky, Saul, (see community organiz-
   ing), 8, 102–104, 130, 144–146
   philosophy of, 102–103, 130
Alperovitz, Gar, xv
Amalgamated Meatcutters Union,
   103–104
American Civic Forum, xiii
American Federation of Labor, 97
American Occupational Therapy
   Association, 179

American Press Institute, 170
AmeriCorps, 196, 198–200
Ames, Michael, xv
Arendt, Hannah, 12, 204–205, 212
   views of labor, 204
   views of public realm, 204–205
   views of work, 204–205
Aristotle, 35
Army Corps of Engineers, 196, 197–198
Articles of Confederation, 38
Augustana Home of Minneapolis, the,
   180–181, 183

Back of the Yards Neighborhood Council
   (BYNC, see community organizing),
   104, 145
   as public space, 103
Back of the Yards, 79–81, 103–104
Bailey, Liberty Hyde, xv, 8, 56, 66, 68–72,
   75, 77, 93, 102, 114–115, 202
   philosophy of education, 68–69
   philosophy of leadership, 69 (see
      also Nehemiah story, chapters 1
      and 10)
   philosophy of science, 70–71

Baker, Ella, 8, 140, 143
"Ballad For Americans," 104
Baltimore Commonwealth, 147,
    149–150, 154, 160–163, 165
Baltimore Teachers Union, 153
Baltimore Urban Coalition, 151
Baltimoreans United in Leadership
    Development (BUILD, see IAF), 147,
    149–150, 150–163, 165
    school campaign, 153, 156–159
Barber, Benjamin, xiv
Bass, Melissa, xiii
Baum, L. Frank, 61
Bayard, Rustin, 140
beat poetry, 131–132
Bellah, Robert, 26–27
Bellamy, Edward, 64
Bender, Thomas, 188
Bennett College, 186–187
    public mission of, 187
Berner, Dave, 31
Bethel AME church, 151–152
Bishop, Steven, 199
Black Ministerial Alliance, 152
Bodnar, John, 101–102
Booth, Heather, 144
Borich, Patrick, 127, 196
Boyte, Craig Evans, xv
Boyte–Evans, Jae Lee, xv
Brandl, John, xiii
Breuer, Rebecca, xiii
Broder, David, 164, 166, 171
Brotherhood of Liberty, the, 151
Brown, Charlotte, 161
Brown, David, xiv
Bruce, Edward, 105
Bryson, John, xiii
Buchan, William, 46

Camp David meeting on democracy, xiv
Campbell, Cole, 169–170
Carls, Jeanne, 30
Carnegie Corporation, 93
Catt, Carrie Chapman, 82
CBS News, 26, 167
Center for Democracy and Citizenship,
    xii–xv, 8, 10, 23–24, 172–173, 175,
    179–180
    mission, 172
    partnerships, 172
    Public Achievement, 175–178
    strategy, 172
    White House project, 172

Central Medical Center (CMC), 183–184
Central Park East schools, 9–10
Chambers, Ed, 145
Charlotte Observer, 168
Chatauqua, 46
Chevalier, Michel, 40
Children's Express, 177
Cisneros, Henry, 162
citizen (see citizenship, public work)
    as customer, 194–195
    as producer, 6, 105, 193, 196, 199, 211
    Greek understanding of, 202–204
    identity, 25–28
Citizenship Education Program (CEP),
    xiii, 140–143
citizenship schools, 29–31, 91, 140–144
    curriculum, 142–143
    definition of citizen in, 142–143
    Highlander origins, 141
    intellectual life in, 142–143
    organizing skills taught in, 142
    philosophy of, 141–143
    public work in, 142
citizenship, 3, 6–7, 21, 25–28, 31–32, 37
    as public work, 6, 21–25, 28–32
    as volunteerism, 6
    centrality to freedom movement, 140
    civics, 26–27
    classes in settlement houses, 91–92
    communitarian, 27
    community 26–27
    youth, 26
City Cares Network, 27
Civic Declaration, xiv
civic education, 29
"civic muscle," 10–11, 81, 181
Civic Practices Network (CPN), xiv
civic virtue, 37–42
    gentry's views, 37–45
civil rights movement, 12, 129, 137–144
    (see also freedom movement)
Civilian Conservation Corps (see New
    Deal), xv, 3, 29, 95, 106–110, 146, 196,
    198
    as citizenship schools, 109
    as public work, 106–107
    benefit to individuals, 106–107
    black experience in, 108–109
    intellectual life of, 107–109
    legacy for country, 106, 107
    organization in 106, 107
    teaching skills and values, 107, 108
Clary, Gil, xiii, 187

Cleveland, Harlan, xi
Cleveland, William, 107–108
Clinton, Bill (President), xiv, 194
Clough, Fred, 65
Cochran Gardens, 134–137
    organizing strategy, 136–137, 177
Cohen, David, xiii, 30
Cohen, Lizbeth, 83
Cohen, Mabel, 135
Coker, Daniel, 151
College of St. Catherine, 127, 186–187
    teaching as public work, 187
Commission on Country Life, 71–72, 196
    philosophy of cooperative exten-
        sion, 71–72
Common Ground, 30
commons, 47–50
commonwealth, 11, 12, 16, 38, 50, 54–55,
    189, 196–200
    biblical tradition of, 192
    cooperative commonwealth, 47–50,
        190–191
    distribution of wealth, 191–192
    Gerald Taylor's philosophy of, 160
    history, 42–45
    language of 49–50, 57–58
    legacy, 50
    legal theory of, 47–49
    public work and, 50
    wealth, 1, 4, 115
commonwealth of freedom, 49, 162, 189,
    194
Communities Organized for Community
    Service (COPS), 145
community organizing movement,
    136–137
community organizing, 103
    as bridge for interracial work,
        137–138
    as public work, 103, 134
    as rebuilding civic confidence, 135–137
    as rebuilding community ties,
        135–136
    as schools for public life, 137–141
    as uplifting the poor, 103
    intellectual vitality of, 138–139
    leadership development in, 139–140
    participation in governance, 140–141
    underlying concepts in, 139–140
    understanding of public space in,
        138–139
    understandings of power in,
        137–138

young people's role in, 136
community service movement, 174–175
    limits, 174–175
Conduct of Life, The, 112
Congress of Industrial Organizations
    (CIO), 97, 102
Constitution Hall, 191
Constitution, 38
consumerism, 61–65, 121–124
    definitions of freedom, 122
    effects on behavior, 123
    homeownership, 122
Cooke, Morris, 99
Cooperative Extension, 72–77, 196–197
    activism of, 76–77
    education for citizenship 75–76, 197
    extension (early years) 39–40, 71–72
    founding of, 72–73
    in New Deal, 76–77
    Liberty Bailey's philosophy of,
        68–71
    public work in, 196–197
    scope of, 76–77
Cornell University, 58, 68, 70, 71
Corporation for National Service, 173
Cortes, Ernesto, 8, 145
Cotton, Dorothy (see citizenship
    schools), xiii, xv, 140–144
Country life movement (see Bailey), 2,
    58–59, 68–69
craft, 128–129
    defined, 128
crisis of citizenship, 5, 14, 23–25
Croly, Herbert, 74
Crowdus, 108–109, 146
Crusade for Citizenship, 140
Currie, Constance, 91

Daedalus, 111
Daley, Richard, 85
Dandridge, Irene, 153
de Graaf, xv
Delli Priscoli, Jerome, 198
democracy (see commonwealth, public
    work, work
    education for, 9–10, 31, 56
    Greek, 35–36, 41, 202–204
    language of as organizing tool,
        99–100
    portable, 54
    relation to farming, 57–61
    theory of, 7–9, 206, 209–213
    uniqueness of American, 36, 57

urban life, 80
women, 42
Democratic Leadership Council, 193
Democratic Vistas, 105
Department of Housing and Urban
Development, 136
Devine, Annie, 138
Dewey, John, 8, 90, 186, 206
Dexter Avenue Bapist Church, 139
Diaz, Bill, xiii
Dietz, Mary, xiii
Dionne, E.J. xii
Dixon, Marian, 156–158
Dobson, Vernon, 152
domestic ideal 117–121
    costs of 119–120
    participation in the labor force,
        117–118
    popular images, 118–119
    pressures to conform, 120
    traditional gender roles, 117, 120–121
Domestic Medicine, 46
Donovan, Dennis, xiii, 176
Dorchester Center, 141
Douglass, Frederick, 151
Drayton, William Henry, 39
Drew Child Development Center, 193
Droker, Howard, 52
Drylongso, 157
Du Bois, W. E. B., 8, 148, 149

East Brooklyn Churches, 17–21
Eddy, Edward, 75
Eley, Geoff, 209
Ellis, James, 54
Ellison, Ralph, 7, 137
Emerald City of Oz, 61
Encyclopedie Methodique, 207
Evans, Sara, xiii
Everett, Edward, 63

Farm Bureau, 75
Farmer Labor Party, 92
Farmers Union, 75
farming, changes in, 75–76
Farr, James, xiii, 176–177
Federal Writers' Project, 106
Federalist Papers, 7, 15, 146
Fellowship of Reconcilation, 151
Ferguson, Janet Chatten, xiv–xv,
    120–121
Fields, LeRon, 198
Fish, Stanley, 210

Fletcher, Michael, 153
Floating Homes Association, 53–55
Fogelman, Edwin, xii
Follett, Mary Baker, 115
Fourteenth Amendment, 49
Frank, Waldo, 123
Frankfurter, Felix, 98
Franklin, Benjamin, 40, 191
Fraser, Nancy, 209
Frederick Douglass High School, 151
freedom movement (see civil rights),
    137–144
    as public work, 138–139
    citizenship schools in, 140–144
    commonwealth themes in, 140
    experience of collective power in,
        137–138
    free spaces in, 138–139
    limitations of, 143
    meaning of freedom in, 137–138
freedom, 4, 138, 190
    as consumerism, 122
    changing definitions of, 122
    Gettysburg Address, 15
    in civil rights, 12
    language of, 49
    quest for, 104
"Freedom's Plow," viii, 104

Gaebler, Ted, 194
Galston, William, xiv
Gandhi, Mahatma, 139
    impact on freedom movement, 139
    Satyagraha, 139
Garland, Hamlin, 58
Garrison, William Lloyd, 151
Gecan, Mike, 18, 157
Gilkey, Bertha, 134–136
Gill, Eric, 128
Ginsberg, Allen, 131–132
Golden Age, The, 64
Gore, Albert (Vice President), xiv,
    194–195
government (see commonwealth, free-
    dom, public leadership), 2–3, 14–16,
    37–39, 194–200
    anger at, 4–5, 14
    as catalyst, 197–199
    founders' views on, 14–16, 191
    loss of civic dimensions in work, 127
    of the people, 4, 16, 76–77, 97–98,
        106–110, 190–191, 192, 193
    reinventing, 194–195

Graf, Arnie, 154–155, 158, 159
Grange, the, 75
Great Depression, 2, 76, 94, 109, 118, 151
Greater Baltimore Committee, 154,
    161–162
Greenberg, Stan, 193
Guetterman, Steve, 198
Gunn, John, 46
Gwaltney, John, 157
Habermas, Jürgen, 205–211
    communicative theory, 208–209
    left–wing criticisms of, 209–211
    public judgment, 208–209
    reemergence of public sphere,
        206–208

Habits of the Heart, 26–27
Hackney, Sheldon, 206
Halberstam, David, 120
Hamilton, Alexander, 38
Hammer, Al, 29
Harbor Place, 153
Harper, Frances, 48, 162
Hartt, Roland Hyde, 66
Hatcher, John, 44
Hayden, Tom, 132
Hayle, Pam, xiii, 180, 183
health, 53, 178–185
    as public work, 178–185
    erosion of civic dimensions in,
        180–181
    impact of public work on providers'
        identity, 184–185
higher education, 185–188
    citizenship education in, 185
    crisis in, 185–186
    extension work, 66–68
    land grant colleges, 66–72
    loss of civic dimension in, 186–187
    organizing strategy, 186–187
Highlander Folk School (see citizenship
    schools), 139, 141
Hillman, Sidney, 98, 186
Hoblitzel, Alan, 152, 159–160, 162
Hofstadter, Richard, 124
Hogg, Kate, xiii
Holbrook, John, 46
Hollywood, 104
Holy Earth, The, 56
Home study circles, 46
homeownership, 114–117
    as American right, 115
    as exclusive enclaves, 116

as spurring consumerism, 116–117
    changing meanings of, 115
    motivations for, 116–117
Horton, Myles, 139
"Howl," 131–132
Hughes, Langston, vii–viii, 3, 7, 104
Hulett, John, 138
Hull House, 34, 78, 86–88, 102, 136, 178
    labor museum, 88
Human Condition, The, 205
Humphrey Institute of Public Affairs,
    xiii, 172
Hurston, Zora Neal, 7
immigrants 79–81, 90
    communal networks, 81–83
    in St. Paul Flats, 88–91
    involvement in public spaces, 81,
        83, 102
    mutual aid, 83–85
    parochialism of, 85
    resistance to exploitation, 83–84
    transition to urban life, 79–81

Industrial Areas Foundation (IAF, see
    community organizing), 17, 31,
    145–147, 155–157, 156–157
    black caucus, 150–151, 165–166
    philosophy of relational power,
        165–166
industrial democracy movement, 97–99
Institute for Water Resources, 198
intellectual capacities of ordinary people,
    46–47, 87
    Jane Addams's view on, 87
    Deborah Meier's views on, 9–10
Institution of Practical Education, 47
Invisible Man, 137

Jackson, Juan, xiii, 175
Jackson, Lillian, 151
Jamieson, Celina, 18
Jefferson, Thomas, 8, 15, 100, 114
Johnson, Carol McGee, xiii
Johnson, Nellie Stone, 92–93, 97, 99
    definition of public work, 92–93
Journal of Democracy, 5
Jungle, The, 79

Kading, Kathryn, 183
Kant, Immanuel, 207–208
Kari, Ana, xv
Kari, John, xiii, xv, 195
Kari, Jonathan, xv

Kautz, Elizabeth, 193
Keller, Robert, 154, 159, 160
Kemmis, Daniel, 59–61, 81
Kemmis, Lily, 59–60
Kemp, Jack, 136
Kerouac, Jack, 131–132
Kettering Foundation, xiv
Khrushchev, Nikita, 122
Kim, Bon Hwan, xv
King, Martin Luther, Jr. (see freedom
   movement), 13, 23, 133, 136, 139–140,
   152
      philosophy of, 139–140
kitchen debate, 122
Klein, Joe, 4
Knapp, Seaman, 73–74
Knights of Labor, 50, 65
Koch, Edward, 19–20
Korean Youth Cultural Center (KYCC),
   xv
Kudrle, Robert, xiii
Kuehn, Bill, 91
labor organizing, 97–98, 99–104
      strategies, 100–104

Lagemann, Ellen, 93
Lake Union, 52–55, 136
Landon, Alfred, 96
Lasch, Christopher, 123
Leach, William, 61
League of Women Voters, 82, 121
Leffingwell, Christopher, 40
"Letter from a Birmingham Jail," 133,
   140
Levitt, William J., 115
Levittown, 115–116
Lewis, John L., 102
Light, Paul, xiii, 127, 194
Lincoln, Abraham, 2, 15–16, 67, 97, 100
      theory of government, 15–16, 97
Lippmann, Walter, 64, 75
Looking Backward, 64
Lord, Russell, 75
Lowell, James Russell, 80
Lowndes County Freedom Party, 138
Loyola University, 161
Lyceum Movement, 46

Mad Magazine, 131
Madison State Journal, 168
Madison, James, 14–15, 37, 146
Main–Traveled Roads, 58
Markowitz, Gerald E., 105

Marshall, Will, xiv
Marx, Karl, 62–63
Maryland National Bank, 152, 162
Massachusetts Fair Share, 144
Massengale, Anthony, xiii, 193
Mathews, David, xiv
Mauer, Jeff, 176
May, Elaine, Tyler, 122
May, Lary, ix, 104
McCarthy, Joseph, 121
McCarthyism, 121
McCormick, Cyrus, 63
McDougall, Harold, xv
McNeil, George, 65
McPike, Liz, 128
Meegan, Joe, 103
Meath, Judy, xiii, xv, 184
Meier, Christian, 35, 203
Meier, Deborah, xiii, 8, 9
Melville, Herman, 7
Merritt, Davis, 166, 167
Metropolitan Council, 195
Michels, Peg, xiii
Michigan State University, 70
Midwest Academy, 144
Miles, Doug, 147, 152, 153, 155–156, 159
Miller, Edward, 44
Minerva Institution, 47
Minnesota Extension Service, 127, 196
Minnesota Farmer Labor Party, 92
Minnich, Elizabeth, xv
Mitchell, Clarence, 151
Mitchell, Miaisha, xiii, 183–184
Mitchell, Parren, 151
Mobley, Barbara, 197
Montana Conservation Corps, 198
Montgomery Bus Boycott, 139
Moreno, Mat, 91
Morgan State College, 151
Morrill Act, 67
Morris, Robert, 47
Morse, Suzanne, xiv
Moses, 150
Mumford, Lewis, 112–113, 116, 202
Musl, Matt, 177
Myers, Christy, xv
Myers, Samuel, xiii
Myers, William, 127
Myrdal, Gunnar, 126

Nathan, Joe, xiii
National American Women's Suffrage
   Association, 82

National Association for the
Advancement of Colored People
(NAACP), 81, 151
National Education Association, 58
National Public Radio, 167
national service, 198–199
Necker, Jacques, 207
Nehemiah, 17–21, 192
Project, 18–19, 162
legislation, 19–20
Neighborhood House (see settlement
houses), 88, 90–91
as public space, 92
citizenship classes in, 91
Nelson, Barbara, xiii
Nelson, Hannah, 157
Nelson, Steve, 100
New Citizenship, xiii, 172
New Deal, 2, 94, 95–99, 104–109
democratization of culture in, 97
Federal Writers' Project, 106
movement, 98
popular art and national renewal,
104–106
promotion of public work, 105
Public Works Administration, 21
new gentry (see professionals, science),
111–114
effects of World War II on, 112
power, 124–125
science of ideology of, 124–127
Newland, Betty, xiv–xv, 120
Newland, Harold, xv
Ninth Amendment, 15
Nixon, Richard, 122, 133, 166
nursing home project (Lazarus Project),
179–183
barriers to public culture, 179–181
organizing strategy, 181–183
concept of public space in, 182
impact of public work on, 183
occupational therapy, 178–180
origins in settlements, 179–180
Reilly's philosophy of, 179
Reilly tradition's impact on Center
for Democracy and Citizenship, 180
loss of civic dimensions of, 180

Ohio Agricultural and Mechanical
College, 68
On the Road, 132
organizing strategies (see practical democratic theory)

as taught in citizenship schools, 141
Back of the Yards, 102–103
BUILD, 154–163
Cochran Gardens, 134–136
College of St. Catherine, 186
labor unions, 100–104
Lake Union, 52–55
Lazarus Project, 179–183
Osborn, David, 194
Overstreet, H. A., 82

Packing House Workers Union, 103
Paine, Thomas, 38, 47, 100
Pampusch, Anita, 187
Park, Marlene, 105
Parks, Rosa, 139
Parton, Dolly, 128
Patterson High School, 161
Penny, Tim, xiii
People's College Association, 66
People's Unemployed League, 151
Perkins, Frances, 98
Peters, Scott, xv
Pettus, Berta, 51, 52
Pettus, Terry, 51–54, 100
Peuchet, Jacques, 207
Pew Health Professions Commission,
185
Phantom Public, The, 75
Phyllis Wheately settlement house, 92
Pinderhughes, Alice, 153, 158–159
populism, 49
People's Party, 65
Port Huron Statement, The, 132–133
Port Office Art Project, 105
power, 162, 209–211
practical democratic theory (see citizen-
ship education, commonwealth,
democracy, freedom, organizing
strategies, public work, work), 7–9
Preacher Red, 143
Preface to Morals, A, 75
prejudice, 66
Pritchett, Henry, 93
professionalism, 111, 124–126, 212
progressivism, 74–77
elitism in, 74–75
democratic elements, 75–77
Project on Public Life and the Press, 167
Provident Bank campaign, 155–156
Pruitt, Iago, 134
public, 11–12, 41–42, 146–147
affairs, 14

changes in self understanding, 12
definitions, 12
multiple perspectives, 12
perceptions of truth, 29–30
talk, 45–47
public culture, 99
New Deal, 104
public journalism, 165–173
relation to democracy, 161, 165–166
professional crisis, 166–167
public work in, 169–172
public leadership, 192–193
public libraries, 46
Public Opinion, 75
public space, 49, 81–83, 149, 161–163,
188, 211
at Central Medical Center, 183–184
BYNC, 103, 192
citizenship education in, 93
in labor movement, 97–99
relation to justice, 83
public sphere (realm), 203–211
Arendt's theory of, 204–205
Greek theory of, 202–204
Habermas's theory of, 205–211
public work corps, 113
public work, 201
absence of in academic theory, 202
and power, 24
as catalyst, 24, 29
as citizenship, 21–25
as cultural creation, 104–106
as political resource for higher education, 71
concept of, 8–9
defined, 2, 9, 16, 23, 202
early usage, 22
erosion of, 16
evaluation of outcomes, 24–25
health, 31
Lemuel Shaw's theory of, 22
philosophy of, 11–12
way of bridging differences, 29–30, 49
Publius, 33
Putnam, Robert, 5
racial division, 149
power of blacks' changed
self–understanding, 156–157,
161–162
strategies based on public work,
149, 159–160, 162–163
strategies based on understanding,
149

Regionalists' movement, 104
Reich, Robert, 128–129
Reilly, Mary, 178–180
Ritchit, Robert, 109
Robbins, I. D, 18, 21
Roberts, Cokie, 167
Robeson, Paul, 104
Rodwell, Gary, 155–156
Rogers, Will, 3, 104
Ronning, James, 95, 108
Roosevelt, F. D. (see government of the
people, New Deal), 2, 21, 95, 96–97,
105–106
theory of government, 97
Tree Army, 106
views on popular art, 105
views on public work and character
building, 106
Roosevelt, Theodore, 58, 71–72, 73, 189,
190
Rosen, Jay, 166, 167, 171–172
Royko, Mike, 84
Ryan, Mary, 209–210

Salzer, Bill, 197
Saunders, Harold, xiv
Schaefer, William Donald, 152–153, 158
Schambra, William, xiii
Scheibel, Jim, 175
Schmoke, Kurt, 161–162
Schön, Donald, 211–212
Schuh, G. Edward, xiii
science, 57–58, 65–66, 70, 124–127
as reframing politics, 126–127
as undermining civic confidence,
125
Bailey's philosophy of, 70–71
expert knowledge, 58, 62, 65–66
impact on work, 126
promise of, 57, 62
remaking of household, 124
scientific management, 65–66
Scott, Gloria, 187–188
settlement houses, 46, 86–94
citizenship classes, 91–92
citizenship schools, 87
education for public work, 86–88
loss of intellectual authority, 93–94
research function of, 86
Shalala, Donna, 186
Sharp Street school, 151
Shaw, Clifford, 102
Shaw, Lemuel, 22, 48, 166

theory of eminent domain, 22
theory of public work by private
    businesses, 166
Shay's Rebellion, 38
Sheldon, Tim, xiii
Shields, Carol, xiii, 197
Shuttlesworth, Fred, 140
Sinclair, Upton, 79
Sirianni, Carmen, xiii–xiv, xv
sit–down strikes, 101–102
Skelton, Nan, xi, xv, xvi, 177
slavery, 41, 49
Slayton, Robert, 79–80
Smith Lever Act, 73
Smith, Adam, 12, 123
Smith, Clarence, 75
Smith, Estus, xiv
Snyder, Mary, 192
Society of Free Inquirers, 47
Souls of Black Folks, The, 148
Southern Christian Leadership
    Conference (SCLC), xiii, 140–143
Spock, Benjamin, 125
St. Bernard's school, 176–177
St. Francis Academy, 151
Stacker, Ralph, 90
Stahl, Leslie, 167
Star Tribune, 168
Steinbrueck, Vitor, 54
Stevenson, Adlai, 117, 119
Stille, Darlene, 128
Stokes, Carl, 153
Strong, Josiah, 66
Student Nonviolent Coordinating
    Committee (SNCC), 140
student movement, 131–133
    cultural stance, 132–133
    impact of freedom movement on,
        131–132
    influence of consumerism on, 133
    New Left, 132–133
    philosophy of, 132–133
suburbia, 114–117
    as loss of public space in, 117
    benefits of, 116–117
    criticisms of, 116
    homeownership, 115–117

Taft, William Howard, 73
Taylor Society, 99
Taylor, Frederick, 65
Taylor, Gerald, xiii, xv, 8, 31, 151,
    160–163

philosophy of democracy, 160–162
Temple of Arts, 47
Tenth Amendment, 15
Tent of the Presence, 150
Terkel, Studs, 22, 101, 129
Thomas, Waymer, 144
Thompson, Bill, 144
Thoreau, Henry David, 64
Thurow, Lester, 191
Times Mirror Center, 174
Times Mirror Company study of the
    press, 167
Tocqueville, Alexis de, 40, 44
Toynbee, Arnold, 126
Treasury Department's Section of Fine
    Arts, 105
Turner, Helen, 88–90
Twenty Years at Hull–House, 78, 173
Tyson, Elisha, 151

Unger, Roberto, 210
University of Michigan, 132
University of Minnesota, xi, 91–92
University of Wisconsin, 186

Veblen, Thorsten, 111
Veronen, Tracy, 176
Virginian Pilot, 168–169
Vlach, John, 41
Volbrecht, Albert, 59–60
voluntarism, 6, 27–28

Wallace, Henry, 98
Walzer, Michael, 10
Warhover, Tom, 169–170
Warren, George, 70
Washington Commonwealth Federation,
    51–53, 100
Watson, Nora, 129
"We the people," 168
wealth, definitions of, 4, 112–113
Weber, Vin, xiii
Webster, Noah, 40
Weil, Simone, 4, 8, 12, 212–213
West, Cornel, 210–211
Wichita Eagle, 166, 167–168
Wiebe, Robert, 64
Wilentz, Sean, 47
Will, George, 199
Willard, Frances, 8, 45
Wilson, Meredith, 75
Wilson, William Julius, 146
Wilson, Woodrow, 73, 98

Winter, William, xiv
WISC TV, 168
Wisconsin Public Television, 168–169
Wolman, Leo, 98
Woman Citizen's Library, 81
Women Employed, 128
Women's Christian Temperance Union,
    45
women's rights crusaders, 49, 82
Women's Empowerment Network, 197
Women's International League for Peace
    and Freedom, 151
women's labor force particiption,
    117–118
women's roles in 1950s
        family oriented, 120
        exceptions, 120–121
Wonderful World of Oz, 61
work (see democracy, freedom, com-
    monwealth, public work),
        changing experiences of, 127–129
        impact of technology on, 128–129
        loss of civic dimension, 128
        loss of craft, 128
        loss of meaning, 3, 190
        meaning of, 7, 12, 201
        relation to democracy, 2, 35–36,

38–42, 190, 211–213
    relation to freedom, 212–213
    relation to power, 4, 10–12, 212–213
    women's, 128
Working People's Social Science Club, 34
    renewed civic meanings, 165
Working, 22, 129
Workmen's Circle, 46
Work of Nations, The, 129
World War II, 112
    effects of, 112

YMCA 26, 31, 81–82
    civic mission of, 82
Young People's Forum, 151–152
Young, Iris, 210
Youngblook, Johnny Ray, 17
Youth and America's Future, 174
youth development as public work,
    173–178
        erosion of productive roles for
        youth, 173–174
            Public Achievement, 175–178
            youth views of public life, 173–174
YWCA, 26, 31, 81
4–H Clubs, 31, 72, 120, 196
    9 to 5, 128